# Leading Issues in ICT Evaluation Research
# Volume 2

Edited by

Shaun Pather

Leading Issues in ICT Evaluation Research
Volume Two

ISBN:    978-1-911218-24-1 (print)


Printed by Lightning Source POD

Published by: Academic Conferences and Publishing International Limited,
Reading, RG4 9AY, United Kingdom, info@academic-publishing.org
Available from www.academic-bookshop.com

# Contents

# About the editor

**Professor Shaun Pather** is based at the University of the Western Cape in South Africa and has spent more than 20 years teaching and researching in the field of ICT management.

His research has focused on the evaluation of Information Systems (IS) effectiveness, particularly within e-Commerce, e-Government and other web enabled contexts. He has developed models for evaluating e-Commerce success, and also has an interest in the application of e-Service Quality evaluation. Shaun has also extended his interest in IS evaluation into practical community engagement and Information Society issues, centered around societal upliftment facilitated by ICT's. He has published in peer reviewed journals and has presented papers at several conferences. He has led several research projects with university and government partners in both the private and public sector. Professor Pather is also a Fulbright Scholar (University of Washington, 2009-2010).

# List of Contributing Authors

*Veronica Adu-Brobbey,* University of Education, Winneba, Ghana

*Foresight Kofi Azumah,* CleverIdeaz Research Consultant, Kumasi, Ghana

*Sven A. Carlsson,* Lund University School of Economics and Management, Sweden

*Steven De Haes,* University of Antwerp, Belgium

*Francis Donkor,* University of Education, Winneba, Ghana

*Aida Hadzic,* University of Gothenburg, Sweden

*Jenny Lagsten,* Swedish Business School at Örebro University, Sweden

*Nick Letch,* The University of Western Australia, Perth, Australia

*Kim Maes,* University of Antwerp, Belgium

*Thanos Magoulas,* University of Gothenburg, Sweden

*Nor Laila Md Noor,* Universiti Teknologi MARA, Shah Alam, Malaysia

*Nazareth Nicolian,* Department of MIS, American Uni-versity of Science and Technology, Beirut, Lebanon

*Simon Gyasi Nimako,* University of Education, Winneba, Ghana

*Ariza Nordin,* Universiti Teknologi MARA, Shah Alam, Malaysia

*Kalevi Pessi,* University of Gothenburg, Sweden

*Martin Read,* University of Portsmouth, UK

*Martyn Roberts,* University of Portsmouth, UK

*Ted Saarikko,* University of Gothenburg, Sweden

*Nikki Smit,* HvA Amsterdam University of Applied Sciences, Amsterdam, The Netherlands

*Xingchen Song,* The University of Western Australia, Perth, Australia

*Olgerta Tona,* Lund University School of Economics and Management, Lund, Sweden

*Geert-Jan van Bussel,* HvA Amsterdam University of Applied Sciences, Amsterdam, The Netherlands

*John van de Pas,* Saxion University of Applied Sciences, Deventer, The Netherlands

*Wim Van Grembergen,* University of Antwerp, Belgium

*Christine Welch,* University of Portsmouth, UK

# Introduction to Leading Issues in ICT Evaluation Research Volume 2

The Electronic Journal for Information Systems Research[1] (EJISE) has a proud seventeen-year tradition of publishing academic research pertaining to the specialist niche of evaluation in relation to Information Systems (IS) and Information and Communications Technologies (ICTs). Volume 2 of the Leading Issues series is a compilation of ten carefully selected EJISE articles published between 2010 and 2015. These articles, when considered as a whole, reflect the *leading issues* in the evaluation of Information Systems over the previous five years, and are therefore invaluable to both the research and practitioner communities. The papers have been selected on the degree to which each contribution advances ICT evaluation with special emphasis on issues typical of the current inter-networked (or *Transfigurate*) era.

Figure 1, providing an overview of keywords found in all articles published in EJISE from 2010 - 2015, is indicative of both the latitude and scope of this published body of knowledge.

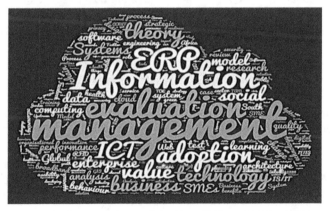

**Figure 1:** Keywords of 110 articles published in EJISE from 2010 to 2015

---

[1] www.ejise.com

Over and above typical words related to this niche field such as *evaluation, information, management* and *ICT*, Figure 1 exhibits the major trends that have underpinned all of the published work in EJISE in the period under purview. These include a focus on Enterprise Resource Planning systems, small and medium enterprises, technology adoption, cloud computing, architecture and social media. The ten papers in this volume thus reflect these trends. The prominence of *management* as a keyword underscores the scope of EJISE which incorporates a focus on research relevant to Information Systems evaluation, with emphasis on organisational and management implications.

### Context of ICT evaluation

The presentation of this second volume of Leading Issues provides an opportune moment to reflect on the big picture in which the ambit of ICT evaluation prevails. Worldwide IT spending is on pace to total a staggering US $3.49 trillion in 2016[2]. Although this reveals a slight decline in expenditure from 2015, the overall expenditure represents a positive growth curve over the past decade. Of this, the largest category of forecasted expenditure is on telecommunications services (41.3%) followed by IT services (26.6%). By and large, this has been the trend the ICT sector has been experiencing since the mainstreaming of the Internet in the 1990s. In this regard, attention is focused beyond just the traditional domain of internal organisational efficiency. Both large and small businesses, and the public sector, reflect constantly evolving models of business, disrupting commercial tradition, and harnessing the ubiquitous presence of ICT and usage thereof. From a research and development perspective, we also see the trends perpetuating technological advances in respect of the cloud, wearable devices, and the Internet of things, for example.

The implication for IS researchers working in the field of IS evaluation is to keep abreast of the evolving environments in which IS are deployed. It is thus hoped that this volume of Leading Issues provides a basis for future work directives. Information Systems have certainly become more complex, and the traditional delineation of what constitutes a *system* is in itself blurred. It is timeous, therefore, to review the various approaches to IS

---

[2] Gartner. 2016. Gartner Says Worldwide IT Spending Is Forecast to Decline 0.5 Percent in 2016. [Online: http://www.gartner.com/newsroom/id/3277517]

evaluation over the years. This necessitates a re-examination of theory, models and frameworks and a realignment of the same through a new set of lenses. Even so, it can undoubtedly be argued that much of the funda-mental rationale for evaluation remains in place. The increasing size of IT budgets still begs robust evaluation, from product, IS design process and service perspectives.

### The relevance of researching the success of Information Systems

*Success* is the underlying concern in ICT evaluation. The fundamental re-search problem, regardless of context, is whether or not expenditure on technology is yielding the desired results. From the first commercial appli-cation of computers, businesses have depended on Information Technolo-gy to varying degrees. Stylianou and Kumar (2000:99) sum up the strategic importance of IS in business quite aptly in arguing that

> *The importance of information technologies and the infor-mation systems function is no longer of debate among business people. The question, rather, is how an organiza-tion can take best advantage of IT in order to support its operations, add value to its products and services, and gain a competitive edge in the marketplace.*

DeLone and McLean (2003:10) have also contributed to this discussion, stating that

> *The measurement of IS success or effectiveness is critical to our understanding of the value and efficacy of IS manage-ment actions and IS investments.*[3]

Thus IS success measurement has been a critical issue of concern both in IS management practice and research. From a macroeconomics perspective, there is an ongoing debate over several years in respect of whether infor-mation technology has contributed to overall productivity of countries. Whilst the jury is still out in that regard, IS researchers are still concerned about success at the system, organizational and inter-organizational level. Research into IS success, though, has posed as a hurdle to the IS communi-

---

[3] The terms *IS Success* and *IS Effectiveness* are used interchangeably in the literature.

ty in that it presents both conceptual challenges and implementation difficulties. Even with numerous researchers investigating these issues over the years, there remains many differing views and stances as to what constitutes *success*.

**A history of the evolving impact of IS on business: from Automate beginnings to the Transfigurate era**

The interest of researchers and business managers in the success of IS has been escalating since the initial commercial deployment of computers. The history of the impact of IS on business over the years provides an important backdrop to this topic in the current Internet-dominated era.
Since the development of the first commercial computer in 1952,[4] the deployment of IS has significantly altered the world of business, attributable to the soaring power and concomitant declining costs of computer technology.[5] The growth in investment in IS in the latter half of the twentieth century increased concerns of executives managing these resources (Hart *et al.*, 2004) with much concern surrounding the benefits associated with IS. Managers had to justify the costs associated with IS, and thus questions pertaining to its success and the evaluation of its benefits shifted to the fore of the research agenda.

There are three phases that describe how our interest in IS success has evolved over the years, mapped against three distinct eras of IS application in business. Laudon and Laudon (2000:15-16) describe the evolution of these eras:

In the 1950s the effects of IS on organisations brought about merely technical changes, only serving to automate clerical procedures. During the 1960s and 1970s, IS had an impact on managerial control, and from the

---

[4] Although the history of computers indicates earlier inventions such as the Z1 Computer in 1936, the Harvard Mark I in 1944, and the ENIAC in 1946, the earliest indications of commercial activity can be attributed to the use of the UNIVAC which was used in 1952 to predict the outcome of the US elections.

[5] This is sometimes referred to as Moore's Law which, named after one of the founders of Intel, stated that semiconductor price/performance would double every two years (Willcocks & Graeser, 2001:195).

1980s onwards IS impacted upon core institutional activities such as products, markets, suppliers and customers.

Zuboff (1988) labelled these phases as Automate, Informate and Transformate:

- *Automate phase*: focused on measurement of technical aspects of IT.
- *Informate phase*: also focused on technical aspects but with a shift towards evaluating the measurement of IS production or IS project management.
- *Transformate phase*: focused on measurement of business benefits with a shift towards a service perspective.

The *Transformate* era still reflects the impact of IS on organisations today. However, in considering the impact of the Internet on the business world, it is clear that organisations are venturing through a special kind of transformation. As the Internet has had a far-reaching impact on the way in which IS are being applied by businesses, the current era can be considered one of spectacular change, or transformation. The term *Transfigurate*, therefore, most aptly describes the current Internet-dominant era, characterised by businesses which operate as global, inter-networked enterprises. Figure 2 summarises the salient aspects of IS benefits and measurement over the years in terms of the Automate, Informate, Transformate and Transfigurate eras.

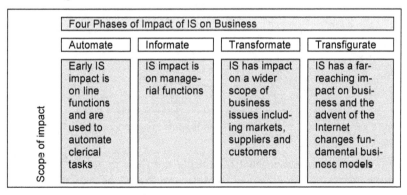

| Four Phases of Impact of IS on Business | | | |
|---|---|---|---|
| Automate | Informate | Transformate | Transfigurate |
| Early IS impact is on line functions and are used to automate clerical tasks | IS impact is on managerial functions | IS has impact on a wider scope of business issues including markets, suppliers and customers | IS has a far-reaching impact on business and the advent of the Internet changes fundamental business models |

(Scope of impact)

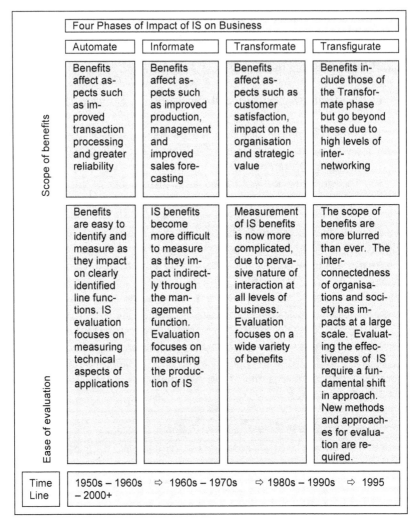

| Four Phases of Impact of IS on Business | | | |
|---|---|---|---|
| Automate | Informate | Transformate | Transfigurate |
| **Scope of benefits** Benefits affect aspects such as improved transaction processing and greater reliability | Benefits affect aspects such as improved production, management and improved sales forecasting | Benefits affect aspects such as customer satisfaction, impact on the organisation and strategic value | Benefits include those of the Transformate phase but go beyond these due to high levels of inter-networking |
| **Ease of evaluation** Benefits are easy to identify and measure as they impact on clearly identified line functions. IS evaluation focuses on measuring technical aspects of applications | IS benefits become more difficult to measure as they impact indirectly through the management function. Evaluation focuses on measuring the production of IS | Measurement of IS benefits is now more complicated, due to pervasive nature of interaction at all levels of business. Evaluation focuses on a wide variety of benefits | The scope of benefits are more blurred than ever. The interconnectedness of organisations and society has impacts at a large scale. Evaluating the effectiveness of IS require a fundamental shift in approach. New methods and approaches for evaluation are required. |
| Time Line | 1950s – 1960s – 2000+ | ⇨ 1960s – 1970s | ⇨ 1980s – 1990s ⇨ 1995 |

**Figure 2:** Evolvement of IS benefits from the Informate phase to the Transfigurate phase

Given the high investment in ICT in the current *Transfigurate* era, catalysed by the commercial adoption of the Internet, the ICT evaluation literature must thus take into account the potential of IS to radically transform modern inter-networked businesses.

Over and above the business domain, ICTs in the current era also have a distinct role to play from a developmental perspective in respect to advancing social and economic transformation. To this end, several countries have passed laws declaring In Internet access basic right, including, amongst others, Finland, France, Greece and Spain. The right to access broadband Internet is also deeply embedded in the United Nation's post MDG agenda. The research which underpins the developmental perspective of ICTs is broadly referred to as ICT for Development (ICT4D). Researchers in the ICT evaluation field must simultaneously channel their energies towards research questions which are equally as vexing as those posed within traditional business environments.

In summary, the following factors support the importance of the ICT evaluation research agenda:

- Firstly, *evaluation* is one of four key management activities, and given the pervasiveness of ICT in organisations today, it is not possible for managers to fulfil their duties if they ignore issues related to IS success.

- Secondly, given the ever-increasing investment in ICTs in the *Transfigurate* era, set against a worldwide economic meltdown, managers are duty-bound to justify such expenditure. Clearly formulated evaluation plans and robust methodologies will assist in making such justifications.

- Thirdly, speculation continues regarding precisely how ICT adds value to business bottom line. Ongoing research pertaining to how IS success should be evaluated will continue to uphold the view that IS investment does indeed contribute towards increased productivity and competitive advantage.

- Fourthly, the emergence of the post-2000 Information Society warrants a special focus on ICT evaluation insofar as ICT support of developmental objectives. Evaluation studies in the ICT4D arena will no doubt come into prominence in the upcoming decade. IS researchers are called upon to join forces with their counterparts in social sciences and humanities to address complex ICT evaluation questions in this area.

In light of the foregoing justification, I hope that the collection of papers in this Leading Issues volume leads us to reflect on the important discoveries of the previous five years, and likewise, encourages us to address with vigour many forthcoming critical ICT evaluation questions.

# References

Delone, W.H. & McLean, E.R. 2003. The Delone and McLean model of information systems success: a ten-year update. *Journal of Management Information Systems*, 19(4):9-30.

Hart, M.L., Berkowitz, S., Ryan, J. & Waspe, K. 2004. Key information systems management issues: a comparative study in South Africa. *South African Journal of Business Management*, 35(4):49-59.

Laudon, K.C. & Laudon, J.P. 2000. Management information systems: organization and technology in the networked enterprise. 6th ed. Upper Saddle River, NJ: Prentice Hall.

Stylianou, A.C. & Kumar, R.L. 2000. An integrative framework for IS quality management. *Communications of the ACM*, 43(9):99-104.

Willcocks, L. & Graeser, V. 2001. *Delivering IT and e-business value*. Oxford: Butterworth-Heinemann.

Zuboff, S. 1988. In the age of the smart machine: the future of work and power. New York: Basic Books.

**Shaun Pather**
Professor of Information Systems
University of the Western Cape
South Africa

# Evaluating Information Systems according to Stakeholders: A Pragmatic Perspective and Method

**Jenny Lagsten**
Swedish Business School at Örebro University, Örebro, Sweden
*Originally published in EJISE (2011) Volume 14, ISS 1*

---

**Editorial Commentary**
This paper makes an important contribution to IS evaluation practice. VISU, the evaluation methodology posited in the paper framed within an interpretive evaluation approach, is grounded in pragmatic knowledge theories. The principal approach of the VISU method is the integration of concerns of all stakeholders of the Information System in systematic dialogue-seminars. The author extends the interpretive philosophical paradigm to one of a 'pragmatic knowledge interest' as she argues that a pragmatic approach from a stakeholder perspective will contribute to change and betterment of the organisations. The importance of this paper as a leading IS evaluation topic is that the roles of stakeholders are shown to be increasingly relevant in determining the effectiveness or success of an Information System. The constantly growing base of users across the globe results in greater demand and higher expectation from IS performance. The elevation of stakeholder-embedded IS evaluation approaches is thus warranted.

---

**Abstract:** In the last decade several researchers have addressed the problem that there does not seem to be much evidence of extensive use of interpretive evaluation approaches in practice. Researchers have though recognized the interpretive evaluation approach as well founded academically and theoretically offering potential advantages such as stakeholder commitment and learning opportunities. One reason for this non-use could be that there are few, if any, interpretive evaluation methods ready at hand for evaluators in practice. An interpretive IS evaluation method means a method in support for doing evaluation as interpretation. This research presents a practical method for doing evaluation of information systems as a joint act of interpretation performed by the stakeholders of the information system in use. In our research we have expanded the interpretive philosophical base to embrace a pragmatic knowledge interest in order to underpin the overall strive for evaluation that is to contribute to change and betterment. The method presented is named VISU (Swedish acronym for IS evaluation for workpractice development). The process of evaluating accordingly to the VISU method has been extensively tested in practice and in theoretical grounding processes and is now considered ready for wider use. The research process for developing VISU has been conducted with canonical action research through parallel work with evaluation and method development in six episodes within two cases. VISU consists of prescribed actions that are anchored in a set of underlying principles stemming from the philosophy of American pragmatism. Evaluation according to VISU is performed in three phases; arrange, evaluate and develop. In the paper VISU is described according to phases, actions, main concepts and principles. The use of VISU is demonstrated through examples from a performed evaluation of an information system in support for social welfare services.

**Keywords:** IS evaluation, stakeholder model, interpretive IS evaluation method, pragmatism, action research

# 1. Introduction

Evaluation of Information Systems (IS) has come to be an important topic for study as well as practice (Irani et al. 2005). As ISs has become more pervasive, complex and interactive evaluation emphasis has, to a degree, shifted to concerns with how and to what extent ISs serve organisational change (Klecun and Cornford 2005). Alternative evaluation approaches to traditional 'scientific' methods has emerged in the field. An interpretative evaluation approach has been reported as a capable evaluation approach with important practical implications (Symons and Walsham 1988; Symons 1991; Avgerou 1995; Farbey et al. 1999; Walsham 1999; Serafeimidis and Smithson 2000; Jones and Hughes 2001). An interpretive IS evaluation model builds basically on Guba and Lincolns (1989) work on constructivist evaluation and could be summarised as: elicitation and articulation of stakeholder concerns, participative process, context dependent criteria, understanding and learning. In spite of a well founded academic and theoretic model, with potential advantages such as stakeholder commitment and learning opportunities, there does not seem to be much evidence of extensive use of interpretative evaluation approaches in practice (Hirschheim and Smithson 1999; Walsham 1999). One reason for the non-use, in the field of IS, could be the lack of practical methodology ready at hand for evaluators and assigners of evaluations which motivates the purpose of this paper that is to provide a comprehensive method in support for doing evaluation as interpretation.

As we see it, one major reason for doing evaluations of information systems is to take actions based on the results of the evaluation. Evaluations should be used; the results of the evaluation should be transformed into change and betterment in the organisation, in the IS and/or in the use of the IS. Evaluation is a process that develops personal and cooperative knowledge through investigating experiences in order to make improvements. Because of the strive towards change and betterment we found the philosophy of American pragmatism in best support for such world view. A pragmatist is interested in change and action. "From a moral standpoint he gives priority to what is conceived as positive changes. The research endeavour is towards knowledge, which makes a positive difference i.e. knowledge which contributes to improvement of IS practices" (Goldkuhl 2004). The interpretive and the pragmatic approach share the concern for understanding and meaning. For a pragmatic IS researcher an interpretive stance is unavoidable, but the pragmatist is, however, not content with making solely interpretive descriptions (Goldkuhl 2004). A pragmatic inquiry goes a step further when, on base of descriptions and understanding, having the interest for change and improvement.

The overall aim of this study has been to develop an interpretative, stakeholder based method for evaluating information systems aiming for change and betterment. The result of the study presented here is the evaluation method VISU. VISU is grounded in pragmatic knowledge theories, evaluation theories (especially the stakeholder model), theories concerning evaluation use and in the school of interpretive IS evaluation. VISU is designed to be used in practical organisational situations where there is a need for evaluation of an information system.

The following section gives an account of the research process. In section 3 the rationale of pragmatic evaluation is presented followed by the description of the VISU method according to the three phases; arrange, evaluate and develop. The VISU method is illustrated by examples from a performed evaluation of an IS supporting social welfare services. The paper concludes with a discussion on implications for practice and research.

## 2. Research process
The research process has been conducted with Canonical Action Research (CAR) (Susman and Evered 1978). Action Research has as goal to solve practical problems at the same time as the researcher study the process

and develop scientific knowledge (Baskerville and Myers 2004). AR has been chosen in order to satisfy the research needs when doing method development. Rigorous method development requires grounding of the method both theoretically and empirically (Goldkuhl 1993; Fitzgerald et al. 2002).

VISU has been designed and tested during several cycles of use through parallel work with evaluation and method development (time period 2001 – 2009). The research has been conducted through six iterative CAR cycles (method development episodes) within two cases. In the first case a method hypothesis was developed parallel with a project evaluation. In the second case, at the social welfare services in a Swedish municipality, the method hypothesis was tested and refined parallel with evaluation of the information system Procapita. Procapita is an off-the-shelf system from a large Swedish ERP vendor and is in use by approximately 150 municipalities in Sweden. In this case Procapita was used by 350 social workers (case handlers) in the daily case handling practice. The method development episodes have investigated different themes due to "what seems to be going on here" (Strauss and Corbin 1998; Baskerville and Pries-Heje 1999). Table 1 and 2 give an overview of episodes, themes, questions and results.

**Table 1:** Method development episode 1-3 at the Swedish Employment Agency.

| Episode | Theme | Questions | Results |
|---------|-------|-----------|---------|
| 1. Model | Evaluation model | What evaluation model satisfies the evaluation needs? | Business needs for usable evaluation results The role of stakeholders in evaluation. |
| 2. Process | Construction of evaluation process | How to design the evaluation process? | Dialogue-seminars Process use of evaluation VISU method draft VISU Principles |
| 3. Method hypothesis | Theoretical grounding of method hypothesis | How to design a method hypothesis from the performed evaluation process that is grounded in theories on evaluation IS evaluation and the American pragmatism? | Multiparadigm model for IS evaluation Grounding of VISU in evaluation theory, IS evaluation theory and American pragmatism VISU method hypothesis |

VISU has been refined in several stages and built originally on Constructivist Evaluation (Guba and Lincoln 1989) and Change Analysis (Goldkuhl and Röstlinger 2005). Constructivist evaluation has contributed with principles on stakeholder perspective, dialectic process and stakeholder generated criteria. Change analysis has contributed with method components and modelling techniques for analysing problems, strengths, goals and with guiding principles on participation.

**Table 2:** Method development episode 4-6 at the Social Welfare Services.

| Episode | Theme | Questions | Results |
|---|---|---|---|
| 4. Method description | Method description | IS the description explicit and easy to use? | Partly validated method description<br>Summary of change needs for VISU |
| 5. Stakeholder model | The evaluation process based on the stakeholder model | Do phases and activities in VISU implement a stakeholder model for evaluation?<br>How does inclusion of stakeholders work in practice?<br>How do VISU questions (activities, problems, strengths, goals) work in dialogue -seminars?<br>How to summarise change requirements and change measures from concerns and issues? | Rationality for pragmatic IS evaluation<br>Adjustments of phases and activities in VISU<br>Mechanism for summarising change requirements and change measures from multiple stakeholders claims and concerns |
| 6. Evaluation use | Results and consequences of the evaluation process | How are results from the evaluation used and how do they contribute to development in the organisation? | Evaluation use model |

# 3. Philosophical and theoretical underpinnings for VISU

Different paradigms (Burell and Morgan 1979; Lewis and Grimes 1999) underpins research in the IS field (Hirschheim and Klein 1989; Orlikowski and Baroudi 1991; Fitzgerald and Howcroft 1998; Braa and Vidgen 1999; Goles and Hirschheim 2000). Research methods are related to evaluation methods as they concern techniques, and the rigor and relevance thereof, for knowledge development through data collection and analysis. IS evaluation approaches are, as well as research methods, anchored in different paradigms (Lagsten and Karlsson 2006). Methods undergo adaption's and changes in use and better understanding could be attained by examination of paradigmatic values of methods (Päivärinta et al. 2010). Explication of basic assumptions and rationale behind methods is helpful for both method users (practitioners) and method developers (researchers) when using and selecting methods in practice and analyzing methods for further precision and sophistication.

Researchers in the field of IS evaluation has begun to recognise the need for grounding evaluation approaches and studies in the ontology and epistemology of relevant paradigms. Different research perspectives has been proposed: political/social constructivist perspective (Wilson and Howcroft 2005), critical theory (Klecun and Cornford 2005), situated practice/interpretative approach (Jones and Hughes 2001), systems-based approach/biology (Jokela et al. 2008), critical realist perspective (Carlsson 2003).

Methods contain prescribed actions to be performed in order to achieve some task or state. Prescribed activities are anchored in values and goals, performance of the activities are believed to give some consequential effects. Figure 1 illustrates the relation between values, prescribed actions and effects. Values and goals exist on a conceptual level. On the action level prescribed actions are turned into action. Method description is interpreted by method users and adapted to the context at hand and actions are taken. On a consequential level action give rise to effects as consequences of the actions that were performed and the way they were performed.

A method establishes a relationship between the conceptual values that underpins the method and the way that those values appear as practical consequences of method use. This relationship could then be understood as the rationale of the method. The rationale of a method means a specific perspective on the evaluation process. The perspective should inform evaluation actions and the way the evaluator approach evaluation actions. To perform evaluation of information systems according to VISU means to work according to a pragmatic rationality.

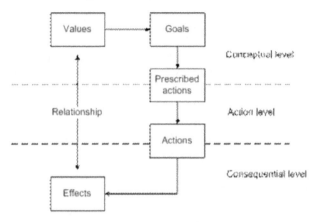

**Figure 1:** Method rationale as the relationship between values in methods and effects of method use (Lagsten 2009) adapted from (Goldkuhl 1993).

A pragmatic evaluation model is founded on five principles drawn from the philosophy of American pragmatism (Peirce 1878/1990; James 1907; Dewey 1931; Rescher 2000). The rationality makes explicit the relation between goals and values that guide prescribed actions in VISU and the effects that are expected as consequences of the action taken. The rationality explains the reasons for why different actions should be carried out by clarifying the connection between values/goals and desired practical effects. This will help evaluators to perform activities in a conscious way and to configure activities according to the situation at hand.

***The Principle of Participation:*** Actors who hold a stake in the information system participate in the evaluation process.

*Values and Goals:* Evaluation is a democratic process where everybody who hold a stake in the IS has the right to be heard. Different stakeholders have different knowledge of the object of evaluation. Different stakeholders have different standards for what is good/bad. Evaluation is an overt and practical process where all decisions are made explicit for all participants.

*Actions:* The evaluation is organised around stakeholders concerns about the IS by the way of dialogue-seminars. The evaluation starts with identifying all stakeholders. The evaluation process is open for inclusion of new stakeholders. Motives and choice of participating stakeholders should be made clear. Stakeholder views are reported separately and jointly. All participants have access to documents produced during the evaluation process.

*Effects:* Comprehensive investigation of the evaluation object. Legitimate evaluation results. The evaluation process establishes a joint view of the evaluation object. Better understanding of the evaluation object as a constellation of conflicting and cooperative interests. Better agenda for action. The evaluation process contributes to shared vocabulary for further dialogue concerning the IS. Understanding and respect between stakeholder groups.

**The Principle of Learning:** Evaluation is carried out as a process of interpretation embodied by dialogue.

*Values and Goals:* Evaluation is a social process carried out through dialogue between individuals. Evaluation is performed as cooperative interpretation where different dialogues are highlighted, between individuals, between stakeholder groups between the IS and the organisation. Genuine dialogue (understandable, truthful, legitimate and sincere assertions, as in Habermas' ideal speech situation) develops reasonable arguments and contributes to individual learning for participants.

*Actions:* Opinions about the IS is generated through dialogues within participating stakeholder groups. The dialogue-seminar starting point is participants' experiences of the IS. Dialogue-seminars are carried out in the condition of genuine dialogue. Dialogue-seminars stimulate learning both within a stakeholder group and between groups.

*Effects:* The evaluation process generates personal knowledge anchored in experiences concerning the IS. Evaluation results grow successively during the process. Evaluation results reflect relevant aspects of the IS within the business context. The character of the evaluation results is customised to participants. Evaluation results are understandable and constitute a basis for individual action.

**The principle of Action:** Evaluation takes actions of individuals as starting point.

*Values and Goals:* Action is significant for everyday knowledge acquisition. Taking action as the starting point means to anchor concepts and abstractions in the practical world. Action should be knowledgeable, knowledge should be actionable.

*Actions:* The evaluation ground in what is being done. The dialogue-seminar is opened with the question of what the participants are doing when using the IS. Evaluation results are marked as measures for action.

*Effects:* Evaluation results are anchored in the practical work with the IS. Evaluation results are relevant. Evaluation results are actionable. Evaluation results guides change through action.

**The Principle of Instrument:** Criteria for the evaluation object are established through the evaluation process.

*Values and Goals:* Values are practical instruments, thinker tools, which help us to live rich and fulfilling lives. Humans strive for change that makes a positive difference. The world is in the making. Values and measures are constantly renegotiated.

*Actions:* Goals and criteria for the IS should be critically scrutinized in the dialogue-seminars. Current goals and criteria for the IS are decided by the stakeholders. Evaluation is a process for deciding upon goals for the IS and measures to reach those goals.

*Effects:* Criteria for the IS represents stakeholder views. The IS is evaluated against current goals and criteria. The IS is evaluated against legitimate goals and criteria. The evaluation results contain the motives for change.

**The Principle of Consequence:** In the evaluation participants take into account consequences of the evaluation.

*Values and Goals:* We as humans investigate our ideas by examining their consequences. The purpose of evaluation is to improve human conditions. Humans are constantly taking actions that change the world and themselves.

*Actions:* Evaluation is a process of intervention. The evaluator count on results produced in the process, from the beginning to the end. The evaluator initially plans the kind and character of results that the process can produce and include activities for transforming results into change and betterment.

*Effects:* The evaluation results in decided change requirements and change measures for different stakeholder groups. The evaluation results in (new) operative knowledge amongst participants. The evaluation results in a joint agenda for action. The evaluation creates arenas for participants to create change and betterment. Evaluation makes change.

By making the paradigmatic values of VISU explicit we hope to enhance learning and use of VISU as well as adaption and elaboration of method components.

# 4. The VISU method

The principal approach in VISU is to ensemble concerns of all stakeholders of the information system in systematic dialogue-seminars. A dialogue-seminar can be compared to a focus group were a special set of questions are addressed and examined by a stakeholder group. The evaluation process is performed in three phases; arrange, evaluate and develop, figure 2.

The process model of VISU put forward an overall view of the evaluation process and the purpose of evaluation to contribute to development and betterment. VISU supports evaluators and assigners to take responsibility of the whole process of evaluation. This is important because initiating activities in the arrange phase to a large extent influence on how the evaluation results later could be used for development. Using evaluation results for development and change consumes time and resources. VISU can be used by an evaluator in order to evaluate an IS in use. In the role as evaluator it is important to have knowledge of ISs, system development and system usage. The evaluator could be a project manager, a skilled system developer or a system manager.

| ARRANGE | EVALUATE | DEVELOP |
|---|---|---|
| Initiate<br>  Form an arena<br>  Understand and describe<br>  the business/practice<br>Identify stakeholders<br>Identify evaluation use<br>Agree on preconditions | Carry out dialogue-seminars<br>Analyse activities, problems,<br>strengths and goals<br>Joint interpretation and valuation | Use evaluation<br>results<br>Report and inform |

**Figure 2:** Process model of VISU

## 4.1    Arrange

In the following section the evaluation process according to VISU is explained by a method description (method-in-concept) and examples from the evaluation of Procapita (method-in-action).

The arrangement phase consists of four main activities:
- Initiate (Form an arena, Understand and describe the business/practice)
- Identify stakeholders
- Identify evaluation use
- Agree on preconditions

***Method-in-concept:***
*Initiate (Form an arena, Understand and describe the business/practice)*
The evaluator creates an arena where the evaluation takes place. Central actors are contacted and the evaluator explains the evaluation process and their role to make sure that the process is comprehensible. The evaluation relies on genuine dialogues and is based on ethics of: openness, participation, stakeholder experience and knowledge, learning, transparent process, critical reflection, comprehensive legitimisation, unconditioned analysis, constructive cooperation and use of evaluation results.

Central actors are those who can assure that knowledgeable stakeholders can participate, in the end of the evaluation they could be involved in implementing the evaluation results. An evaluation board should be set up with experts of the domain. The board assists the evaluator with domain knowledge as work content, documents, tools, laws, rules, routines and contacts. Board members should have knowledge, commitment and mandate to act on information from the evaluation. They also communicate and anchor the evaluation process within other agencies of the organisation. Doing entrée and getting established as evaluator in the organisation is also about building trust. Different actors could have reasons to conceal important information. Trust takes time to build and the evaluator has to openly deal with questions and issues that is raised.

The evaluator need to understand and describe the domain of the IS. The evaluator is not the domain expert – the stakeholders are. But the evaluator is responsible for depicting the IS-domain in a knowledgeable way. A description, as a rich picture, of the IS-domain is helpful when communicating the evaluation process, identifying relevant questions and issues and identifying participating stakeholders. Different techniques or models could be used for the initial description depending on the choice of the organisation or the evaluator.

*Identify stakeholders*

An IS has a multitude of stakeholders. A stakeholder is a person or group that hold a stake in the IS (or in the evaluation). In the evaluation problems, strengths, goals, change requirements and change measures concerning the IS, as seen by its stakeholders, will be reproduced and analysed. Choosing which stakeholders that should participate also means a choice of interests and perspectives that will influence future situation. As many stakeholders as possible should be included in the evaluation process; but the evaluation party has limited recourses. The inclusion of stakeholders is a balance between the need of a rich description and available recourses. Guba and Lincoln (1989) define 3 categories of stakeholders; agents, beneficiaries and victims. People involved with systems development or systems maintenance could be agents, system users could be beneficiaries but they could also be victims. Initially a catalogue of preliminary stakeholders is established, preferably by a brainstorming procedure in the evaluation board. This catalogue is exposed in different contexts (presentations, interviews, dialogue-seminars) and is adjusted and approved during the process. The evaluation is a knowledge creating process; it should be possible to include more stakeholders during the process, reasons for inclusion should be communicated.

*Identify evaluation use*

The question of how to make use of the evaluation results should be addressed from the beginning. Evaluation is pointless if resulting knowledge is not transformed into practice, this transfer needs to be planned. Questions to ask are: Who could make use and maintain the knowledge created in the evaluation? Who will receive the evaluation results and be responsible for transforming them into effects as change and betterment? What ways of working and documenting are possible and available in order make enhance use? Making use of results takes time and consumes recourses, a strategy and plan for transformation of results into effects should be made.

*Agree on preconditions*

Necessary evaluation preconditions is summarised in a document that establishes a frame for the evaluation and a contract.
1. Name of evaluation project.
2. *Assigner.* The name of the person/group that sponsors the evaluation.

3. *Evaluator.* Name and contact information.
4. *Purpose of the evaluation.* VISU supports evaluating ISs from a multi-stakeholder perspective. The initial questions from assigners and an overall purpose are clarified. Assigners are regarded as one stakeholder. The evaluation is open for new questions throughout the process.
5. *Information system.* The definition of the IS embrace both a traditional notion (a software intense system which assembles, stores, processes and delivers information) and social notion (a human activity system relying on technology). The evaluation object should be tentatively defined; it is likely that the evaluation redefines the idea of the IS.
6. *Stakeholders.* Participating stakeholders are specified and the reasons for inclusion, further stakeholders could later be included.
7. *Method and process.* The evaluation method, process and basic values should be described, a timetable is made. The overall process i summarised in figure 3: i) Identify all stakeholders of the IS ii) Through dialogue make an inventory of activities, problems, strengths and goals as seen by stakeholders iii) Summarise change requirements and suggest change measures iv) Establish a joint interpretation and evaluation of the IS.
8. *Evaluation results.* Character and types of evaluation results. A brief plan for use of results.
9. Budget.

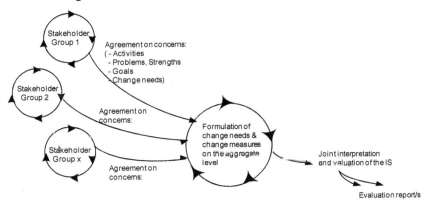

**Figure 3:** Overall evaluation process in VISU

**Method-in-Action**

In the evaluation of Procapita the evaluator put an effort in understanding the IS-domain by meetings with maintenance personnel and the social welfare committee, participating in Procapita education, and studying central documents. A model of the case handling practice was created together with social workers and a rich picture of the IS-domain was depicted (figure 4).

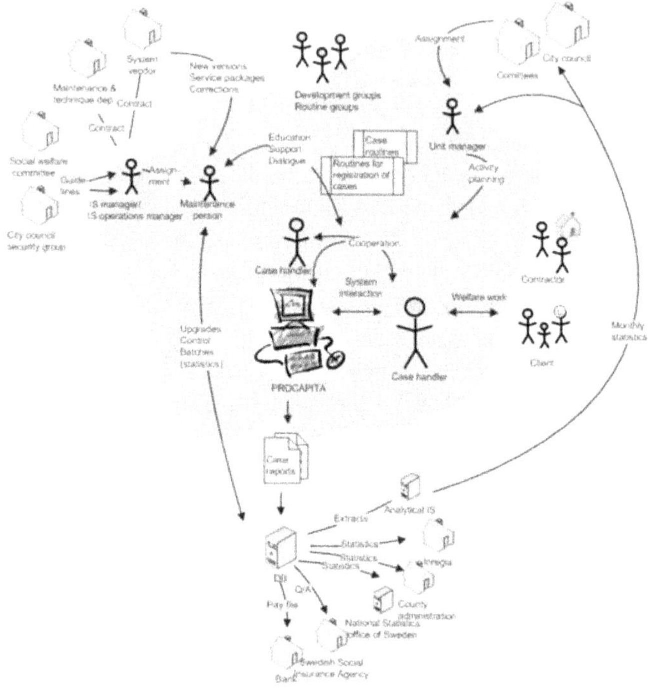

**Figure 4:** The information system Procapita from a stakeholder perspective.

The evaluator informed managers and administrative personnel about the process and they were asked to organise stakeholder participation in the forthcoming dialogue-seminars. An evaluation board was established consisting of the IS manager, the IS operations manager and maintenance people. A stakeholder catalogue was made within a brainstorming procedure in the evaluation board and further refined in presentations and discussions throughout the evaluation (table 3).

Stakeholders were chosen on basis of on their crucial interests in Procapita and their ability to answer the evaluation questions. A contract was drawn stating preconditions of the evaluation. The evaluation object was defined as "the use of Procapita in the case handling practice" and the aim was "to evaluate Procapita as seen by (all) its stakeholders".

The questions that the municipality wanted to resolve was defined as well as method, participating stakeholders, type of results and a timetable. The main question for the IS manager (assigner) was if it was time to terminate Procapita or if the system satisfied the organisational needs. A number of sub questions were also specified: How is the system perceived by its users? Do they have relevant education in system usage? How do unit managers perceive their responsibility for the use of Procapita and the resulting documentation? Why is not all cases handled in Procapita as decided by city council? Is the organisation prepared for eventually terminating Procapita?

**Table 3:** Stakeholders of Procapita

| | | |
|---|---|---|
| System users at financial support unit | IS operations manager | Assigners |
| System users at family homes unit | City council security group | Contact persons |
| System users at family law unit | Central maintenance and technique department | Contact families |
| System users at treatment units | Development group | Family homes |
| System users at investigation unit | Routine group | The Swedish Social Insurance Agency |
| System users at refuge introduction | Care and Social services committees | The bank |
| System users at emergency service unit | Clients | Different Courts |
| Planning officers | Families of clients | National Board of Health and Welfare |
| Unit managers | System vendor | Inregia |
| Elected politicians | Economists | National Statistics office of Sweden |
| Social services committees (east, west) | Measurement people | The union |
| Social welfare committee | County administrative board | Other information systems |
| Maintenance team | | |
| IS manager | | |

## 4.2 Evaluate

The evaluation phase consists of three main activities:

- Carry out dialogue-seminars

- Analyse activities, problems, strengths and goals
- Joint interpretation and valuation

**Method-in-concept:**
*Carry out dialogue-seminars*
In this phase the actual evaluation is carried out through dialogue-seminars. Central organisers of stakeholder concerns are four specific VISU-questions elaborated in the seminars: What do you do while using Procapita? What problems do you perceive? What good does the system do for you? What are the goals you try to achieve?

Participating stakeholders are invited to dialogue-seminars. A dialogue-seminar can be compared to a focus group. The group consists preferably of 5-8 persons that legitimately represent the wider stakeholder group. The seminar builds on the principles of genuine dialogue, participants are assumed to be understandable, truthful, legitimate and sincere. Participants in one seminar should be working with similar tasks and have the same organisational positions. It is not wise to mix persons with employer declarations and employees because of the risk that the employer is given expert power in the group (Wibeck 2000).

A seminar goes on for about 1,5 hour. Depending on the ambition and complexity two (or more) seminars could be held. The routine for each stakeholder group:

- Choose participants from the larger stakeholder group.
- Book a room.
- Send invitation and process description to participants.
- Conduct seminar 1.
- Analyse and summarise working report.
- Send working report to participants for feedback.
- Conduct seminar 2.
- Send working report to participants for validation.
- Publish working report available to all stakeholder groups.

The room should be equipped for drawing/writing together and showing slides; an oval table contribute to an intimate environment. All groups should have the same possibilities to present their concerns.

The routine in each seminar:

- Presentation of participants.
- Presentation of evaluation process/preconditions and task for the dialogue-seminar.
- Dialogue on basis of the VISU-questions.
- Prioritising of problems, strengths and goals.
- Instruction for next seminar.

It is important to start the session with the question on activities, what participants do while using the system, what tasks they perform through the system. Activities are the starting point for the dialogues. In the dialogue insights are given, understanding is raised, concepts are defined, situations are identified, misconceptions are clarified, agreements are held, purposes and objectives are negotiated, conclusions are drawn, actions are planned, language and grammar for the conversation is developed. The process in the seminar is a joint interpretive investigation into the participants concerns of the system based on their situated experience (figure 5).

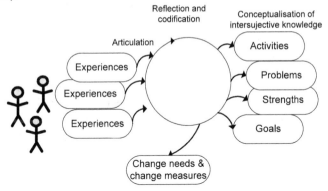

**Figure 5:** The dialogue-seminar in VISU.

*Analyse activities, problems, strengths and goals*
Central organisers of concerns in seminars are four specific VISU-questions:

- What do you do while using Procapita? (Activities)
- What problems do you perceive? (Problems)
- What good does the system do for you? (Strengths)
- What are the goals you try to achieve? (Goals)

Those questions are elaborated in dialogue-seminars and later organise the analysis on an aggregate level. The VISU-questions are other than the evaluation questions and works as tools for gathering information to answer those. VISU-questions build on method components in the method change analysis (Goldkuhl and Röstlinger 2005). In activity analysis activities and their relations into processes are identified. A problem is something unsatisfactory (an itch), a strength is something that is positive/unproblematic and a goal is a desired state. Having described activities, problems, strengths and goals for each stakeholder group it is time to form change requirements and change measures. The overall process of the joint interpretation process is described in figure 6. A change requirement is a need for something to be changed; it is the difference between a problem situation and the corresponding goal situation. A change requirement comprises a step between problem and measure. Formulating change requirements give opportunity for alternative measures and a frame for creating different change proposals (Goldkuhl and Röstlinger 2003).

Identification of change requirements and measures has already begun in the dialogue-seminars. The last step in the evaluation is to identify change requirements for each stakeholder group and to form change measures aggregated for all participating stakeholders. This could be done either in a closing dialogue-seminar with representatives from all participating stakeholder groups or by the evaluator herself or in the evaluation board. A seminar is to prefer to establish a confirmed overall picture. The evaluator needs to prepare documentation that illuminate and structure stakeholder concerns.

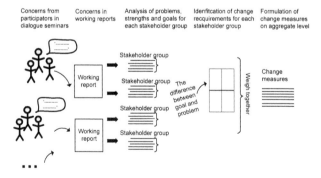

**Figure 6:** The joint interpretation process in VISU.

18

**Method-in-action:**
In the evaluation phase 16 dialogue-seminars were held. The stakeholders represented were users (five different groups), unit managers, maintenance, and IS management. Each group (3-7 individuals) had two seminars taking two hours in general. Each seminar was documented in a working report articulating stakeholder concerns arranged by activities, problems, strengths and goals. In between the first and second seminar participants got the report by e-mail. In the second seminar the group made refinements and validated the report. All reports were successively published on the Intranet. Parallel with the ongoing dialogue-seminars the evaluation board analysed the reports and some immediate changes were made.

After the dialogue-seminars were carried out the evaluator analysed the working reports according to statements on activities, problems (400 altogether), strengths (50) and goals (70). For each stakeholder an account was written. For example, users (case handlers) carried out 40%-80% of their working hours through Procapita, main activities were to: document errands, write journal notes, make investigations, take decisions, follow-up decisions and search for information. Main concerns (problems, strengths and goals) for users are shown in table 4. Change requirements for the four stakeholders were described as in table 5.

**Table 4:** Main problems, strengths and goals recognised by Users

| Problems (main areas) | Strengths | Goals |
|---|---|---|
| Procapita (P) consumes time and energy<br>P takes time to learn<br>The GUI brings a cognitive workload<br>Functions have unclear consequences<br>Week models for standard cases in P<br>Functions are missing/poor<br>Lack of support for document handling<br>Data are saved on local discs<br>Wrong information is saved in P<br>Unclear rules for content in case documentation<br>Sometimes P is not accessible<br>Maintenance routines do not fully support user needs<br>Information from P is not fully reliable | Good functionality for statistics<br>Provide legal security.<br>Give overview of cases<br>Provide good coordination of cases<br>Good support organisation<br>Necessary functionality<br>Simple<br>General positive judgements (i.e. works good for me) | Correct help to clients<br>High legal security for client<br>Correct statistics<br>Effective routines for cases<br>Good coordination of cases<br>Correct data in P<br>Correct documentation of case<br>Good knowledge of handling P for case handlers |

**Table 5:** Change requirements of Users, Unit managers, Maintenance team and IS managers.

| Users | Unit managers |
|---|---|
| Better GUI<br>Better support for handling documents in P<br>All templates should be implemented and be correct<br>Improvement of some of the functions in P<br>Deepened knowledge on case registration<br>More and adjusted education<br>Handle corrections in case documentation<br>Uniform case documentation<br>Clear case models<br>Access to handle templates in P<br>Test cases<br>Bettered computer skills<br>Practical information security skills<br>Information on status of Procapita maintenance activities | Fine-tune statistical information to fit the units<br>Better knowledge on the statistical tool in P<br>Modified access to cases to enable cooperation |
| **Maintenance team** | **IS managers** |
| Bug-free versions and fixes from the vendor<br>Information on status of Procapita maintenance from vendor<br>Few wrongly registered cases /less correction work<br>More case handlers following the education<br>Adjust their P courses to fit different user groups<br>More straight client-contractor model<br>More effective work in the development group | Increased undertaking of P from the units<br>Explicit interface between maintenance team and unit managers<br>More rigor in inquiries before ordering of new functions from vendor<br>Accuracy in judgements concerning if P satisfies the needs in the organisation |

Having identified change requirements of the different stakeholders change measures aggregated for all stakeholders were formed. A range of change measures were identified and described under following labels:

1. Wash away usability problems from the interface
2. Develop adjusted education
3. Develop conceptual models for cases and registration
4. Demand bug-free versions and fixes from the vendor
5. Establish an arena for communication between units and maintenance
6. Explicate the interface between practice and maintenance
7. Assess and evaluate continuously.

## 4.3 Develop

The development phase consists of two main activities:

- Use evaluation results
- Report and inform

*Method-in-concept:*
*Use evaluation results*
One major reason for doing evaluations is to take actions based on the results and therefore the phase of development is emphasized in VISU. The results produced in the evaluation should be used in order to develop the IS and the practice. As shown in figure 7 the evaluation process is a temporary practice related to several continual practices. (Findings on evaluation results and uses have earlier been reported from the study in Lagsten and Goldkuhl 2008).

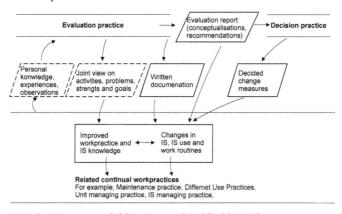

**Figure 7:** Evaluation use model (Lagsten and Goldkuhl 2008)

Continual practices could be system maintenance, different sub practices use of the IS, management and management of the IT function. The evaluation practice is concerned with these continual practices and is furnished with knowledge from them through the participating stakeholders. Stakeholders/participants go back and forth between the temporary evaluation and their respective ordinary workpractice. They bring experiences from their practices to the evaluation and they gain insights from the evaluation dialogue-seminars which they bring back to their workpractices. The evaluation produces gradually written documentation which participants also can bring back. Participation in the evaluation yields learning about their workpractice. These new insights may be turned into changed behaviour in

21

workpractices and even in immediate changes in routines, IS uses or in the IS. There is a flow of knowledge from the evaluation practice to the ordinary workpractices during the conduct of evaluation. People may not wait until the evaluation process has come to an end and a formal report is written to start changing their workpractices. New insights are often imperative to action. What is described here is process use during the evaluation. One essential result from the evaluation is, of course, the written evaluation report which comprises documented learnings about the evaluation object and recommendations for future actions. Such report is often handled in some official decision context, a decision practice. Decision makers make deliberations based on the report and produce formal decisions, which often will be change measures to be implemented in the ordinary workpractices.

*Report and inform*

In the process, working reports from dialogue-seminars has been produced. An overall evaluation report describes the different stakeholders interpretations and concerns for the IS and the context from their point of view. The purpose is to offer understanding for different stakeholders concerns and change requirements. It is important that readers of a report can make their own sense and judgements of the situational context and suggestions. A traditional report might not always be recognized as the most useful way of communicating results for different audiences especially if the aim of the evaluation is formative. The way of reporting should be adapted for the audience to facilitate use. Results can be reported as working reports, requirement specifications, routine descriptions, use cases, term catalogues, risks, problem analysis, design proposals, glossaries, revised plans, goal analysis, information/decision meetings, PowerPoint presentations, specifications for education etc. Reports should have apparent receivers and evident purpose for use.

The way of communicating results should be discussed at the end of the evaluation phase. The use of evaluation results demands resources that should have been planned in the arrangement phase that may need some adjustments. Participating stakeholders should be informed about communication and use of results.

**Method-in-action:**
Each dialogue-seminar produced a working report that gave account of the stakeholder groups concerns, these reports were successively published on the Intranet available to all staff. The evaluation board had also analyzed all working reports and identified and documented change requirements for maintenance, some changes were made immediately. An evaluation report was written containing a comprehensive model of the system from a multiple-stakeholder perspective, accounts of problems, strengths and goals for the different stakeholders. The report concluded with identified measures and discussion on the initial evaluation questions. Seminars were held to discuss the findings. The evaluator finally gave a presentation of the evaluation report for the social welfare committee and the IS manager got the assignment from the committee to write a detailed plan on how to act upon findings and knowledge from the evaluation.

Changes and development steamed out from the evaluation process. In a follow-up of the dialogue-seminars participants stated that "it has contributed to reflective thinking about Procapita", "you get to learn new ways and shortcuts on how to handle Procapita", "gives the side-effect that we discuss case handling in the group" and "gets a joint and overall picture of the system". A person from maintenance expressed "it has been a long journey and I have struggled back and forth with my opinion but now I feel satisfied with the system. It's a good system". The IS manager meant that "the maintenance personnel have adopted a new approach – they have taken on a user perspective". Several projects were planned and some begun during the evaluation (concerning roles, templates, education, logging, text editing). The maintenance team delivered more precise demands on the vendor and performed more careful investigations in ongoing projects. Some fixes were also made in Procapita.

The IS manager decided not to terminate the system but to renegotiate the contract with the vendor. The evaluation process gave rise to diffusion in other areas than the focal matters of the evaluation. An information security education for 250 managers within the municipality were held, the IS-manager explained "the insights from the evaluation gave me the extra strength to negotiate the funding for the education that was not planned for in this budget". Another example was that a new element, evaluation, was incorporated in the business plan for the maintenance unit.

# 5. Implications for practice and research

For a long time there has been a call for interpretive IS evaluation methods. This research contributes with a comprehensible method, VISU, for doing evaluation of an information system as a joint act of interpretation. VISU is one way to operationalise an interpretive evaluation approach. VISU has shown to be a useful method for conducting an evaluation that gives answers to relevant questions, VISU also supports use of evaluation results.

There is also an interesting philosophical issue raised in this paper. We have suggested that by enveloping the interpretive IS evaluation model in the philosophy of pragmatism the interpretive IS evaluation model acquire a foundation for change and betterment that makes the interpretive model more efficient and uncomplicated to operate into a method for practical use. Making paradigmatic values explicit enhances learning and use of evaluation methods as well as configuration and further elaboration of method components.

The process model of VISU can stimulate researchers in the IS field to better understand and study the process of evaluation. In the model the evaluation phase is enclosed by an arrangement phase and a phase of development supporting the use of the evaluation in the practical setting. VISU emphasizes that evaluation is to be understood as a process carried out by people and that evaluation is an intervention with its own set of activities. This is in line with the Evaluation Logic Model (Mark and Henry 2004) which describes evaluation according to inputs, activities, outputs and utilization.

The evaluation use model is useful when planning evaluation processes in order to provide understanding on what kind of results an evaluation can produce and how to make use of these results. The model gives a contribution to the research on IS evaluation as well by shedding light on how evaluation influences on people and practices.

Overall it seems like people, through participating in the evaluation process, elaborate on the importance of needs and changes and develop the final motives that make up their minds on which changes to go on and work with.

# References

Avgerou, C. (1995). "Evaluating Information Systems by Consultation and Negotiation." International Journal of Information Management 15(6): 427-436.

Baskerville, R. and M. D. Myers (2004). "Special Issue on Action Research in Information Systems: Making IS Research Relevant to Practice - Foreword." MIS Quarterly 28(3): 329-335.

Baskerville, R. and J. Pries-Heje (1999). "Grounded action research: a method for understanding IT in practice." Accounting Management & Information Technology 9: 1-23.

Braa, K. and R. Vidgen (1999). "Interpretation, intervention, and reduction in the organizational laboratory: a framework for in-context information system research." Accounting Management and Information Technologies(9): 25–47.

Burell, G. and G. Morgan (1979). Sociological paradigms an organisational analysis. London, Heinemann.

Carlsson, S. A. (2003). Advancing Information Systems Evaluation (Research): A Critical Realist Approach. European Conference on Information Technology Evaluation (ECITE-2003), Madrid.

Dewey, J. (1931). The development of American pragmatism. Philosophy and Civilization.

Farbey, B., F. Land and D. Targett (1999). "The moving staircase Problems of appraisal and evaluation in a turbulent environment." Information Technology & People 12(3): 238-252.

Fitzgerald, B. and D. Howcroft (1998). "Towards Dissolution of the IS Research Debate: From Polarisation to Polarity." Journal of Information Technology Special issue on research methods.

Fitzgerald, B., N. Russo and E. Stolterman (2002). Information Systems Development: Methods in Action. Berkshire, McGraw-Hill.

Goldkuhl, G. (1993). Välgrundad metodutveckling, Linköpings universitet.

Goldkuhl, G. (2004). Meanings of pragmatism: Ways to conduct information systems research. ALOIS (Action in Language, Organisations and Information Systems) 2004, Linköping, Sverige, Linköpings universitet.

Goldkuhl, G. and A. Röstlinger (2003). The significance of workpractice diagnosis: Socio-pragmatic ontology and epistemology of change analysis. ALOIS (Action in Language, Organisations and Information Systems) 2003, Linköping, Sverige, Linköpings universitet.

Goldkuhl, G. and A. Röstlinger (2005). Change Analysis – Innovation and Evolution. Invited paper to the 14th International Conference on Information Systems Development (ISD), Karlstad, Sweden.

Goles, T. and R. Hirschheim (2000). "The paradigm is dead, the paradigm is dead...long live the paradigm: the legacy of Burell and Morgan." The International Journal of Management Science, OMEGA 28: 249-268.

Guba, E. and Y. Lincoln (1989). Fourth Generation Evaluation. Newbury Park, SAGE.

Hirschheim, R. and H. K. Klein (1989). "Four paradigms of information systems development." Communications of the ACM 32(10): 1199-1216.

Hirschheim, R. and S. Smithson (1999). Evaluation of Information Systems: a Critical Assessment. Beyond the II Productivity Paradox. Willcocks and Lester. Chichester, John Wiley & Sons.

Irani, Z., A. M. Sharif and P. E. D. Love (2005). "Linking knowledge transformation to Information Systems Evaluation." European Journal of Information Systems 14: 213-228.

James, W. (1907). What pragmatism means. Pragmatism, A New Name For Some Old Ways of Thinking. New York.

Jokela, P., P. Karlsudd and M. Östlund (2008). "Theory, Method and Tools for Evaluation Using a Systems-based approach." The Electronic Journal of Information Systems Evaluation 11(3): 197-212.

Jones, S. and J. Hughes (2001). "Understanding IS evaluation as a complex social process: a case study of a UK local authority." European Journal of Information Systems 10: 189-203.

Klecun, E. and T. Cornford (2005). "A Critical Approach to Evaluation." European Journal of Information Systems 14: 229-243.

Lagsten, J. (2009). Utvärdera informationssystem – Pragmatiskt perspektiv och metod. (Doctoral thesis in Swedish, Evaluating Information Systems: Pragmatic perspective and method), Department of Management and Engineering, Linköping Universitty Linköping University Electronic Press.

Lagsten, J. and G. Goldkuhl (2008). "Interpretive IS Evaluation: Results and Uses." Electronic Journal of Information Systems Evaluation (EJISE) 11(2): 97-108.

Lagsten, J. and F. Karlsson (2006). Multiparadigm analysis - clarity into information systems evaluation. ECITE, European Conference on Information Technology Evaluation, Italy, Genoa.

Lewis, M. W. and A. J. Grimes (1999). "Metatriangulation: Building Theory from Multiple Paradigms." Academy of Management Review 24(4): 672-690.

Mark, M. and G. Henry (2004). "The Mechanisms and Outcomes of Evaluation Influence." Evaluation 10(1): 25-57.

Orlikowski, W. J. and J. J. Baroudi (1991). "Studying information technology in organizations: research approaches and assumptions." Information Systems Research 2(1).

Peirce, C. S., Ed. (1878/1990). Hur våra idéer kan göras klara. Pragmatism och kosmologi. Göteborg, Daidalos.

Päivärinta, T., M. K. Sein and T. Peltola (2010). "From ideals towards practice: paradigmatic mismatches and drifts in method deployment." Information Systems Journal 20: 481-516.

Rescher, N. (2000). Realistic Pragmatism - An Introduction to Pragmatic Philosophy. Albany, State University of New York Press.

Serafeimidis, V. and S. Smithson (2000). "Information systems evaluation in practice: A case study of organizational change." Journal of Information Technology(15): 93 - 105.

Strauss, A. and J. Corbin (1998). Basics of Qualitative Research. Techniques and Procedures for Developing Grounded Theory. Thousand Oaks, USA, Sage Publications.

Susman, G. and R. Evered (1978). "An assessment of the Scientific Merits of Action Research." Administrative Science Quarterly 23(4): 582-603.

Symons, V. (1991). "A review of information systems evaluation: content, context, process." European Journal of Information Systems 1(3): 205-212.

Symons, V. and G. Walsham (1988). "The evaluation of information systems: a critique." Journal of Applied Systems Analysis 15.

Walsham, G. (1999). Interpretive Evaluation Design for Information Systems. Beyond the IT Productivity Paradox. Willcocks and Lester. Chichester, John Wiley & Sons.

Wibeck, V. (2000). Fokusgrupper. Om fokuserade gruppintervjuer som undersökningsmetod. . Lund, Studentlitteratur.

Wilson, M. and D. Howcroft (2005). "Power, politics and persuasion in IS evaluation: a focus on 'relevant social groups' " The Journal of Strategic Information Systems 14(1): 17-43.

# Confirmatory factor analysis of service quality dimensions within mobile telephony industry in Ghana

Simon Gyasi Nimako[1], Foresight Kofi Azumah[2], Francis Donkor[1] and Veronica Adu-Brobbey[1]
[1]University of Education, Winneba, Ghana
[2]CleverIdeaz Research Consultant, Kumasi, Ghana

*Originally published in EJISE (2012) Volume 15, ISS 2*

## Editorial Commentary

Mobile telephony is fundamental to Africa's growth, as evidenced by the rapid penetration levels experienced on the continent since the early 2000s. In 2014, GSMA (www.gsma.com) reported that Sub-Saharan Africa (SSA) has been the fastest growing region over the last five years, in terms of both unique mobile subscribers and connections. Models for using service quality approaches for evaluating IS, evident in the literature from the 1990s, have been the subject of much debate. In essence, such approaches provide a user-oriented perspective of various facets of IS quality. Models for evaluating mobile telephony service on the African continent are therefore critical to ensure that customers are able to harness the benefits of mobile service given that there is evidence of links to both social and economic development. This paper takes an important step towards this. Models such as the one posited in this paper will likely provide a tool for regulators to harness the proposed instrument to monitor the effectiveness of operators. Importantly, the evaluation of service-side telecommunications will point to key technical and hardware side issues. The operation and mainstreaming of such models will also be able to inform policy development in the telecommunications space.

**Abstract:** Due to the increasing importance and investment in modern information systems (IS) technologies, the evaluation of service quality (SQ) in information system environments has attracted significant attention and debate in the literature. Much effort has been made by scholars and practitioners to use IS service quality criteria and dimensions in different industry contexts. Not much attention has been devoted to using other SQ model criteria and dimensions to evaluate information systems in the mobile telephony industry (MTI) context. This study fills the gap, and contributes to the body of knowledge in the area SQ in the MTI environment.

This paper, which was a part of a larger study, sought to empirically validate SQ dimensions that are relevant to the mobile telephony industry in Ghana. It used Confirmatory Factor Analysis (CFA) to detect the underlying latent variables that significantly determine SQ in Ghana's MTI. 1000 customers were sampled from four mobile telecom operators in Ghana in a cross-sectional survey that used a self-administered structured questionnaire for data collection. The findings indicate that four emerged SQ dimensions relevant to Ghana's MTI were labelled as: Customer relations, Image, Tangibles and Real network quality. Cronbach alpha reliability for all items indicated a high value of 0.918. Service providers could conveniently use the derived instrument items for measuring service quality in Ghana Mobile Telephony industry. It concludes that aside the popular SERVQUAL, alternative SQ models model, like one conceptualised in this study, could be useful in determining SQ dimensions relevant to MTI. Limitations and directions for research are discussed.

**Keywords:** Service quality, SERVQUAL model, Technical and Functional Quality Model, mobile telephony industry, factor analysis.

# 1. Introduction

The need for business organisations to focus on improving service quality in order to remain competitive and influence customer behaviour has long been recognised in the literature (Grönroos 1990; 2001; Kotler & Keller 2006; Lovelock & Wirtz 2007). Service quality has been noted in many studies as a significant antecedent of customer satisfaction and customer loyalty (Parasuraman, Zeithaml, & Berry 1988; Rust and Oliver 1994; Spreng & Mackoy 1996; Voss, Rosenzweig, Blackmon & Chase 2004; Zeithaml & Bitner 2003). SQ evaluation from consumer's perspective was described by Grönroos (1982) as Consumer Perceived Quality (CPQ). CPQ has been differently conceptualised by many authors and has resulted in the proliferation of many models of service quality, each of which is context specific with unique features (Nitin Deshmukh & Vrat 2005). While existing literature on service quality for mobile telephony in emerging economies context is limited, those that exist are country specific. Therefore the purpose of this paper is to identify the latent variables for service quality dimensions most relevant to MTI in Ghana using factor analysis.

# 2. Literature Review and Conceptual Framework

## 2.1 The Mobile Telephony Research Context

Many previous studies suggest that further research is required to investigate whether the service quality dimensions proposed in service quality models apply to other different industry contexts (April & Pather 2008; Molla & Licker, 2001; Nitin et al. 2005; Newman & Cowling 1996; Parasuraman, et al. 1988). The mobile telephony industry like many service organisations has unique features that are relevant to customer requirements different from the traditional goods industries. Though MTI could be classified as an Information System (IS) environment for which IS-service quality models may be applicable, it is argued that, the industry is a unique wireless electronic environment with unique mobile services delivery from mobile network operators to individual consumer (B2C) and industrial customers (B2B). Such uniqueness may have relevant implications for what quality of network services consumers (B2C) expect from service providers and the relative worth of each service quality dimension. The uniqueness of MTI, apart from its distinctiveness as a sector, lies in terms of the impact of the industry on consumer life. It appears that it is one industry among the information systems category that is ubiquitous, giving access to the use of mobile telecommunication services to the largest number of individuals in both developed and developing countries (ITU, 2010). Mobile telecommunication service in Ghana is not only becoming a necessity for business and social life, but also it is one of the information system services category that is easy to use and has been widely used by illiterates and literates everywhere in cities, rural and urban communities.

The deregulation of Ghana's mobile industry since 1994 has allowed new private mult-national entrants into Ghana MTI, which has contributed to the fierce competition among the service providers in the industry (Addy-Nayo 2001; Frempong & Henten 2004; Ghana NCA 2010). Delivering high SQ has, therefore, become a major concern for the mobile network operators in Ghana. The SQ of the industry may include dimensions different from other service contexts studied in the literature. Thus, customers may expect many different dimensions of the SQ relating to service quality expected to be delivered by mobile network operators. It would be a useful contribution to increase understanding of the constructs and dimensions of SQ relevant to the MTI in Ghana in the B2C context.

## 2.2 Service Quality Concept

The literature is filled with proliferation of different definitions for service quality from different perspectives. It is defined as the extent to which a service meets customers' needs or expectations (Asubonteng, McCleary, & Swan 1996). In Parasuraman et al. (1988), SQ is defined as a form of attitude, which could be related to satisfaction but not equivalent to it that results from a comparison of expectations with perceptions of performance. SQ as perceived by consumers is often termed consumer-perceived quality (CPQ). Grönroos in 1982 was the first to define the CPQ as the confirmation (or disconfirmation) of a consumer's expectations of service compared with the customer's perception of the service actually received. In the work of Edvardsson (2005:128), the author noted that "customer perception of service quality is beyond cognitive assessment as it is formed during the production, delivery and consumption of services and not just at the consumption stage." This is achieved as customers play their role as co-producers by carrying out activities as well as being part of interactions that influence both process quality and outcome quality. The concept of SQ from the customer perspective, therefore, includes not only what (outcome) the consumer expects, but also how the consumer is served (Grönroos 2001:151).

SQ is not just a corporate offering, but a competitive weapon which is necessary for corporate profitability and survival (Anderson, Fornell, and Lehmann 1994; Grönroos 1990; Newman & Cowling 1996; Rosen, Karwan, & Scribner 2003). Successful modern organisations no longer compete only on cost but more importantly on service/product quality. In a competitive environment like the MTI, delivering quality service is seen as a key differentiator and has increasingly become a key element of business strategy (Heskett, Sasser & Schlesinger, 1997; Kotler & Keller, 2006).Thus, in most service context, SQ is a critical business requirement (Voss, 2003, Voss et al. 2004) that is driven by employee satisfaction, which also drives customer satisfaction, which in turn drives customer loyalty and retention that eventually leads to profitability and growth, as proposed in the Service-Profit Chain (Heskett, Jones, Loveman, Sasser, Schlesinge 1994).

# 3. Service Quality in Information Systems Context

There have been several attempts by scholars to understand, evaluate and identify key factors that determine quality of information systems from the end-user perspective. As a result, some significant effort has been made by scholars and practitioners in the information systems literature on electronic service quality (E-service quality). E-service, according to Rowley (2006), refers to deeds, efforts, or performances whose delivery is mediated by information technology. Generally, it can be described as an interactive content-centered and internet-based customer service that is driven by customers and integrated with the support of technologies and systems offered by service providers, which aim at strengthening the customer-provider relationship (Cronin 2003; Zeithaml, Parasuraman, Malhotra 2000). Given the technology quality dimensions of e-service quality that are different from the traditional service context, e-service quality has been regarded having the potential to not only deliver strategic benefits but also to enhance operational efficiency and profitability.

A review of existing literature indicates that, results from many previous studies identified different dimensions for e-service quality in different research contexts (Li and Suomi 2009; Ho and Lin 2010). DeLone and McLean (1992) developed their first IS model and classified IS effectiveness measures into six categories. Later they revised it to include service quality in their Updated D&M IS success model (DeLone & McLean 2003). Dabholkar (1996) also found the following e-service quality aspects: site design, reliability, delivery, ease of use, enjoyment and control in the context of E-service. Zeithaml et al (2000) found these six critical dimension factors: Efficiency, reliability, fulfillment, privacy, responsiveness, compensation, and e-service quality dimensions in the online retailing context. Moreover, Zeithaml et al. (2000) proposed a 7-dimension instrument for measuring e-service quality called E-S-QUAL using the SERVQUAL in the traditional distribution channels in a study on internet service quality.

Zeithaml et al. (2002) again conducted a study in which they compared the SERVQUAL and the E-S-QUAL and concluded that though some traditional SERVQUAL dimensions can be applied to e-service quality, there are other unique dimensions of e-service quality that related to technology. The original E-S-QUAL consisted of 11 dimensions and later condensed into 7 by Parasuraman et al. (2005), which were split into core dimensions and the recovery dimensions. The core dimensions, termed E-S-QUAL, are: efficiency, system availability, fulfilment and privacy. The recovery dimensions, termed E-RecS-QUAL are: responsiveness, compensation and contact (Parasuraman et al. 2005). Yoo and Douthu (2001) also found that ease of use,

31

aesthetic design, processing speed and security were important factors in online retailing.

Moreover, Wolfinbarger and Gilly (2003) found these four e-service quality aspects: web site appearance, communication, accessibility, credibility, understanding and availability as critical factors in online retailing. Lee and Lin (2005) developed e-service model including web site design, reliability, responsiveness, trust, and personalization in the online retailing context. Furthermore, Field, Heim & Sinha (2004) identified website design, reliability, security and customer service aspects of e-service dimensions. Kim et al. (2006) identified nine e-service quality items, being: efficiency, fulfilment, system availability, privacy, responsiveness, compensation, contact, information and graphic style in online retailing. More recently, in Li and Suomi (2009) eight dimensions of e-service quality were proposed, which were: website design, reliability, responsiveness, security, fulfilment, personalization, information and empathy. In empirical work of Cristobal (2007) and Ho and Lin (2010) the following service quality dimension were found in Internet banking context, these were: web design, customer service, assurance, preferential treatment and information provision. Pather & Usabuwera (2010) also identified and proposed seven items for e-service quality items, namely: reliability, security, appearance/aesthetics, availability/access, ease of use, responsiveness and communication.

The above review shows that different dimensions have been found in different industry context in the IS literature, and that very little attention has been devoted to understanding IS service quality criteria and dimensions in mobile telephony context.

# 4.   Evaluating Service Quality in IS Contexts

## 4.1   SERVQUAL-based IS Service Quality

Many studies have generally found useful the inclusion of service quality perspective to IS user satisfaction research, some such as Kim (1990), Watson et al. (1993) and Pitt et al. (1995) specifically recommend the SERVQUAL as a measure of IS success. Kettinger and Lee (1997) developed and empirically validated, using factor analysis methods, a condensed 13-item scale called IS-SERVQUAL based on the 22-item SERVQUAL instrument for the IS environment, to reflect IS specific issues such as software, hardware and computer technology. In this regard, DeLone and McLean (1992) after developing their first DeLone and McLean (D&M) IS success model for classifying the multitude of effectiveness measures into six categories, revised it to include service quality in their Updated D&M IS success model (DeLone & McLean 2003). Their conceptualisation of SQ was based on SERVQUAL model by Parasuraman et al. (1988).

The basis of the IS service quality model in many previous studies (e.g. DeLone & McLean 2003) was the SERVQUAL model that was originally proposed by Parasuraman, Zeithaml and Berry in 1985 and modified in 1988 in the Extended GAP model (Figure 1).

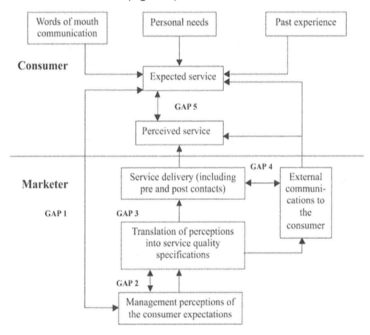

Source: Parasuraman *et al.* (1985)

**Figure 1:** The Extended Gap Model of Service Quality

In their model, the authors conceptualised service quality as a five dimensional construct, to develop the popularly known SERVQUAL instrument. The five SERVQUAL dimensions are: Tangibles, Empathy, Assurance, Reliable, and Responsiveness. Tangibles are the physical facilities, equipment, and appearance of personnel. Empathy refers to the caring, individualised attention the firm provides its customers. Assurance means knowledge and courtesy of employees and their ability to inspire trust and confidence. Reliability is the ability to perform the promised service dependably and accurately, and Responsiveness refers to willingness to help customers and provide prompt service. The items for each of the dimensions have been modified in many previous studies to suit a particular context as noted by Parasuraman et al. (1988:31) that the SERVQUAL instrument could be *"adapted or supplemented to fit the characteristics or specific research needs of a particular organisation".*

However, other researchers such as van Dyke et al. (1997) have controverted the validity and usefulness of SERVQUAL in the IS environment. Again the use of the SERVQUAL model itself has received several criticisms from many authors (Asubonteng et al. 1996; Babakus and Boller 1992; Cronin & Taylor 1992) for different scores, its dimensionality, applicability and the lack of validity of the model, notably the dependence or independence of the five main variables.

Whereas in many IS contexts, the SERVQUAL model-based IS Service Quality criteria and dimensions have been used extensively in evaluating IS service quality (Kettinger and Lee 1997; Kang and Bradley 2002; Park and Kim 2005), little attention has been given to the use of other alternative models of service quality in evaluating IS quality in the mobile telephony context.

*Alternative Service Quality Model for Mobile Telephony Industry*
In the empirical work of Nitin, Deshmukh and Vrat (2005) on service quality models, the authors found nineteen models of service quality that have been postulated by different authors in different service contexts with different but equivalent dimensions. The earliest model the authors found was the Technical and Functional Quality Model of Christian Grönroos (1984). In his model, SQ is conceptualised as a three-dimension construct, namely: technical quality; functional quality; and image (see Figure 2). He believes that the customer evaluations of perceived performance of service against his/her perceived service quality result in a measure of service quality. He explains Technical Quality as the quality of what consumer actually receives as a result of his/her interaction with the service firm and is important to him/her and to his/her evaluation of the quality of service. Functional quality is how he/she gets the technical outcome. This is important to him/her and to his/her views of service he/she has received.

Image, which could be referred to as reputational quality, is very important to service firms and this can be expected to build up mainly by technical and functional quality of service including factors such as tradition, ideology, word of mouth, pricing and public relations. Although, this model has not been widely adopted and applied in many research contexts as compared to the SERVQUAL of Parasuraman et al. (1988), few authors like Bozorgi (2007) and Gi-Du and James (2004) who applied it recommended for different settings.

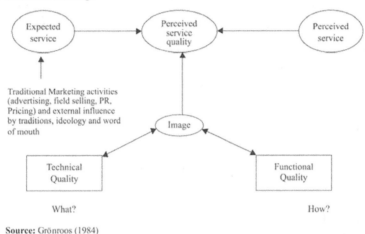

**Source:** Grönroos (1984)

**Figure 2:** Grönroos Model of Service Quality

## 4.2 Justification for the Alternative SQ model

After reviewing many service quality models, Grönroos' (1984) model of service quality was selected in understanding service quality dimensions that may be relevant to the mobile telephony industry. The Model was deemed most appropriate for the study for three reasons. First it is comprehensive in that it includes not only functional quality as portrayed by Parasuraman *et al.* (1988) but also technical quality as well as image, which is more realistic of today's dynamic global marketplace than what functional-quality-only models portray. Gi-Du and James (2004: 266) applied the model in a similar mobile telecom setting and concluded that, "The results from a cell phone service sample revealed that Grönroos' model is a more appropriate representation of service quality than the American perspective (SERVQUAL model) with its limited concentration on the dimension of functional quality." Second, the model is more suitable for mobile telecommunication context. Nitin, et al (2005: 946) noted that "the service quality outcome and measurement is dependent on type of service, setting, situation, time need, etc. factors." The mobile telecom market is a type of service industry in which customers place much importance not only on how they are served (functional quality), but also and more importantly, on outcome or nature of services they receive and experience which constitute technical quality variables like network quality (Wang & Lo 2002; Gi-Du and James 2004). Third, the model is empirically validated by Gi-Du and James (2004) and has been applied by Bozorgi (2007) who recommends it for different mobile telecom context. The validated model is displayed in Figure 3.

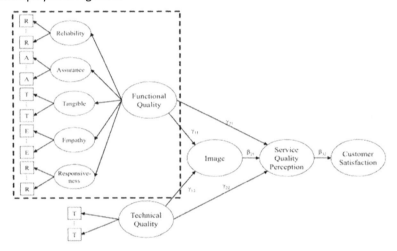

**Figure 3:** Grönroos Service Quality Model

*Source: Grönroos (2000 cited in Gi Du & James 2004: 269).*

For the above reasons, service quality is conceptualised to include all three dimensions of Grönroos' SERVQUAL model, namely: functional quality, technical quality and image or reputational quality.

Rust & Oliver (1994), and more recently also Hume & Mort (2008) contend that 'value' is a significant dimension of SQ that significantly affects customer satisfaction. Value is considered what the consumer gives in exchange for what he gets. "Value" could be described as the value for money or how economical services are to customers. Consequently, "value" will be termed "economy" dimension, and in this study, will be included separately as a fourth dimension of service quality. Therefore, the conceptual framework for this study has four dimensions of SQ, namely: Functional, Technical, Image and Economy SQ dimensions (Figure 4). A factor analysis approach is applied to determine the relevant dimensions in mobile telecom context.

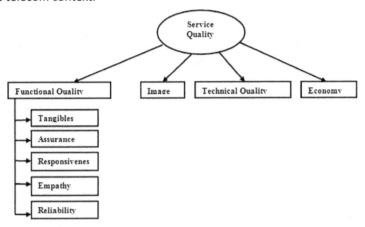

**Figure 4:** Emerged Framework

*Source: Based on Grönroos (1984); Parasuraman, Zeithaml & Berry (1985); Hume & Mort (2008) and Rust & Oliver (1994)*

# 5. Methodology

## 5.1 Sampling

In order to collect data of high quality that reflect customers' opinion, a survey was conducted from the four mobile telecom networks in Ghana in 2008; namely: Scancom Ghana Limited operators of MTN, Millicom Ghana Limited operators of Tigo, Ghana Telecom operators of Onetouch, and Kasapa telecom. For anonymity, each of the four companies used in this study is represented by a letter (A, B, C and D). A convenient sample size of 1000 respondents was selected from the four networks. Conscious effort was made to select literate respondents. The survey yielded a response rate of 93.7%, of which 601 customers were from Company A, 140 customers from Company B, 40 from Company C and 156 customers from Company D. These numbers were adequate since a minimum sample of 30 is considered a large sample size for statistical analysis (Cooper and Schindler, 2006).

Research Instrument Design

A self-administered, structured questionnaire was used to collect data from respondents as recommended for a large survey (Saunders 2000; Cooper and Schindler 2006; Malhotra & Birks 2007). Based on the recommendations of Danaher and Haddrell (1996), Devlin, Dong & Brown (1993) and Rust & Oliver (1994) we appropriately adopted five-point disconfirmation scales to measure dimensions of perceived service quality since personal contact was to be used and high predictive validity was a major concern: The Likert scale ranged from much better expected to much worse than expected, coded 1-5 respectively. This present study was part of a larger study so the questionnaire had five 5 items related to respondents' identification data, and included eight dimensions of SQ with thirty-six items. The five Functional Quality items were basically based on constructs initially developed by Parasuraman et al. (1988), but modified for the research context. Thus Functional Quality is defined in terms of five main variables: tangibles, reliability, responsiveness, assurance and empathy. Technical quality and image constructs were developed by the researchers guided by similar previous studies, and specific indicators for each Functional Quality variable were based on previous research (Gi-Du and James 2004; Parasuraman et al. 1988; Wang & Lo 2002). The items were then modified within the context of the Ghana MTI settings. The main dimensions and their specific indicators are depicted in Table 1.

The questionnaire was pre-tested to a sample of twenty (20) subscribers purposively selected. This small size was guided by the suggestion by Fink (2003b in Saunders, Lewis, Thornhill 2007) that the minimum of ten (10) members for pre-testing is adequate. Finally, adjustments were made to get more effective instruments, the initial reliability test for the dimension items yielded a Cronbach alpha from 0.68 to 0.86 (Table 2). The questionnaire was administered to the target population through personal contact by research assistants for nearly two weeks. To improve representativeness, it was administered in three selected cities in three zonal divisions in Ghana, namely: Tamale for the Upper Zone, Kumasi for the Middle Zone and Accra for Southern Zone.

**Table 1:** SQ Dimensions and indicators

| CODES | DIMENSION AND INDICATORS |
|---|---|
| | **TANGIBLES** |
| TA1 | Network's ability to give you access to information, SIM card (chip), reload cards |
| TA2 | Provision of visually attractive, offices, equipment and materials like starter packs and reload cards |
| TA3 | Network's ability to providing variety of entertainment facilities, etc. |
| TA4 | How appealing the appearance and uniforms of employees are. |
| | **RELIABILITY** |
| RL1 | How timely is the delivery of SMS, MMS, Voice message and other services of network. |
| RL2 | How mobile network is truthful (keeping to promises) |
| RL3 | How dependable and consistent network i in solving customers' complaints |
| RL4 | How able network is to perform services right the first time |
| RL5 | How able is your network to insist on error-free records. |
| | **RESPONSIVENESS** |
| RS1 | How network is able to tell customers exactly when services will be performed |
| RS2 | How network is able to give prompt customer services and attend to customers' needs/problems |
| RS3 | How employees' are willing to help customers in emergency situations |
| RS4 | How the employees are approachable and easy to contact |
| RS5 | Employees' ability to communicate clearly to customers. |
| | **EMPATHY** |
| EM1 | Having convenient periods & terms for activation, recharge, and accounts suspension, free call times. |
| EM2 | Having operating hours convenient to all customers. |
| EM3 | Having sound loyalty programme to recognise you as a frequent customer. |
| EM4 | Having the customer's best interest at heart. |
| EM5 | Giving individual customer attention by employees. |
| EM6 | Efforts to understand specific customer needs. |
| EM7 | Apologising for inconvenience caused to customers. |
| | **ASSURANCE** |
| AS1 | Ability to provide variety of value added services- Music, internet access, SMS,etc. |
| AS2 | Sincerity and patience in resolving customers' complaints/problems. |
| AS3 | The behaviour of employees in instilling confidence in customers. |
| AS4 | Employees' use of required skills and knowledge to answer customers' questions. |
| | **ECONOMY** |
| EC1 | How economical the use of mobile telecom network's is services in terms of: Reloading cards and their denominations |
| EC2 | How economical the use of mobile telecom network's services is in terms of: The call charge per minute/second |
| | **TECHNICAL QUALITY** |
| TQ1 | Successful in completion of calls, SMS, MMS, line activation, credit reloading, etc |
| TQ2 | Employees have technological knowledge and skills in solving customer problems. |
| TQ3 | Network clarity and speed for call and other services. |
| TQ4 | Network innovativeness – ability to use current technology to improve services. |

*Source: Developed based on Based on Grönroos (1984); Parasuraman, Zeithaml & Berry (1985); Hume & Mort (2008) and Rust & Oliver (1994).*

**Table 2:** Reliability test showing Cronbach alpha from 0.68 to 0.86

| Multi-Item Scale (Dimensions) | Cronbach Alpha | Number of items |
|---|---|---|
| Tangibles | 0.715 | 4 |
| Reliability | 0.780 | 5 |
| Responsiveness | 0.830 | 5 |
| Empathy | 0.850 | 7 |
| Assurance | 0.800 | 4 |
| Economy | 0.680 | 2 |
| Technical quality | 0.820 | 5 |
| Image | 0.838 | 4 |
| All items for 8 dimensions | 0.860 | 36 |

Table 2 Scale Reliability
Source: Field data, SPSS output

# 6. Data Analysis

Demographics, factor analysis and item/scale reliability were analyzed using SPSS version 16.0 for Windows.

## 6.1 Demographic Data

The characteristics of the respondents are presented in Table 3. In terms of gender, 55% of the respondents were males and 45% were females. 50% of the respondents were within the ages of 20-39 years and 13% were between 40 and 49 years, implying that majority of them were in the economically active population.

Occupation-wise, most of them (63%) were students, 24% were public servants, 4 % were business persons, while 9% belong to other professions. In terms of income, 98% of respondents earned monthly income below GH¢300 of which 31% earned between GH¢100 to ¢200 while 30% earned virtually no monthly income indicating that most of them earned considerably lower incomes. All respondents were educated with 75% of them having tertiary education, while 25% had Senior High School (SHS) and post-SHS education levels.

**Table 3:** Respondents' characteristics (n = 937)

|  |  | Frequency | % | $\bar{x}$ | Std Dev |
|---|---|---|---|---|---|
| Gender | Male | 520 | 55.5 |  |  |
|  | female | 417 | 45.5 |  |  |
| Occupation | Civil/Public | 222 | 23.7 |  |  |
|  | Student | 592 | 63.2 |  |  |
|  | Business Person | 35 | 3.7 |  |  |
|  | Other | 88 | 9.4 |  |  |
| Age | <20 | 16 | 1.7 |  |  |
|  | 20-29 | 470 | 50.2 |  |  |
|  | 30-39 | 316 | 33.7 | 31 | 0.8 |
|  | 40-49 | 121 | 12.9 |  |  |
|  | ≥50 | 14 | 1.5 |  |  |
| Income | <100 | 93 | 9.9 |  |  |
|  | 101-200 | 277 | 29.6 |  |  |
|  | 201-300 | 195 | 20.8 | 130.8 | 1.4 |
|  | >300 | 79 | 8.4 |  |  |
|  | Non-income Earner | 293 | 31.3 |  |  |
| Education Level | SHS | 74 | 7.9 |  |  |
|  | Post SHS | 162 | 17.3 |  |  |
|  | Tertiary | 701 | 74.8 |  |  |

*Source: Field data, 2008*

## 6.2 Factor Analysis

Factor Analysis (FA) is a data reduction technique that uses correlations between data variables. It assumes that some underlying factors exist that explains the correlations or inter-relationships among observed variables (Chatfield and Collins 1992). It has been used extensively in psychology, econometrics, marketing, sociology, and education (Bollen 1989; Doll, Xia,

Torkzadeh 1994; Li, Tan, and Xie 2002). Statistical data analysis for this study for FA followed the approach similar to the one used by Kettinger and Lee (1995) and April and Pather (2008). Basically the steps involved are:

1. Exploratory factor analysis
2. Regrouping of items
3. Confirmatory factor analysis
4. Testing the validity and reliability of the emerged dimensions

### 6.2.1 Exploratory factor analysis (EFA)

EFA is fundamentally used to reduce large number of variables down to a smaller number of components. It is a method that aims at extracting maximum variance from the dataset within each factor (Chatfield and Collins 1992). In the empirical work of Costello and Osborne (2005) on best practices in exploratory factor analysis, they strongly recommended the use of Principal Component Analysis (PCA) since it has the potency of revealing the underlying structure of the latent variables with an appropriate rotation method. On rotation methods they advice that "In general, ML(Maximum Likelihood) or PAF (Principal Axis Factoring) will give you the best results, depending on whether your data are generally normally-distributed or significantly non-normal, respectively (2005: 2). They further recommend preference for the use of Oblique rotation over Orthogonal since the former "will reproduce Orthogonal solution but not vice versa" (2005: 7). Therefore, for the present study since the sample was large and the items were generally normally distributed (0.952 ≤ SD ≤ 1.20), ML extraction method with Oblique or Oblimin Rotation Method was chosen for EFA. This was performed on all eight dimensions with thirty-six items. For simplicity of analytical purpose each statement of the questionnaire was coded as TA1, TA2, RL1, RL2 and so on (see Table 1). On the criteria for selecting factor loading, generally factor loading above 0.6 is considered high while factor loading greater than or equal to 0.3 is considered moderately high (Klien 2005). Therefore the cut-off for analysing factor loading was 0.50 ± 0.03. Next no items (row) should have multiple factor loadings greater or equal to 0.50 ± 0.03. Lastly, no factors (columns) should have only one high loading item. Other factor loadings that do not satisfy the above criteria are considered meaningless and can be safely removed, while the high loading factors are critical factors and therefore can be retained.

The results of the EFA show a high value of 0.966 for the Kaiser-Meyer-Olkin Measure and indicate the suitability of the research data for structure detection, i.e. the proportion of variance in the items that might be caused by underlying factors. Thus, generally the data is useful for factor analysis. This is confirmed by the significance of the Bartlett's test of sphericity tests (X2: 15881.357, df: 630.000, Sig.: 0.000) indicating that the variables are not unrelated and therefore suitable for structure detection. Table 4 indicates that five factors or components emerged but the fifth factor had no significantly high loading items. Therefore, the fifth factor was eliminated together with fifteen items because they did not satisfy the criteria set for factor loading selection; these are indicated with strike-throughs. Only three dimensions of SQ were not affected at all (Tangibles, Economy and Image) while the other five dimensions were affected.

**Table 4:** Exploratory Factor Analysis

| | | | | | | | | | | |
|---|---|---|---|---|---|---|---|---|---|---|
| **Pattern Matrix** | | | | | | | | | | |
| Item Loading | Factor | | | | | Item loading | Factor | | | |
| | 1 | 2 | 3 | 4 | 5 | | 1 | 2 | 3 | 4 | 5 |
| TA1 | -.069 | -.078 | .602* | .006 | -.070 | EM5 | .662* | -.078 | -.019 | -.009 | -.116 |
| TA2 | .023 | -.017 | .795* | -.104 | .021 | EM6 | .581* | -.092 | .004 | .049 | -.133 |
| TA3 | .061 | .027 | .503* | .103 | -.013 | EM7 | .565* | .037 | .059 | .083 | -.064 |
| TA4 | .051 | .008 | .531* | -.053 | .004 | ~~AS1~~ | ~~.336~~ | ~~-.038~~ | ~~.262~~ | ~~.170~~ | ~~.171~~ |
| ~~RL1~~ | ~~-.042~~ | ~~-.105~~ | ~~.350~~ | ~~.136~~ | ~~-.270~~ | AS2 | .693* | -.007 | .040 | .093 | .055 |
| ~~RL2~~ | ~~.114~~ | ~~-.017~~ | ~~.229~~ | ~~.158~~ | ~~-.362~~ | AS3 | .714* | .029 | .028 | .146 | .161 |
| ~~RL3~~ | ~~.311~~ | ~~-.060~~ | ~~.104~~ | ~~.040~~ | ~~-.333~~ | AS4 | .588* | -.092 | .058 | .138 | .131 |
| ~~RL4~~ | ~~.125~~ | ~~-.089~~ | ~~.216~~ | ~~.079~~ | ~~-.341~~ | EC1 | .116 | -.094 | -.014 | .489* | .021 |
| ~~RL5~~ | ~~.064~~ | ~~.045~~ | ~~.189~~ | ~~.194~~ | ~~-.352~~ | EC2 | .067 | -.016 | -.052 | .538* | -.104 |
| ~~RS1~~ | ~~.147~~ | ~~-.085~~ | ~~.157~~ | ~~.118~~ | ~~-.396~~ | TQ1 | -.007 | -.177 | .197 | .476* | -.011 |
| ~~RS2~~ | ~~.331~~ | ~~-.109~~ | ~~.087~~ | ~~-.003~~ | ~~-.429~~ | ~~TQ2~~ | ~~.356~~ | ~~-.122~~ | ~~.116~~ | ~~.275~~ | ~~.028~~ |
| RS3 | .610* | -.109 | .035 | -.114 | -.176 | TQ3 | -.007 | -.118 | .049 | .572* | -.128 |
| RS4 | .699* | -.008 | .051 | -.110 | -.102 | ~~TQ4~~ | ~~.075~~ | ~~-.228~~ | ~~.128~~ | ~~.466~~ | ~~.077~~ |
| RS5 | .710* | -.042 | .033 | -.137 | -.026 | ~~TQ5~~ | ~~-.042~~ | ~~-.286~~ | ~~.065~~ | ~~.381~~ | ~~.007~~ |
| EM1 | ~~.289~~ | ~~-.097~~ | ~~.159~~ | ~~.192~~ | ~~.006~~ | IM1 | -.007 | -.690* | .087 | .042 | .036 |
| ~~EM2~~ | ~~.302~~ | ~~-.059~~ | ~~.055~~ | ~~.239~~ | ~~-.141~~ | IM2 | .007 | -.900* | -.052 | -.061 | .004 |
| ~~EM3~~ | ~~.325~~ | ~~-.002~~ | ~~-.028~~ | ~~.241~~ | ~~-.188~~ | IM3 | .035 | -.771* | -.015 | -.026 | -.001 |
| ~~EM4~~ | ~~.402~~ | ~~-.017~~ | ~~.026~~ | ~~.239~~ | ~~-.237~~ | IM4 | .020 | -.535* | .021 | .162 | -.039 |

Extraction Method: Maximum Likelihood. Rotation Method: Oblimin with Kaiser Normalization. *Retained factor loadings

## 6.2.2 Regrouping of Items

As shown in Table 5, Components 2 and 3 have only Image and Tangibles items respectively. While component/factor 1 contains a mixture of 3 items each from Responsible, Empathy and Assurance, component 4 contains a blend of 2 items each from Economy and Technical quality items, all of which are found in the original set of eight SQ dimensions in the conceptual framework for the study. These derived dimensions were then relabelled. The labels were intuitively chosen based on the meaning suggested within the context of mobile telephony industry. These are consistent with labelling and coding textual data (See Strauss & Corbin 1998; Wilkin & Castleman 2003). The justifications for these labels are as shown in Table 5:

**Table 5:** Regrouping of questionnaire items

| Emerged Component/Factor | Retained Items | Labels for Component Dimensions |
|---|---|---|
| 1 | RS3, RS4, RS5, EM5, EM6, EM7, ASS2, AS3 and AS4 | Customer relations |
| 2 | IM1, IM2, IM3, and IM4 | Image |
| 3 | TA1, TA2, TA3 and TA4 | Tangibles |
| 4 | EC1, EC2, TQ1 and TQ2 | Real Network quality |

*Factor 1* is a good combination of Responsiveness, Empathy and Assurance items. Responsiveness items are: How employees' are willing to help customers in emergency situations (RS3), how employees are approachable and easy to contact (R4), and employees' ability to communicate clearly with customers (R5). Empathy items are: Giving individual customer attention by employees (EM5). Efforts to understand specific customer needs (EM6) and Apologising for inconvenience caused to customers (EM7). Assurance items are: Sincerity and patience in resolving customers' complaints/problems (AS2), the behaviour of employees in instilling confidence in customers (AS3), and Employees' use of required skills and knowledge to answer customers' questions (AS4).

These items basically relate to a firm's interactions with customers, and suggest the quality of informed and empathic responses of the service provider to customers that communicates the firm's concern, readiness, sensitivity and ability to satisfactorily address concerns, and meet the needs and requirements of customers. These items focus on the customers' perception of the service provider's knowledge and behaviour towards handling customers' need and complaints, based upon which service provider's sincere and appropriate responses are effectively communicated to customers in such a manner that lead to wining customers' confidence and loyalty. Therefore, the appropriate label for this component was Customer relations of service quality aspects of the service provider towards its customers.

*Factor 2* contained only items from the original Tangibles dimension. None of the original Tangibles items was eliminated, so it could be retained as Tangibles dimension. This refers to the visible appearances of all representations of the service provider to the outside world seen in such things as employees' uniforms, firm support materials, and appealing nature of buildings and office environment.

*Factor 3* had only items from the original Image dimension. None of the Image items was removed, so it was retained as Image or reputational quality. They include SQ aspects of being a successful firm, socially responsible, having good reputation and brand name.

Factor 4 had a mixture of Economy and Technical quality items. The two Economy items basically relate to how affordable the services are in terms of various recharging rates (EC1) and the call charge per minute/second (EC2). The Technical quality items are: Successful in completion of calls, SMS, MMS, and line activation, credit reloading (TQ1), and network clarity and speed for call and other services (TQ3).

These items represent the real value customers get for their money in patronising the services of the firms. It shows the ability of the service provider to deliver excellence services, at considerably affordable prices to different customer groups. In mobile telephony context, it could specifically entail providing high network quality that enables clarity and speed for call completion and all network services to the customers. Customers expect to get maximum value in the sense of Technical quality (outcome of the service usage) for every sacrifice they make towards the firm in the form of money, time, efforts, and so on. An appropriate dimension label for these items was Real Network quality, reflecting the ability of the service provider to provide quality network services at affordable rates to give customers greater value for their money.

### 6.2.3 Confirmatory factor analysis (CFA) on the remaining 21 items

The next step in the data analysis was to perform a CFA on the remaining 21 items using Maximum Likelihood extraction method with Oblimin rotation to confirm the dimensionality of the derived instrument. The CFA was run based on the procedure explained above. The results are presented in Table 5. With factor loading values above 0.4, three dimensions items - TA3, TA4, TQ1, and TQ2 - could be considered as moderately high. With factor loading equal to and above 0.5, three dimensions, TA1, AS4 and IM4, could be described as high. Finally, 15 dimension items are considered strong with values above 0.6 (Garson 2007; Kline 2005). Thus, the results of the CFA provide strong evidence to confirm the derived dimensions of the EFA in Table 4.

### 6.2.4    *Validity and reliability of derived instrument*

Instrument validity refers to whether the statistical instrument measure what it is intended to measure, i.e. accuracy of measurement of content (Saunders 2000; Straub, Boudreau & Gefen 2004) Content validity or sampling validity refers to whether a measurement instrument has adequate and representative coverage of the concepts in the variables being measured (Straub *et al.* 2004). It is usually achieved by seeking opinion of other investigators or experts. Construct validity has to do with measuring an instrument to an overall theoretical framework in order to determine whether the device confirms a series of hypothesis derived from an existing theoretical framework. In this work, the questionnaire items for this study were based on literature reviews and experts' review to ensure its content and construct validity. The survey instrument items were grounded in Grönroos' (1984) framework for SQ and other similar validated SERVQUAL instruments applicable to mobile industry (Gi-Du &James, 2004).

Straub *et al.* (2004) maintain that the two main aspects of Construct Validity, being, convergent Validity and discriminant validity, can be deduced from the CFA results. Since the items converge strongly to the derived dimensions, good convergent validity is indicated in the "strong" factor loadings. Also discriminant validity can be deduced because the factor loadings indicate that the items do not overlap across different dimensions.

Reliability refers to whether a measurement instrument is able to yield consistent results each time it is applied. It is the property of a measurement device that causes it to yield similar outcome for similar inputs. Statistically, a Cronbach alpha measurement can be used to determine reliability of a measurement instrument (Straub *et al.* 2004). A Cronbach alpha value of 0.7 and greater is considered reliable (Straub *et al.* 2004). The

Cronbach alpha values from the SPSS output (see Table 6) for each component are greater than 0.7, and the composite alpha for all twenty-one items is 0.918, thus indicating good reliability.

**Table 5:** Confirmatory Factor Analysis for Derived Dimensions

| Item | Factor | | | | Item | Factor | | | |
|------|------|------|------|------|------|------|------|------|------|
| | 1 | 2 | 3 | 4 | | 1 | 2 | 3 | 4 |
| TA1 | -.047 | -.073 | .588 | .054 | AS2 | .701 | -.027 | -.025 | .061 |
| TA2 | -.026 | .021 | .866 | -.062 | AS3 | .659 | .018 | -.038 | .142 |
| TA3 | .072 | .006 | .476 | .098 | AS4 | .563 | -.119 | -.012 | .095 |
| TA4 | .079 | .014 | .481 | -.027 | EC1 | .049 | -.041 | -.014 | .620 |
| RS3 | .689 | -.038 | .067 | -.063 | EC2 | .029 | .056 | -.002 | .680 |
| RS4 | .767 | .061 | .049 | -.057 | TQ1 | .003 | -.173 | .188 | .480 |
| RS5 | .772 | .013 | -.010 | -.103 | TQ3 | .070 | -.142 | .078 | .481 |
| EM5 | .718 | -.036 | .016 | -.006 | IM1 | .005 | -.676 | .095 | .025 |
| EM6 | .643 | -.053 | .020 | .073 | IM2 | .026 | -.910 | -.058 | -.077 |
| EM7 | .603 | .022 | .025 | .072 | IM3 | .022 | -.748 | .005 | .011 |
| | | | | | IM4 | .025 | -.520 | .044 | .166 |

*Extraction Method: Maximum Likelihood. Rotation Method: Oblimin with Kaiser Normalization.*

**Table 6:** Reliability Statistics

| Emerged SQ Dimensions | Number of Items | Cronbach Alpha |
|------|------|------|
| Customer relations | 9 | 0.899 |
| Image | 4 | 0.838 |
| Tangibles | 4 | 0.715 |
| Real Network quality | 4 | 0.759 |
| All Dimensions | 21 | 0.918 |

# 7. Discussion and Implementation

The results of the study show that out of the eight SQ dimensions with *thirty-six* instrument items developed from the literature, only *five* of the eight SQ dimensions are relevant in the context of mobile telephony industry in Ghana. There are *twenty-one* instrument items in the five derived dimensions. Tangibles, Image and Economy SQ dimensions in the original SQ dimensions found in literature were retained, while the rest received considerable modification through the FA and subsequently labelled appropriately. The meaning and implications of derived dimensions are discussed as follows:

*Customer relations:* This label describes the blend of responsiveness, assurance and empathy which are all functional quality items that relate specifically to how customers' needs and concerns are handled effectively by employees based on each customer's unique needs and complaints, personality and demographic characteristics. Thus, *customer relations* include all staff-customer interactions of service quality aspects of the service provider towards its customers. This is very significant in the MTI since customers will want to contact their service operators often for many issues regarding their needs and complaints about mobile network services. These findings are consistent with the work of April and Pather (2008) who found that Responsiveness, Assurance and Empathy are collectively a significant component of Information Systems service quality criteria and dimensions that are applicable  not only in large brick-and-mortar organisations, but also to SME e-Commerce businesses in the tourism sector in South Africa. They, however, labelled this component appropriately in their model as *Supportiveness* for their research context.

Many previous studies such as (Edvardson 2005; Lovelock & Witz 2007) have similarly discussed customer relation factors as the core of delivering effective customer services that highlights how customers would want to be handled and treated by the staff of service providers. Customer service was found to be an important e-service quality factor in the work of Cristobal (2007). Without effective customer relations the service providers are likely to find it difficult in attracting new customers, retaining existing customers and establishing effective long-term mutually beneficial relationship with customers (Edvardson 2005; Lovelock & Witz 2007).

The implication of this dimension is that marketing management need to focus on establishing and improving customer relationship management in the organisation. In this regard, the management of mobile telecom networks should ensure that their employees seek to influence customers positively through quality staff-customer interactions. It means that service providers in the MTI should establish effective customer service centres to manage all customer touch points, staff-customer interactions, handle customer complaints, and establish good rapport with customer while being sensitive to customers' changing requirements (Kotler & Keller 2006; Lovelock & Wirtz 2007).

Some of the key factors identified in the literature that fosters effective interaction between staff of service providers and customers are trust and reliability, effective communication and friendliness (Bansal, Irving, & Taylor 2004; Pather & Usabuwera 2010). In view of this, service providers should endeavour to use varieties of means to communicate to consumers effectively regarding new rates for calls, apologies for delay services and technical problems in network connectivity, new promotions and new products. Employees should pay attention to customer complaints and demonstrate expert knowledge in handling customer problems in order to build trust, assurance and reliability perceptions in customers. Again, staff should endeavour to develop, establish and maintain socially beneficial, friendly relationship with customers in order to elicit customers' positive feelings towards the service provider as a way of establishing affective loyalty bonds between the organization and its customers (Bansal *et al.* 2004).

*Tangibles:* This label concerns the visible appearances of all representations of the service provider to the outside world seen in such things as employees' uniforms, firm support materials, and appealing nature of buildings and other physical facilities. The attractive nature company's representations may have considerable influence in inviting existing customers to approach the service provider's customer service centres, and more importantly in eliciting positive perceptions of the service provider in the minds of potential customers. This dimension was similarly retained in the work of April and Pather (2008).

Previous studies have found that the quality of the firm's representations could influence customer satisfaction and behaviour intentions (Keaveney 1995). Customers are more likely to be identified with a service provider who they think has good and appealing nature of buildings, employees' uniforms, materials and vehicles, and other physical facilities.

The implication of this dimension is that managers should focus on improving and developing good and appealing physical facilities to improve customer perception of the firm, its staff and physical facilities. Managers should not only be concerned with the delivery of expert services but also they should seek to improve upon customer perception of their physical facilities and representation that appear to the general public. As customers patronize firms' offerings, they are not only interested in their problems being solved, but also they would want to feel proud of their companies for having good and appealing physical facilities and representation. Intuitively, this could not only have an indirect positive impact on customer loyalty but also on attraction of new customers through positive word-of-mouth communication from customers to their social and business groups, which in turn could attract more new customers.

*Image or reputational quality:* This dimension involves issues such as having good reputation, good brand name, and being socially responsible and well-known as a successful company in the minds of the customer and the public. Image or reputation quality has been found in previous studies to be one of the factors that could influence word-of-mouth communications, consumer perceived quality of service provider, consumer satisfaction, and eventually customers' loyalty to service provider (Kotler & Keller 2006; Lovelock & Wirtz 2007). Where customers have favourable image or good reputation of a service provider, they are more likely to have favourable service quality perceptions, high expectations for satisfaction and strong eagerness to recommend the service provider to family, friends and business partners.

The implication is that marketing management need to focus on creating favourable image of the service provider through effective promotional activities and the delivery of functional and technical quality (Grönroos, 1994). Service providers should, therefore, demonstrate the ability to deliver and exceed customer expectations not only with how they deliver the services (functional quality), but also and more importantly with what is delivered (technical quality). These two quality categories are able to influence customers' image of the service provider (Grönroos, 2001). Aside this, the management of the mobile telecom networks should focus on building good reputational quality through effective implementation of corporate social responsibility, and show their compliance with industry code of ethics. Service providers, in particular the mobile operators in Ghana, must avoid unethical corporate behaviour and scandals as it may have repercussions on their reputational quality, which in turn could influence consumers' intention to switch to other service providers (Keaveney 1995).

*Real Network quality:* This emerged SQ dimension fundamentally refers to ensuring Technical quality at affordable prices. Network quality represents fundamentally core service as far as mobile telecommunication is concerned. And consumers expect to experience this quality factor at a value equal to what they sacrifice for it. Thus, customers expect to have success in completion of calls, SMS, MMS, and line activation, credit reloading and network clarity and speed for call completion and other services, while expecting that the services received offer them real value for their sacrifices in money paid and time spent for the services. The difference between what consumers spent on the network services and the quality of the services they received should be equivalent, otherwise, customer value decreases.

The implication is that mobile network providers should focus on providing excellent network quality at affordable prices. This could in turn influence positively customer perceived value as customers perceive the benefit derived from the services to be greater than the cost of sacrifice (e.g. money) they lose in exchange for the services. Real network quality should be significantly evidenced in all core mobile telecom services and at affordable prices in terms of recharging rates, the call charge per minute/second, reconnection rates, number portability fees, among others. Where this quality is poorly delivered to consumers it could result in influencing their commitment to the service provider (Bansal et al. 2005), induce intention to switch and negative word-of-mouth (Gerrard, & Cunningham 2004; Keaveney 1995).

Finally, the study implies that the emerged dimensions could serve as useful criteria and dimensions for evaluating service quality in mobile telephony industry context.

The items in the emerged dimensions are summarised in Figure 2 and Table 7.

**Table 7:** Derived Dimensions of SQ for Mobile Telephony Context

|  | **TANGIBLES** |
|---|---|
| TA1 | Network's ability to give you access to information, SIM card (chip), reload cards |
| TA2 | Provision of visually attractive, offices, equipment and materials like starter packs and reload cards |
| TA3 | Network's ability to providing variety of entertainment facilities, etc. |
| TA4 | How appealing are the appearance and uniforms of employees? |
|  | **CUSTOMER RELATIONS** |
| RS3 | How the employees are willing to help customers in emergency situations |
| RS4 | How the employees are approachable and easy to contact. |
| RS5 | Employees' ability to communicate clearly with you. |
| EM4 | Service provider having the customer's best interest at heart. |
| EM5 | Service provider giving individual customer attention by employees. |
| EM6 | Service provider's efforts to understand specific customer needs. |
| EM7 | Service provider's apology for inconvenience caused to customers. |
| AS2 | Employees' sincerity and patience in resolving customers' complaints/problems. |
| AS3 | The behaviour of employees in instilling confidence in customers. |
| AS4 | Employees' use of required skills and knowledge to answer customers' questions. |
|  | **ECONOMY (VALUE)** |
| EC1 | How economical the use of mobile telecom network's services is in terms of rates for reloading cards and their denominations. |
| EC2 | How economical the use of mobile telecom network's services is in terms of rates for the call charge per minute/second. |
|  | **TECHNICAL QUALITY** |
| TQ1 | Successful in completion of calls, SMS, MMS, line activation, credit reloading, etc |
| TQ3 | Network clarity and speed for call and other services. |
|  | **IMAGE** |
| IM1 | How *successful* mobile network company is |
| IM2 | The *reputation* of your mobile network service provider |
| IM3 | The *brand image* of the services. |
| IM4 | How service provider is *socially responsible* |

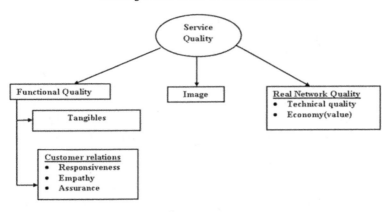

**Figure 2:** Derived SQ dimensions for MTI Context

# 8. Conclusion

In many IS contexts, the IS Service Quality criteria and dimensions that have been used extensively in evaluating IS service quality are based on SERVQUAL developed by Parasuraman et al. (1985), little attention has been given to the use of other alternative models of SQ in evaluating IS service quality in the mobile telephony context. This paper attempts to fill this gap by drawing on Technical and Functional quality model (Grönroos 1984, 2000), through CFA approach, to propose a framework of latent factors that are critical for understanding SQ in IS evaluation in mobile telephony context. It contributes to the extant literature on information systems evaluation and advances our knowledge of critical factors that describe and reflect end-user evaluation of IS service quality specifically in the mobile telecommunication industry in developing country context. It also provides practitioners with a general framework as a guide for developing marketing and management strategies for effective management of IS service quality in mobile telecommunication contexts.

The four emerged dimensions with twenty-one items, being Customer relations, Tangibles, Image and Real Network Quality could be used by mobile network operators as critical factors in evaluating SQ in MTI. This, however, doesn't mean all the other five underlying dimensions in Reliability that were eliminated and the other fifteen items of Empathy and Assurance, Responsiveness and Technical quality are not important for Ghanaian customers. This instead indicates that it is necessary to modify the items to capture these 15 dimensions for service quality scale in Ghana mobile telephony industry. It concludes that alternative SQ models aside the popular SERVQUAL model, like one conceptualised in this study, could be useful in determining SQ dimensions relevant to MTI.

It is cautioned that the results of the present study should be interpreted within in the context of Ghana mobile telephony industry, and similar studies should be done in similar context in different countries to compare the results before generalisations could be made. The factors identified in this work for evaluating SQ dimension applicable to MTI are not exhaustive; they do not include factors such as security and ease of use which have been recently suggested in the work of Pather & Usabuwera (2010) to be important in end-user evaluation of information systems contexts. Future research should explore these and other critical factors in B2B industry context for a better understanding of service quality dimension relevant to both B2C and B2B telecommunication contexts in IS discipline.

# References

Addy-Nayo, C.(2001) 3G mobile policy: The case of Ghana. Retrieved on 10th August 2008 from www.itu.int/osg/spu/ni/3G/casestudies/ghana/ghanafinal.doc.

Anderson, E. W., Fornell, C. & Lehmann, D. R. (1994) "Customer Satisfaction, Market Share and Profitability: Findings from Sweden," Journal of Marketing, 58(3), 53-66.

April G. D. & Pather S. (2008) Evaluating Service Quality Dimensions within e-Commerce SMEs , Electronic Journal Information Systems Evaluation, Volume 11 Issue 3 (109-124)

Asubonteng, P., McCleary, K.J. & Swan, J. E. (1996) "SERVQUAL revisited: a critical review of SERVICE QUALITY", Journal of Services Marketing, 10 (6), pp. 62-81.

Bansal, H. S., Irving, P. G., & Taylor, S. F. (2004). A three-component model of customer commitment to service providers. Journal of the Academy of Marketing Science, 32, 234-250.

Bollen, K. A. (1989), Structural Equation with Latent Variables, John Wiley & Sons, New York, NY.

Bozorgi, M. M. (2007) Measuring Service quality in the Airline Using SERVQUAL model - (Case of IAA), Masters Thesis LTU, Sweden., AALTU-PB-07046-SE

Chatfield, C. & Collins, A. J. (1992) Introduction to Mult-variate Analysis, Chapman & Hall, London.

Cooper, D. R. & Schindler, P. S. (2006) "Business Research Methods: empirical investigation", Journal of Service Research, 1 (2), pp. 108-28.

Costello & Osborne (2005) Exploratory Factor Analysis, Practical Assessment Research & Evaluation, Vol. 10, No 7 2

Cristoal, E., Flavian, C., & Guinaliu M. (2007), "Perceived e-service quality: Measurement validity and effects on consumer satisfaction and web site loyalty", Managing Service Quality, Vol.      17 No. 3, pp. 317-340.

Cronin, J.J. Jr. & Taylor, S.A. (1992) "Measuring Service: a re-examination and extension", Journal of Marketing,  56, pp. 55-68.

Cronin, J.J. Jr. (2003) "Looking back to see forward in services marketing: some ideas to  consider", Managing Service Quality, Vol. 13(5) pp. 332-337.

Dabholkar, P. (1996), "Consumer evaluations of new technology-based self-service options: an investigation of alternative modes of service quality", International Journal of Research in Marketing , Vol. 13 No. 1, pp. 29-51.

Danaher, P. J. & Haddrell, V. (1996) "A comparison of question scales used for measuring customer satisfaction", International Journal of Service Industry Management, 7 (4), pp. 4-26. MCB University Press.

DeLone, W.H. & McLean, E.R. (1992) Information systems success: the quest for the dependant variable. Information Systems Research, 3(1):60-95.

DeLone, W.H. & McLean, E.R. (2003) The DeLone and McLean model of information systems success: a ten-year update. Journal of Management Information Systems, 19(4):9-30.

Devlin, S. J., Dong, H. K. & Brown, M. (1993). "Selecting a Scale for Measuring     Quality."Marketing Research: A magazine of Management and Applications, 5(3): 12-17

Doll, W. J., Xia, W. D. & Torkzadeh, G. (1994), "A confirmatory factor analysis of the end- user computing satisfaction instrument", MIS Quartely, December, pp. 453-461

Edvardsson, B. (2005) "GURU'S VIEW, Service quality: beyond cognitive assessment", Managing Service quality, 15 (2), pp. 127-131.

Field, J.M., Heim, G.R. & Sinha, K.K. (2004), "Managing quality in the e-service system:Development and application of a process model", Production and Operations Management,Vol. 13 No. 4, pp. 291-306.

Frempong, G. & Henten, A. (2004) "Telecom Developments and Investments in Ghana",  WDR Dialong Theme 2003, Discussion Paper, WDR 0305.

Garson, G.D. (2007) Factor analysis. [online]http://www2.chass.ncsu.edu/garson/pa765/factor.htm [16 March 2008].

Gerrard, P., & Cunningham, J. B. (2004) Consumer switching behavior in the Asian banking-market. Journal of Services Marketing, 18, pp. 215-223.

Ghana National Communication Authority (Ghana NCA) (2010) Report for 2009 accessed at: http://www.nca.org.gh/index.php?option=com_content&view=article&id=204&Itemid=100 [20 April, 2010).

Gi-Du, K. & James, J. (2004) "Service quality Dimensions: An Examination of Grönroos' Service Quality Model", Managing Service Quality  14(4), pp. 266–277.

Grönroos, C. (1982) 'An Applied Service Marketing Theory', European Journal of     Marketing 16(7):30-41.

Grönroos, C. (1984) "Service model and its marketing implications", European Journal of Marketing,  18 (4), pp. 36-44.

Grönroos, C. (1990) "Service Management: A Management Focus for Service Competition", International Journal of Service Industry Management,  1(1), pp 6-14

Grönroos, C. (1994) "From Marketing Mix to Relationship Marketing. Towards a     Paradigm Shift Marketing" Asia - Australia Marketing Journal, 2(1), 9 – 30.

Grönroos, C. (2000) Service Management and Marketing, Lexington Books, Lexington, MA.

Grönroos, C. (2001) "The Perceived Quality Concept: a mistake?" Managing Service quality 11(3), pp. 150-152

Heskett, J. L., Jones, T. O., Loveman, G. W., Sasser W. E., Jr., & Schlesinge L. R (1994) "Putting the service-profit chain to work", Harvard Business Review, March/April, pp. 164-174.

Heskett, J. L., Sasser E., & Schlesinger, L. (1997) The Service Profit Chain, Free Press,     New York, NY

Ho, B.C. & Lin W. (2010) Measuring the service quality of internet banking: scale     development and validation, European Business Review, Vol.22 (1). Pp. 5-24

Hume, M. & Mort, G. S. (2008) "Satisfaction in performing arts: the role of value"     European Journal of Marketing 42 (3/4), pp. 311-326.

*Simon Gyasi Nimako et al*

ITU World Communication (2010) The World in 2010, ICT facts and figures [online],retrieved from (http://www.itu.int/ITU) on 10th June, 2011

Kang, H. & Bradley, G. (2002) Measuring the performance of IT services: an assessment of SERVQUAL. International Journal of Accounting Information Systems, 3(1):15    164.

Keaveney, S. M. (1995). Customer switching behavior in service industries: An exploratorystudy. Journal of Marketing, 1995, 2-71.

Kettinger, W.J. & Lee, C.C. (1997) Pragmatic perspectives on the measuring of information systems service quality. MIS Quarterly, 21(2):223-241.

Kim, K. K. (1990) User Information Satisfaction: Toward Conceptual Clarity. Proceedings of the International Conference on Information Systems (ICIS), Copenhagen.

Kim, M., Kim, J-H. & Lennon S.J. (2006), "Online service attributes available on apparel retail websites: An E-S-QUAL approach", Managing Service Quality, Vol. 16 No. 1, pp. 51-77.

Kline, R. B. (2005). Principles and practice of structural equation modeling (2nd ed.). New York: Guilford.

Kotler, P. & Keller K. (2006) Marketing Management, 12th Edition, Pearson Education Inc, New Jersey.

Lee, G-G & Lin, H-F. (2005), "Customer perceptions of e-service quality in online shopping", International Journal of Retail & Distribution Management, Vol. 33 No. 2, pp. 161-176.

Li H. & Suomi R. (2009) A Proposed Scale for Measuring E-service Quality    International Journal of u- and e-Service, Science and Technology Vol. 2, No. 1, pp. 2-9

Li, Y. N., Tan, K. C. & Xie, M. (2002) Measuring Web-based Service quality", Total    Quality Management, Vol. 13 No. 5, pp. 686-699.

Lovelock, C. & Wirtz J. (2007) "Services Marketing: People, Technology, Strategy" (6th    Ed.) Pearson Prentice Hall, New Jersey.

Malhotra, N. K. & Birks, D. F. (2007) Marketing Research: An applied Approach (3rd Ed.), Prentice Hall, Incorporated.

Molla, A. And Licker, P.S. (2001) E-commerce systems success: An attempt to extend andrespecify the Delone and Mclean model of IS success. Journal of Electronic Commerce Success Vol.2 (4) p.1-11.

Newman, K. & Cowling, A. (1996), 'Service quality in retail banking: the experience of two British clearing banks', International Journal of Bank Marketing, Vol. 14, No. 6 pp.    3-11

Nitin, S., Deshmukh, S.G. & Vrat, P. (2005) "Service quality Models: A review" International Journal of Quality and Reliability Management, 22(9), pp. 913-949q

Parasuraman, A., Zeithaml, V.A., & Berry, L. L. (1988) "SERVQUAL: A multiple item scale  for measuring customer perceptions of Service quality", Journal of Retailing, 64, pp.12-40.

Parasuraman, A., Zeithaml, V.A., & Malhotra, A. (2005) "E-S-QUAL: A multiple item scale for electronic service quality", Journal of Service Research, 7(3), pp.213-233.

Park, J. & Kim, J. S. (2005) The impact of IS sourcing type on service quality and maintenance efforts. Information & Management, 42(1):261-274.

Pitt, L.F., Watson, R.T. & Kavan, C.B. (1995) Service quality: a measure of information    systems effectiveness. MIS Quarterly, 19(2):173-188.

Rosen, L. D., Karwan, K.R. & Scribner, L. L. (2003) "Service quality measurement and the disconfirmation model: Taking care in interpretation", Total Quality Management,    14 (1), pp.314 – 317

Rowley, J. (2006), "An Analysis of e-Service literature: towards a research agenda", InternetResearch, Vol. 16(3) pp.339-359.

Rust, R.T. & Oliver, R.L. (1994) "Service quality: Insights and Managerial Implications from the Frontier", in Rust, R. and Oliver, R. (Eds), Service quality: New Directions in Theory and Practice, Sage Publications, Thousand Oaks, CA, pp. 1-20.

Saunders, N. K. (2000) Research Methods for Business Students, (2nd Ed.), Financial Times/Prentice Hall, Essey,England.

Saunders, M., Lewis, P. & Thornhill, A. (2007) Research Methods for Business Student (6thedn), Pearson Education Limited

Spreng, R. A. and Mackoy R., (1996) An Emperical Examination of a Model of Perceived Service quality and Satisfaction. Journal of Retailing, 72(2).

Straub, D., Boudreau, M. & Gefen, D. (2004) Validation guidelines for IS positivist research.communications of the Association for Information Systems, 13:380-427.

Strauss, A.L. & Corbin, J. (1998) Basics of Qualitative Research: Techniques and Procedures for Developing Grounded Theory, 2nd ed. London: Sage.

Van Dyke, T.P., Kappelman, L.A. & Prybutok, V.R. (1997) Measuring information systems service quality: concerns on the use of the SERVQUAL questionnaire. MIS Quarterly, 21(2):195-208.

Voss, C. Roth A.V., Rosenzweig, E.D., Blackmon, K. & Chase, R.B. (2004), "A Tale of Two Countries' Conservatism, Service Quality, and Feedback on Customer Satisfaction", Journal of Service Research, Vol 6(3), No 3 pp. 212-23

Voss, C., (2003).The Experience Profit Cycle, Research Report, Center for Operations and Technology Management, London Business School, London.

Wang, Y. & Hing-Po Lo. (2002) Service quality, customer satisfaction and behaviour intentions: Evidence from China's telecom Industry. Info 4, 6 pp. 50-60.MCB UP Ltd

Watson, W.T., Pitt, L.F., Cunningham, C.J. & Nel, D. (1993) User satisfaction and service quality of the IS department: closing the gaps. Journal of Information Technology, 8:257-265.

Wilkin, C. & Castleman, T. (2003) Development of an Instrument to Evaluate the Quality of Delivered Information Systems. Proceedings of the 36th Hawaii International Conference on System Sciences, Big Island, HI, USA, 6-9 January 2003.

Wolfinbarger, M.F. & Gilly M.C. (2003), "ETAILQ: Dimensionalizing, measuring and predicting e-tailing quality", Journal of Retailing, Vol.79 No.3, pp. 183-198.

Yoo, B. & Donthu, N. (2001), "Developing a scale to measure perceived quality of an Internet shopping site (SITEQUAL)", Quarterly Journal of Electronic Commerce, Vol. 2 No. 1, pp.31-46.

Zeithaml, V. & Bitner, M.J. (2003) Services Marketing: Integrating Customer Focus across the Firm, (3rd ed.), McGraw-Hill, New York, NY.

Zeithaml, V.A. (2000), "Service quality, profitability and the economic worth of customers: what we know and what we need to learn", Journal of the Academy of Marketing Science, Vol.28 .No. 1, pp. 67-85.

Zeithaml, V.A., Parasuraman, A., & Malhotra, A. (2000) "e-Service quality: definition, dimensions and conceptual model", working paper, Marketing Science Institute, Cambridge, MA

Zeithaml, V.A., Parasuraman, A., & Malhotra, A. (2002) "Service quality through websites: acritical review of extant knowledge" Journal of the Academy of Marketing Science, Vol. 30(4) pp. 362-375.

# Alignment in Enterprise Architecture: A Comparative Analysis of Four Architectural Approaches

**Thanos Magoulas, Aida Hadzic, Ted Saarikko and Kalevi Pessi**
**Department of Applied IT, University of Gothenburg, Sweden**
*Originally published in EJISE (2012) Volume 15, ISS 1*

**Editorial Commentary**
The increasing implementation of ERP systems across public and private sectors amongst organisations of all sizes implies that ERP-related evaluation issues will feature prominently on the future agenda. The importance of this paper is that the authors unravel the complex issue of architectural alignment with all facets of the organisation. The paper suggests that current approaches to Enterprise Architecture provide sufficient guidance for structural and functional alignment, but less so for 'infological' or 'socio-cultural' alignment. Thus this paper establishes an important framework for the future of IS evaluation within the ERP environment. The issues relating to socio-cultural alignment of ERP architecture, in particular, will warrant further investigation as Information Systems demand alignment to this oft-forgotten element of organisations. This paper thus secures a foundation for future IS evaluation studies which must seek to develop holistic evaluation approaches for assessing ERP alignment with an architectural framework.

**Abstract:** As modern organizations struggle with the complexity and dynamicity of their business environments, they increasingly turn to Enterprise Architecture as a means to organize their capabilities. However, adopting Enterprise Architecture is hardly a straightforward matter as the practical guidance available is plagued by disparity in nomenclature as well as content. The purpose of this paper is to take a first step in remedying the dearth of rational appraisal of approaches to Enterprise Architecture by closer examining a handful of guides and frameworks. Our ultimate aim in this paper is to provide knowledge about the various dimensions of enterprise architectures that demand alignment between its constitutionals parts. Therefore the efforts of our study were focused on elucidating the following issue: How are the various forms and aspects of architectural alignment treated by the investigated approaches to Enterprise Architecture? Due to the lack of commonalities between the assorted approaches, an independent metric is required. We therefore utilize the concept of alignment and analyze how the various forms and aspects of architectural alignment are treated by formalized approaches to Enterprise Architecture. This methodology was applied to the Zachman Framework, The Open Group Architecture Framework (TOGAF), the Extended Enterprise Architecture Framework (E2AF) and the Generalised Enterprise Reference Architecture and Methodology (GERAM). Our investigation clearly demonstrates that: 1) Approaches to Enterprise Architecture provide guidance for structural and functional alignment, but not for infological or socio-cultural alignment. 2) The area of contextual alignment is described in a simplistic manner. 3) None of the investigated approaches discuss the mutual interdependence that exists between the various forms of alignment. Our work serves to further the understanding of multi-dimensionality of Enterprise Architecture in general and architectural alignment in particular.

**Keywords:** enterprise architecture, architectural alignment, Zachman framework, TOGAF, GERAM, E2AF

# 1. Introduction

The organizations of today are facing a world fraught with uncertainty. Increasingly capricious and demanding consumers necessitate careful consideration in to which products or services to offer at any given time. Meanwhile, competition is no longer limited to a geographical region as corporations are able to vie for business on a global market. The traditional modus operandi based on command and control is no longer able to satisfy the needs of the modern enterprise in this brave new world of opportunism and innovation.

It is clear that the modern organization needs a new blueprint in order to stay ahead of the game – or at the very least stay in the game. To this end, much attention has been paid to Enterprise Architecture over the past couple of decades – not just as a means to improve competitiveness, but also to reduce complexity, increase changeability, provide a basis for evaluation et cetera.

A literary review by Schöenherr (2009) clearly shows that the level of interest in Enterprise Architecture is indeed increasing. Although the term architecture was limited to information systems when originally adopted by John Zachman (1987), the concept has since then been expanded to encompass the entire enterprise and interpreted by academia as well as the private and public sectors. The different views on how to approach Enterprise Architecture are often documented and compiled into "guides" or "frameworks" which are intended to instruct practitioners in how to apply this concept to their organization. However, the numerous approaches all present disparate views on what exactly Enterprise Architecture entails and how it is best administered (Rood, 1994; Whitman, Ramachandran & Ketkar, 2001; Sessions, 2007; Schöenherr, 2009). This essentially leaves the practitioner in the dark as the approaches offer virtually no common ground, no common language and no common orientation on which to base a comparison.

The purpose of this paper is to take a first step in remedying the dearth of rational appraisal of approaches to Enterprise Architecture by closer examining a handful of guides and frameworks. Due to the lack of commonalities, we intend to utilize the concept of alignment as a metric. Alignment is said to describe the condition of IS/IT being in harmony with business needs (Henderson & Venkatraman, 1992). This would not only ensure full utilization of resources, but also drive synergic effects (Luftman, 1996; Papp, 2001) – a situation very much in conformity with the aims of Enterprise Architecture. Succinctly put, we wish to analyze following question: How are the various forms and aspects of architectural alignment treated by the investigated approaches to Enterprise Architecture? In pursuing this line of inquiry, we wish to expand the current stream of research into Enterprise Architecture. Furthermore, we would like to emphasize architectural alignment in particular.

## 2. Related research

While it is not within the scope of this paper to provide a comprehensive literary review, we have identified certain streams of research into alignment that carry relevance to our own research. Furthermore, we have reviewed alternative avenues to evaluate and contrast architectural approaches in order to illustrate the lack of academic convergence.

### 2.1 Alignment

With the diffusion and decentralisation of processing power (via the personal computer) in the 1980s, many companies invested heavily in IT without deriving expected benefits. This gave rise to what was often referred to as the productivity paradox (Brynjolfsson, 1993). Henderson and Venkatraman (1992) claimed that part of the reason for this state of affairs was the lack of alignment between IT and business which prompted them to present their Strategic Alignment Model (SAM). SAM was not the first conceptualization of alignment, but it has certainly dominated subsequent research efforts into the field. SAM stresses the importance of integration between business and IT, as well as the need to adapt the internal structure of the enterprise to marketing and strategy. In order to achieve this, the business strategy must be accompanied by an IT strategy. There are a number of subtle differences in how these may influence one another, but Henderson and Venkatraman stress the constancy of business as the driver and IT as the enabler.

While research into alignment to a large degree has followed in the path set by SAM (often referred to as Business-IT alignment), there are several authors that view this model as limited. Ciborra (1997) offers one of the more astringent criticism as he dismisses SAM outright, claiming that lines and shapes on a diagram hold no real bearing on the realities of business. Maes, Rijsenbrij, Truijens & Goedvolk (2000) claim that SAM is overly simplified and ignores the middle ground that ties strategy with operations and business with IT. They therefore expand upon SAM by adding the interim layer structure between strategy and operations as a means to emphasize the importance of architecture in modern enterprises. Furthermore, business and IT represent different professions – each with their own sense of culture and expertise. One must therefore take care to facilitate the exchange of information between the two areas. The importance of fostering inter-departmental communication has also been highlighted by Luftman (2000) as well as Walentowitz, Beimborn, Schroiff and Weitzel (2011).

Baker and Jones (2008) take an interest in sustaining strategic alignment as opposed to merely viewing it as either a process or an end-state. They pursue this line of inquiry through expanding upon SAM by recognizing five different types of alignment needed to fully acknowledge the complexity faced by the modern enterprise. They refer to these types of alignment as business alignment, IT alignment, contextual alignment, structural alignment and strategic alignment. By widening the strategic discourse among stakeholders, the authors theorize that a wider understanding of the enterprise will prove beneficial to sustaining strategic alignment.

Chan and Reich (2007) distinguish between several dimensions of alignment based on an extensive literature review. These are enumerated as the strategic and intellectual dimension, structural dimension, social dimension and cultural dimension. The authors note that research into alignment is heavily biased towards strategy and structure as these dimensions of alignment form a more direct causal link to performance. While social and cultural issues should not be overlooked, they are typically perceived as contextual issues rather than integral components of alignment.

Based on our review, we may draw the following assumptions regarding alignment. First, the concept has been heavily influenced by SAM over the past decade. Therefore, research into alignment has been focused on realising formal business strategies. Second, the scope of alignment is often limited to the duality between IT and business. Even though some authors have highlighted the need for a more multi-dimensional perspective, the focus is still on extrinsic values such as performance whilst omitting intrinsic values like comprehension and acceptance.

## 2.2 Approaches to Enterprise Architecture

The past decade has seen several attempts to juxtapose architectural approaches. Given the diverse nature of available frameworks and methodologies, such an undertaking carries with it an inherent difficulty in that one runs the risk of "mixing apples and oranges." Consequently, the roads travelled are almost as winding and diverse as the approaches they seek to analyze. Please note that we utilize the term architectural approach as a generic term for the assorted frameworks and methodologies that strive to guide the practice of Enterprise Architecture.

A relatively direct analytical technique entails simply mapping one or more approaches(s) onto one another. This avenue has been pursued by Urbaczewski and Mrdalj (2006) as well as Noran (2003). Urbaczewski and Mrdalj analyze several frameworks employed by practitioners by mapping them against one another based on views, abstractions and life cycle. They arrive at the conclusion that the Zachman framework possesses the most comprehensive guidance due to its explicit description on stakeholder viewpoints. Noran follows a narrower – yet profoundly deeper – procedure when he maps the Zachman framework onto GERAM. His analysis is based on enterprise modelling and to what extent the Zachman framework corresponds to the extensive provisions offered by GERAM in that department. His conclusions are limited to ascertaining that although explicit comparisons are difficult, one may make implicit connections based on content rather than nomenclature.

Other juxtapositions have been undertaken based on less direct forms of comparison. Leist and Zellner (2006) also take a specific interest in enterprise modelling – albeit not from the point of any specific architectural approach. Their evaluation is based on the premise that the chief purpose of architecture (the authors do not specify type of architecture) is to reduce perceived complexity and increase comprehensibility. Following this line of reasoning, their analysis is based on the extent to which architectural approaches provide guidance regarding meta-models, procedure models, modelling techniques, participating roles and specification documents. Based on their evaluation, Leist and Zellner conclude that none of the frameworks included in their analysis meet all the desiderata for an architectural approach.

Franke, Höök, König, Lagerström, Närman, Ullberg, Gustafsson and Ekstedt (2009) utilize a meta-framework in order to provide a common platform for evaluating architectural approaches. This framework – designated Enterprise Architecture Framework Framework (EAF2) – is based on a selection of several existing architectural approaches. These are put through an iterative cycle of analysis where entities are identified, extracted, defined in general terms and consolidated into the final meta-framework. The authors assert that this meta-framework is a viable means to not only compare architectural approaches, but also combine them as EAF2 stipulates the provisions and omissions of each approach.

Several authors have adopted external metrics that are inherently independent from the terminology and methodology of any single approach as a means for juxtaposition. Tang, Han and Chen (2004) evaluate several approaches based on what they specify in terms of goals, inputs and outcomes. Based on these metrics, they conclude that the architectural approaches covered in their analysis can be delineated into those that are suitable for Enterprise Architecture, and those that are more suited to Software Architecture. Abdallah and Galal-Edeen (2006) adopt a somewhat similar research methodology, but in addition to goals, inputs and outcomes they add a fourth metric which they aptly designate "other". The authors refrain from drawing any definitive conclusions beyond stressing the need for adaption to individual needs regardless of which architectural approach one adopts. Odongo, Kang and Ko (2010) take this basic approach even further by establishing eleven separate metrics on which to base an evaluation as well as an algorithm to perform the analysis of architectural approaches. By weighing and subsequently ascribing a numeric value to each metric, the prospective user is then able to aggregate the numbers for each approach analyzed and thus see which one is better suited to one's needs.

Sessions (2007) provides a practitioner perspective on a few of the more widely adopted architectural approaches. Based on his comprehensive – albeit pragmatic – analysis, the author surmises that none of the approaches are sufficiently comprehensive by themselves. They all feature strengths and weaknesses that may or may not be relevant to the practitioner. Based on this conclusion, Sessions urges prospective users to develop their own architectural approach in order to meet the specific circumstances facing each enterprise.

Given the diverse avenues pursued and conclusions reached through the various analyses outlined above, it is obvious that there is no clear-cut consensus to be found. We may however highlight two salient points. First, the majority of evaluations adopt a relatively mechanistic perspective and perceive enterprise Architecture as a means to design and govern artefacts rather than consider how they relate to the enterprise as such. Second, most evaluations bring up the need for adapting architectural approaches (as well as the analysis thereof) to the idiosyncrasies of the individual enterprise. What these idiosyncrasies entail is however usually addressed in a perfunctory manner or not at all.

## 3. Research model

Given the inherent difficulties in the comparison this paper seeks to carry out, we feel that previous efforts to evaluate architectural approaches fail to the requirements of the enterprise as a whole. The same can be said for the bulk of the stream of SAM-based research into alignment. Instead, the most meaningful approach would in our opinion be to analyze architectural approaches to actual organizational needs and practices. Furthermore, we will present an alternate view on alignment that will encompass a wider view of the enterprise than just the business strategies.

As a baseline for our evaluation, this comparison will utilize the MIT1990s framework for organizational research (Morton, 1991). Furthermore, we will expand upon this model using research by Dahlbom (1996), Magoulas and Pessi (1998), and Spanos, Prastacos and Poulymenakou (2002).

Our research model defines the realized architecture of an enterprise in five basic areas of interests. They are: (1) the area of goals, objectives and values, (2) the area of enterprise activities and their management, (3) the area of decisional rights and responsibilities, (4) the area of primary stakeholders and lastly, (5) the area of information systems and the corresponding ICT. These resources together define the information infrastructure of the enterprise.

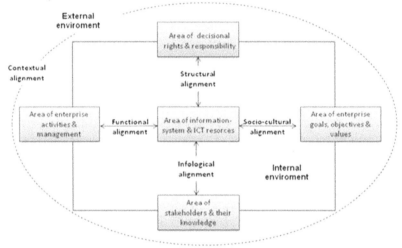

**Figure 1:** Model for research

## 3.1   The area of enterprise goals, objectives and values

Whereas goals and objectives usually take the shape of a hierarchy, other aspects like values, norms, culture et cetera define the conditions under which this hierarchy is formed. Thus, within the context of informatics, the structure of goals may be either asymmetric hierarchies or symmetric networks since they are established through negotiations (Hedberg, 1980; Langefors 1975, 1986). Furthermore, the social organization should not limit its concerns to profitability, but must also promote a favourable environment for the individuals that work towards collective goals (Ackoff, 1967; Hedberg, 1980). Failure to do so may lead to dispassionate employees which would certainly impede progress in the long term. The individual must therefore feel that his or her own goals are accommodated by the organization.

## 3.2 The area of enterprise activities and management

A process may be defined in terms of a group of activities organised in such way as to produce a certain product or service. Thus, any form of process transforms a certain object from a certain state to another desired or expected state. In the same sense the knowledge to do such a thing is called technology (Mackenzie, 1984). Hence, the concepts of process and technology are integrated to each other and the interdependence of the involved activities becomes the subject matter of coordination. In the same sense, several activities of processes may share the same kind of resources. This fact creates another requirement for coordination. The transformation may employ different kinds of tools and may be either structured or unstructured. In any case, every form of process states the requisite for both skills and knowledge. Processes may be described as being of a coordinative, evaluative, innovative or developmental character; which in turn affects their need for functionality, flexibility, efficiency, quality, et cetera.

## 3.3 The area of decisional rights and responsibilities

Usually, social structure is the result of design rather than cultivation. This is either achieved through the decomposition of enterprise ends into a comprehensible structure of elementary task-based units (Simon, 1962, 1969), or the integration of existing task-based units into a comprehensible structure of authority and responsibilities (Churchman, 1971).

The shape of the social structure depends on the situational characteristics of the environment such as legal and ethical responsibility. Therefore, at any moment in time the structure is expected to meet expectations from society while simultaneously satisfy systemic desirability (Checkland, 1981, 1985; Hedberg, 1980; Magoulas & Pessi, 1998). The concept of social structure covers such aspects as the division of work, structures of power, patterns of communication, allocation of authorities and responsibilities, et cetera.

## 3.4 The area of stakeholders and their knowledge

The stakeholders are the backbone of all organizations. They may be executives, employees, support staff, customers, suppliers, shareholders, local communities or other groups concerned with the enterprise. The stakeholders are the source of knowledge and experience as well as conflict due to their individuality. The individuality of the stakeholder may clash with the participatory nature of systems. Lastly, the most significant aspect of stakeholders may be given in terms of collaboration, communication and commitment (Ackoff, 1967; Checkland, 1981).

### 3.5    The area of information systems and ICT resources

From the perspective of alignment, information systems and Information and Communication Technology (ICT) forms a natural centre as this area permeates all aspects of the enterprise. While information systems today tend to be computerized, the essential feature is its emphasis on proper procedure (Putnam, 1966). If collectively viewed, the information systems architecture (not to be confused with Enterprise Architecture) defines those systems that provide the enterprise with information and services. These may be transactional, relational, informative, decisional or innovative in nature (Magoulas & Pessi, 1998). This area covers activities such as project planning, project management, modelling, architectural design and simulation.

## 4.    Aligning the constitutional parts of an Enterprise Architecture

The concept of alignment has been expressed in several ways. As a result, alignment is treated synonymously to the following ideas: (1) fit, (2) link, (3) harmony, (4) balance, (5) fusion, (6) integration, (7) relationship, (8) compatibility and (9) conformity (see for instance Avison, Jones, Powell & Wilson, 2004). However, within the context of informatics, the concept of alignment is given in terms of harmonious relationships between two areas of interest in general and the enterprise as a whole in particular. In the latter case, the alignment is called contextual and we discuss it briefly later on.

### 4.1    A sense of socio-cultural alignment

Socio-cultural alignment is reflected in the harmonious nature of relationships between the areas of information systems and the areas of goals, objectives and values. The crucial assumption here is that information and knowledge is the glue that holds business and/or social communities together (Magoulas & Pessi, 1998). Such alignment can be defined as:

**Stakeholders Expectation (Time) = Delivered contributions (Time)**

The notion is to determine how shared values, mutual goal-commitments and collaborative behaviour are addressed within the enterprise. The soundness of the socio-cultural alignment may be expressed and assessed in terms of cultural feasibility, i.e. shared values and priorities, social feasibility, co-determination, shared visions, shared goals as well as continuity of mutual commitments. Furthermore, it is of profound interest to determine the manner in which the organization settles upon its common goals.

## 4.2  A sense of functional alignment

Functional alignment is a state of harmonious relationships between the area of information systems and the area of activities and processes. The fundamental assumption here is that information and knowledge are critical and in many cases strategic resources (Magoulas and Pessi, 1998). Such an alignment can be defined in the following manner:

**Required information capabilities (Time) = Available information capabilities (Time)**

The equation represents the essentials of Galbraith's (1973, 1977) contingency theory, and essentially expresses the necessity for the enterprise to satisfy its need for information in a timely manner.

Any form of informational activity performed by the systems may be seen as a non-separated part of an enterprise activity. In several approaches, enterprise processes are treated as the "creator" as well as "user" of information. In other words, while the quality of information systems depends on the quality of enterprise processes, the quality of enterprise processes depends on the quality of information systems.

The dimension of functional alignment ultimately boils down to issues of coordinated development, i.e. how the development of the information systems has been synchronized with the development of enterprise processes. The soundness of functional alignment should therefore be based on process effectiveness; support, flexibility, inter-dependency, quality improvement, degree of required co-ordination, degree of required synchronisation and economy.

## 4.3    A sense of structural alignment

Structural alignment defines and integrates the area of information systems with the area of power, i.e. sources of authorities and responsibilities. The crucial assumption here is that information and knowledge are significant sources of power (Magoulas & Pessi, 1998). Therefore the concept of "Information Politics" used by Davenport (1997) reflects the very same issues as structural alignment. In any case, structural alignment concerns the harmonious relationships between the structure of power and the information systems. Such alignment can be defined as:

### Established structure = Accepted structure

A balanced equation means that the established structure is accepted by the stakeholders of the enterprise. A misaligned structure can manifest itself in terms of conflicts, alienation, absenteeism, et cetera (Hedberg, 1980; Davenport, 1997). However, this form of alignment is impacted by the requisites of comprehensibility. A lack of comprehensibility leads to inability to manage both processes and information. Therefore, rather than technological sophistication, the requisite of simplicity (and efficiency) of processes should dominate the structuring of the enterprise. Furthermore, the structure of information-flows should map the boundaries of responsibilities. Unclear, complex and incomprehensible information structures lead to loss of manageability. There is a broad consensus regarding the various models that promote or inhibit the structural alignment. Among the more commonly referenced are: Business monarchy, IT-utopia, federalism, feudalism, dualism and anarchism (Davenport, 1997; Ross, Weill & Robertson, 2006; Boddy, 2009).

## 4.4    A sense of infological alignment

Infological alignment reflects the harmonious relationships between the area of information systems and the area of the individual stakeholders. The basic assumption in this case is that information is knowledge communicated through our language (Langefors, 1975, 1986).

Infological alignment expresses the requisites for locality, comprehensibility and meaningfulness. Cognitive distance, working styles, decision styles, communicative styles and perspectives can be seen as significant factors for the actors' willingness to use and accept the information systems. Such alignment can be expressed as:

**Required information = Provided information + extra information**

However, information is knowledge communicated through the use of data. Accordingly, infology comprises different approaches to further sound communication. Yet communicating information outside its natural (local) boundaries can be problematic (Langefors, 1975, 1986; Hugoson, 1989, 1990; Magoulas & Pessi, 1998). In many cases the communication of information requires additional information. Furthermore, the value of information and information systems depend entirely on the effects that these tools have on the individual and his social surrounding.

Not all kinds of information can be universally communicated. The globalisation of information should receive specific treatment and should be established through negotiation (Hugoson, 1989). Information systems should support the learning processes that take place within the functions of the organisation. Hence, standard operating procedures should be avoided as much as possible – especially in dynamic environments. In a situation where information gathering and storage becomes institutionalized, there is a clear risk of encountering what may be referred to as the information paradox. This paradox is characterized by a situation where there is a vast amount of data in the information systems, yet none of it is relevant or useful. Concomitantly, the information that actually is needed is not accessible as it is merely present in the minds of employees or in unsanctioned, "feral" information systems (Houghton & Kerr, 2006).

Lastly, the goodness of infological integration can be measured in terms of infological completeness; that is to say a clear and unequivocal understanding of means and ends. A state of infological alignment can thus be demonstrated when information conforms to the tacit knowledge of actors in terms of validity, functionality and relevance (Langefors, 1975, 1986; Mendelson, 2000; Argyris, 1980; Hewitt, 1986; Ackoff, 1967; Simon, 1962, 1969).

## 4.5   A sense of contextual alignment

Contextual alignment concerns the harmonious relationships between the enterprise as a whole, its information systems and its external environment. The concerned relationships have only an indirect impact on the information systems and the different areas of interests. These areas may at first glance seem unrelated, but since the flow of information permeates the organization, it is necessary to be mindful of the subtle manner in which different areas influence one another. Contextual alignment also includes the enterprise's boundaries as well as its interaction with its environment (Tichy, 1983). Although it may be difficult (or even impossible) for the organization to affect any change beyond the limits of its enterprise areas, one should be mindful of opportunities and impediments as they are usually the impetus for organizational change. Such alignment can be defined as:

**Expected enterprise behaviour = Observed enterprise behaviour**

Those factors that relate to the indirect interaction between organizational areas as well as environmental circumstances are critical to attaining contextual alignment.

# 5. Comparative analysis of approaches

The approaches addressed in this paper are the Zachman Framework, The Open Group Architecture Framework - TOGAF, the Extended Enterprise Architecture Framework – E2AF and the Generalised Enterprise Reference Architecture and Methodology - GERAM. The first and second of these frameworks were elected due to their popularity, E2AF due to its explicit focus on the extended enterprise and GERAM due to its focus on customization.

The Zachman Framework (Zachman, 1987; Sowa & Zachman, 1992) was originally developed by John Zachman and extended to its current scope with the aid of John Sowa. In its inception, the purpose of the framework was to steer organizations away from the widespread practice of viewing the enterprise through static and disconnected models.

The Open Group Architecture Framework (The Open Group, 2009) was originally released in 1995. At the time, it was based upon TAFIM, a framework for information management developed by the United States Department of Defense. Currently in its ninth revision, TOGAF has gradually expanded its scope from strict management of IT towards a broader business orientation.

The Generalised Enterprise Reference Architecture and Methodology (Bernus & Nemes, 1994; IFIP-IFAC Task force on Architectures for Enterprise Integration, 2003) is the product of the IFAC/IFIP Task Force on Architectures for Enterprise Integration, founded in 1990. GERAM is designed so that the practitioner is able to combine different frameworks or methodologies in order to custom design a new architecture. Consequently, it is an extensive standard that includes meticulous descriptions of reference architectures, modeling languages, techniques and tools.

The Extended Enterprise Architecture Framework was created by Jaap Schekkerman in 2001. Rather than any unified documentation, E2AF is documented in several separate documents that are incremented in a piecemeal fashion. E2AF assumes a holistic approach to architecture, stating that an enterprise that is to function as a whole must be designed as a whole (Schekkerman 2006:b). Strong emphasis is also placed on contextual awareness and stresses constant awareness of threats and opportunities in the environment (Schekkerman 2006:a, 2006:c).

The study at hand has been conducted using the best, first-hand literary sources available. It is however possible that some documentation regarding these approaches is unavailable due to reasons pertaining to intellectual property or fragmented documentation.

The tables below express the manner in which the investigated approaches address the various forms of alignment. "Clear" denotes the presence of explicit guidance regarding architectural alignment whereas "unclear" denotes the absence or lack of salience.

## 5.1   Socio-cultural alignment

A state of socio-cultural alignment reflects the harmonious contribution of the information systems & ICT to the ever changing expectations of internal as well as external stakeholders of the enterprise. In many cases, the lack of socio-cultural guidelines can be attributed to the underlying paradigms of the investigated approaches. That is to say, some approaches presuppose that information resources should be treated as independent of organization and culture.

**Table 1:** Results of analysis vis-à-vis socio-cultural alignment

|  | ZACHMAN | TOGAF | GERAM | E2AF |
|---|---|---|---|---|
| Clear |  |  |  |  |
| Unclear | Insufficient guidance regarding relationship between IS and objectives of planner and owner. | Insufficient details offered regarding concept "enterprise benefits". | Alignment based on requirements of IT and rather than objectives of business. | Advocates satisfaction of collective needs of the extended enterprise, but offers little practical guidance. |

## 5.2 Functional alignment

The functional alignment concerns the harmonious contribution of available information systems & ICT capabilities to the information, service, transactions, and relations required by either the business processes or business units of the enterprise. Lack of clarity is often based on the fact that architectural approaches refer to the architecture as a singular information system that serves the whole enterprise and its surroundings. Another cause for concern is the fact that the investigated approaches tend to describe the processes and activities in isolation rather than their relationships to other areas of the enterprise.

**Table 2:** Results of analysis vis-à-vis functional alignment

|  | ZACHMAN | TOGAF | GERAM | E2AF |
|---|---|---|---|---|
| Clear |  | Alignment ensured by operational contracts between customers of and providers. | Harmonization between required IS services and provided IS services. | Alignment between business processes & IS ensured through basic principles. |
| Unclear | Insufficient guidance regarding business processes and the area of IS & ICT. | Insufficient guidance on how services are integrated into business processes and subsequently implemented. | Insufficient practical guidance regarding the modelling of the various entities of an enterprise. |  |

## 5.3   Structural alignment

Structural alignment reflects a situation where information systems & ICT capabilities are characterized by a clear, comprehensible, and accepted form of authority and responsibility. Unclear guidance regarding structural alignment is often derived from the propensity of approaches to describe responsibilities in themselves rather than in relationship to area of information systems. Another source of potential misgivings is the paradigm underlying each one of investigated approaches. Much like with socio-cultural issues, some approaches presuppose that information resources should be treated as independent of organization and structure.

**Table 3:** Results of analysis vis-à-vis structural alignment

|         | ZACHMAN | TOGAF | GERAM | E2AF |
|---------|---------|-------|-------|------|
| Clear   |         | Based on governance contracts, IT responsibility, data trustees, ownership of common applications. | Clear view of responsibilities & roles of functional areas. | Offers guidance based on level of influence of concerned stakeholders. |
| Unclear | Insufficient or missing guidance regarding the areas of authority and responsibilities with the areas of IS & ICT. | Insufficient guidance regarding the relationship between the area of responsibility and the business objectives. | Insufficient guidance regarding harmonization of operations with capabilities of IS & ICT. | |

## 5.4   Infological alignment

Infological alignment concerns the sound use of available information systems & ICT capabilities to satisfy the required informational, transactional and relational needs of human stakeholders. In many cases, infological ambiguity can be a presumption by architectural approaches that facts are always facts. By assuming this position, issues like cognitive distance and occupational proficiencies are in effect ignored.

**Table 4:** Results of analysis vis-à-vis infological alignment

| | ZACHMAN | TOGAF | GERAM | E2AF |
|---|---|---|---|---|
| Clear | | | | Collective un-derstanding advocated through commu-nication between internal and external stake-holders. |
| Unclear | Insufficient guidance re-garding how information requisites such as quality, availability, comparability, consistency, etc. are treated. | Insufficient guidance on how to avoid information paradox and still promote sharing and availability of data. | Insufficient guidance on how to align stakeholders to IS & ICT.<br><br>Insufficient guidance on aligning hu-man capabili-ties, mental models, etc and IS capabil-ities. | |

## 5.5   Contextual alignment

The most essential property of contextual alignment is given in terms of harmony between the external and internal environments of the enter-prise. Since the enterprise is unable to directly control its environment, it is only natural for architectural approaches to focus on guidance concerning internal assets. Contextual harmony fills in the blanks with regards to the plurality of legal regulations, rules of intellectual property and political issues that surround the enterprise.

**Table 5:** Results of analysis vis-à-vis contextual alignment

|  | ZACHMAN | TOGAF | GERAM | E2AF |
|---|---|---|---|---|
| Clear |  | Alignment between EA and governance established through operational and governance contracts.<br><br>Stipulates enterprise conformance with regulations, laws and intellectual property. | Securing architectural alignment between areas of enterprise by crossing functional barriers.<br><br>Integration and interoperability between the heterogeneous environments of enterprise. | Advocates economic, legal, ethical and discretionary viewpoints.<br><br>Strong emphasis on external partners. |
| Unclear | Insufficient guidance regarding how IS relates to the enterprise and its surrounding environment.<br><br>Unclear guidance as to how the parts of the architecture fit together.<br><br>Unsatisfactory guidance regarding how the architecture differentiates between physical possibilities and system rules. | Framework does not cover issues of alignment between business & IT strategy.<br><br>Insufficient guidance regarding how the alignment between EA and enterprise mission is established.<br><br>Scarce guidance regarding how the alignment between EA and its implementation is managed. | Insufficient guidance regarding how the role of IS promotes the responsiveness of the enterprise to environmental changes. | Lack of guidance regarding how to manage conflicting expectations and viewpoints of partners. |

# 6. Discussion

The common denominator of any enterprise architecture is given in terms of various forms of sound alignment between its constitutional parts. Thus, without alignment any sense of architecture disappears. Hence, the ultimate aim of our efforts was to improve the existing body of knowledge regarding architectural alignment and how it is treated by a handful of architectural approaches: Zachman framework, TOGAF, GERAM and E2AF. Each one provides a collection of concepts, principles, guidelines and/or values that is intended to support any effort in the process of designing, developing implementing and evaluating an enterprise architecture that is capable of maintaining alignment between its constitutional parts. Thus, our focus has been to clarify how each one of the investigated approaches treats the issues associated with alignment. We will now briefly discuss the manner and extent to which the investigated approaches offer guidance on socio-cultural, functional, structural, infological, and contextual alignment.

Our investigation into the socio-cultural dimension shows that none of the architectural approaches covered in this paper provide clear guidance with regards to socio-cultural alignment.

Our analysis of the functional issues indicates that three of the four approaches – TOGAF, GERAM and E2AF – offer clear guidance on the different aspects of functional alignment. However, the Zachman framework offers little support and may therefore be considered unsatisfactory in terms of attaining architectural alignment.

Moving on to the structural dimension, our evaluation suggests that the situation is to a large extent the same. That is to say, three of the four approaches - TOGAF, GERAM and E2AF – offer strong practical support on attaining structural alignment. Again, the Zachman framework is lacking in guidance for structural issues.

The analysis of the infological dimension shows that only one of the investigated approaches – E2AF – offers suitable guidance with regards to infological alignment. The support offered by the three remaining approaches – Zachman framework, TOGAF and GERAM – is either doubtful or brief with few clear guidelines.

Finally, the analysis of the contextual dimension shows that three of the investigated approaches – TOGAF, GERAM, and E2AF – provide comprehensive, albeit somewhat simplistic, support regarding contextual alignment. Again, the Zachman framework does not provide any discernible guidelines. It does bear mentioning that among the architectural approaches evaluated; only E2AF offers what may be considered a somewhat nuanced view of contextual issues. By and large, the environment is simply seen as a source of requirements such as legal restrictions and contractual obligations. This is perhaps no great surprise given the sheer complexity of our world at large. However, given that the "outside world" is the source for many of the challenges faced by modern enterprises, one would assume that some manner of guidance would be in order.

It is prudent to point out that this evaluation rooted in the Scandinavian school of informatics which carries with it explicit consideration of hard (mechanistic) & soft (humanistic) aspects of systems thinking. This also extends to our view of organizational design in general and alignment of Enterprise Architecture in particular. Practical examples of architectures that align hard and soft aspects of the enterprise can also be found within international companies such as Xerox (Howard, 1992).

Set against a delineation of Enterprise Architecture into hard and soft aspects, we can discern that the architectural approaches which we have analyzed seem to gravitate towards the hard aspects of architectural design. Hence, these approaches offer a great deal of guidance regarding enterprise activities and formal responsibilities. This provides a stark contrast to the soft aspects of architectural design where very little practical support is offered. It is not within the scope of this article to formulate advice or guidelines to practitioners, but we would suggest caution against underestimating the humanistic aspects of architectural design. Stakeholder discontentment, lack of comprehension and a myopic focus on requirements rather than goals may prove equally (if not more) crippling compared to poor process management or unclear responsibilities.

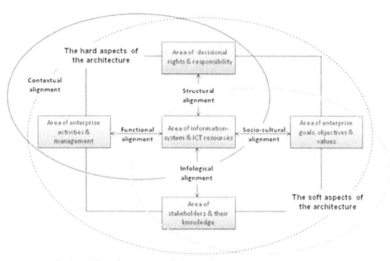

**Figure 2:** The hard & soft aspects of the architecture

# 7. Conclusions

The primary aim of this paper has been to ascertain how the various forms and aspects of architectural alignment are treated by formalized approaches to Enterprise Architecture. This issue has been investigated with respect to socio-cultural, functional, structural, infological and contextual alignment. Our study has provided us with the following conclusions:

Firstly, our investigation clearly demonstrates that approaches to Enterprise Architecture provide guidance for structural and functional alignment, but less so for infological or socio-cultural alignment. A possible explanation may be that investigated approaches follow a paradigm that demands the independence of information and information systems from cognitive, organizational and technological aspects (as explained by Brancheau & Wetherbe, 1986). Another feasible interpretation is that investigated approaches are derived from a tradition of engineering design rather than architectural design. This would account for the focus on requirements and constraints found in the "hard" aspects of the enterprise, rather than the "softer" aspects such as goals and decision making that characterizes architectural design.

Secondly, the area of contextual alignment is described by all investigated approaches as being relatively simplistic and stable. Some forms of contextual alignment are established through contractual agreements while others are dictated through laws and regulations. This is presumably in response to the heterogeneity inherent to most environments.

Finally, none of the investigated approaches discuss the mutual interdependence that exists between the various forms of alignment. However, the architectural patterns of the enterprise are the result of organizational forces rather than rationality. This follows previous research by Mintzberg (1989).

# References

Abdallah, S & Galal-Edeen, G.H. (2006) Towards a framework for enterprise architecture frameworks comparison and selection. Proceedings of the Fourth International Conference on Informatics and Systems.

Ackoff, R. L. (1967). Management Misinformation Systems. Management Science, 4 (4), 147-156.

Argyris, C. (1980). Some Inner Contradictions in Management Information Systems. In The Information Systems Environment (Lucas, I H., Land, F., Lincoln, T. and Supper, K. Eds.), 15-35, North-Holland, Amsterdam.

Australian Government Information Management Office. (2011). Australian Government Architecture Reference Models, version 3.0. Australian Government Information Management Office, Canberra.

Avison, D., Jones, J., Powell, P. & Wilson, D. (2004). Using and validating the strategic alignment model, Journal of Strategic Information Systems, 13 (3), 223-246.

Baets, W. (1992). Aligning information systems with business strategy. The Journal of Strategic Information Systems, 1(4), September 1992, 205-213.

Baker, J. & Jones, D. (2008). A Theoretical Framework for Sustained Strategic Alignment and an Agenda for Research. Proceedings of JAIS Theory Development Workshop. Sprouts: Working Papers on Information Systems, 8 (16).

Bernus, P. & Nemes, L. (1994). A Framework to Define a Generic Enterprise Reference Architecture and Methodology. In Proceedings of the International Conference on Automation, Robotics and Computer Vision (ICARCV'94), Singapore, November 10–12, 1994.

Boddy, D., Boonstra, A. & Kennedy, G. (2009). Managing Information Systems, Strategy and Organisation. 3rd Edition. Pearson Education, Essex.

Brancheau, J.C. & Wetherbe, J.C, (1986). Information Architectures: Methods and practice, Information Processing & Management, 22 (6), 453-463.

Brynjolfsson, E. (1993). The productivity paradox of information technology. Communications of the ACM 36 (12) (December 1993), 66-77.

Chan, Y, E. & Reich, B. H. (2007). IT alignment: what have we learned? Journal of Information Technology, 22, 297–315.

Checkland, P. (1981). Systems Thinking, Systems Practice. John Wiley & Sons, New York.

Churchman C.W. (1971). The design of inquiring systems: Basic concept of systems and organization, Basic Books, New York.

Ciborra, C. (1997). De Profundis? Deconstructing the concept of strategic alignment. Scandinavian Journal of Information Systems, 9 (1), 67-82.

Dahlbom, B. (1996). The new informatics. Scandinavian journal of Information systems, 8 (2), 29-48.

Davenport, T. (1997). Information ecology: Mastering the information and knowledge environment. Oxford University press, New York.

Franke, U., Hook, D., Konig, J., Lagerstrom, R., Narman, P., Ullberg, J., Gustafsson, P., & Ekstedt, M. (2009). EAF2- a Framework for Categorizing Enterprise Architecture Frameworks. Proceedings of the 10th ACIS International Conference on Software Engineering, Artificial Intelligences, Networking and Parallel/Distributed Computing. 327-332.

Galbraith, J. R. (1973). Designing Complex Organizations. Addison-Wesley, Boston.

Galbraith, J. R. (1977). Organizational Design. Addison-Wesley, Boston.

GAO – US Government Accountability Office. (2005). The US Government's Performance Reference Model 1.0. US Government Accountability Office, Washington DC.

IFIP-IFAC Task force on Architectures for Enterprise Integration. (2003). The Generalised Enterprise Reference Architecture and Methodology: Version 1.6.3 (Final). In Handbook on Enterprise Architecture (Bernus, P., Nemes, L. and Schmidt, G. Eds.) Springer-Verlag, Berlin.

Hedberg, B. (1980). Using Computerized Information Systems to Design Better Organization and Jobs. In The Human Side of Information Processing (Bjørn-Andersen, N. Ed.), 19-33, North-Holland, Amsterdam.

Henderson, J. & Venkatraman, N. (1992). Strategic Alignment: A model for organizational transformation through information technology. In Transforming Organizations (Kochan, T. & Unseem, M. Eds.), 97-117, Oxford University Press, New York.

Hewitt, C. (1986). Offices are Open Systems. ACM Transactions on Office Information Systems, Vol. 4 (3), 271-287.

Houghton, L. & Kerr, D. (2006). A study into the creation of feral information systems as a response to an ERP implementation within the supply chain of a large government-owned corporation. International Journal of Internet and Enterprise Management 4(2), 135-147.

Howard, R. (1992). The CEO as Organizational Architect: An Interview with Xerox's Paul Allaire. Harvard Business Review, 70 (5), 106-121.

Hugoson, M-Å. (1989). A System of Systems: A theory of information systems Architecture and Interaction. Strukturering av informationsystem, Chalmers tekniska högskola, Göteborg, SVING & SVIG. (In Swedish)

Hugoson, M-Å. (1990). Versamhetsbaserad Systemstrukturering. Principer och tilläpmningar, Göteborg, Programator AB. (In Swedish)

Hugoson, M-Å., Magoulas, T. & Pessi, K. (2008). Interoperability Strategies for Business Agility. In Advances in enterprise engineering I. Lecture notes in business information processing, 10 (3), 108-121, Springer-Verlag, Berlin.

Langefors, B. (1975). Control Structure and Formalized Information Analysis in Organizations. In Information Systems and Organizational Structure (Grochla, E. & Szyperski, N. Eds.). Walter de Gruyter, New York & Berlin.

Langefors, B. (1986). Information and Management Systems. In Erhvervs Økonomisk Tidsskrift. Reprint. Published by Foreningen af Danske Civiløkonomer.

Leist, S. & Zellner, G. (2006) Evaluation of current architecture frameworks. Proceedings of the 2006 symposium on Applied computing, 1546-1553.

Luftman, J. N. (1996). Applying the Strategic Alignment Model. In Luftman, J.N. (Ed.) Competing in the Information Age: Strategic Alignment in Practice. Oxford University Press, New York.

Luftman, J. N. (2000). Assessing Business-IT Alignment Maturity. Communications of the AIS, 4, 1–50.

Maes, R., Rijsenbrij, D., Truijens, O. & Goedvolk, H. (2000). Redefining business-IT alignment through a unified framework. PrimaVera Working Paper 2000-19, Universitet van Amsterdam.

Magoulas T. & Pessi K. (1998). Strategisk IT Management. Doctoral Dissertation, University of Gothenburg, Department of Informatics. (In Swedish)

McKenzie, K.D. (1984). A Strategy and desiderata for organizational design. Human Systems Management 4, 201-213.

Mendelson, H. (2000). Organizational Architecture and Success in the Information Technology Industry. Management Science, 46 (4), 513-529.

Mintzberg, H. (1989). Mintzberg on Management. Free Press, New York.

Morton, M.S.S. (1991). Introduction. In Morton, M.S.S (Ed.) The Corporation of the 1990s: Information Technology and Organizational Transformation. Oxford University Press, New York.

National Institutes of Health. (2011). NIH Enterprise Architecture Framework. [online] Available at: < http://enterprisearchitecture.nih.gov/About/Approach/Framework.htm > [Accessed 29 November 2011].

Noran, O. (2003). An analysis of the Zachman framework for enterprise architecture from the GERAM perspective. IFAC Annual Reviews in Control 27(2), 163-183.

Odongo, A.O., Kang, S. & Ko, I-Y. (2010). A Scheme for Systematically Selecting an Enterprise Architecture Framework. Proceedings of the 9th IEEE/ACIS International conference on Computer and Information Science, 665-670.

Office of Management and Budget. (2007). FEA Consolidated Reference Model Document, version 2.3. Office of Management and Budget, Washington DC.

Papp, R. (2001). Strategic Information Technology: Opportunities for Competitive Advantage. IDEA Publishing Group, Hershey.

Putnam, A. O., Barlow, E. R. & Stilian, G. N. (1966). Samordnad företagskontroll - totala informationssystem i praktisk belysning. Translated from English by Heinmetz, E. J. Beckmans bokförlag, Stockholm. (In Swedish)

Rood, A. M. (1994). Enterprise Architecture: Definition, content and utility. In Proceedings of the third workshop on enabling technologies: Infrastructure for Collaborative Enterprises, 106-11, IEEE computer society press, Los Alamitos.

Ross, J.W., Weill, P. & Robertson, D.C. (2006). Enterprise Architecture as Strategy: Creating a Foundation for Business Execution. Harvard Business Press, Boston.

Schekkerman, J. (2006:a). Enterprise Architecture Assessment Guide: Version 2.2. Institute For Enterprise Architecture Developments, Amersfoort.

Schekkerman, J. (2006:b). Extended Enterprise Architecture Framework Essentials Guide: Version 1.5. Institute For Enterprise Architecture Developments, Amersfoort.

Schekkerman, J. (2006:c). Extended Enterprise Architecture Viewpoints Support Guide. Institute For Enterprise Architecture Developments, Amersfoort.

Schöenherr, M. (2009). Towards a Common Terminology in the Discipline of Enterprise Architecture. In Service-Oriented Computing --- ICSOC 2008 Workshops, Lecture Notes In Computer Science, Vol. 5472 (Feuerlicht, G. and Lamersdorf, W. Eds.), 400-413, Springer-Verlag, Berlin.

Sessions, R. (2007). A Comparison of the Top Four Enterprise Architecture Methodologies. ObjectWatch Inc.

Simon, H. (1962). The Architecture of Complexity. Proceedings of the American Philosophical Society, 106 (6), 467-482.

Simon, H. (1969). The Sciences of the Artificial, The MIT Press, Cambridge, MA.

Sowa, J.F. & Zachman, J.A. (1992). Extending and Formalizing the Framework for Information Systems Architecture. IBM Systems Journal 31 (3), 590-616.

Spanos, Y.E., Prastacos, G.P. & Poulymenakou, A. (2002). The relationship between communication technologies adoption and management. Information and Management 39, 659-675.

Tang, A., Han, J. & Chen, P. (2004). A Comparative Analysis of Architecture Frameworks. Proceedings of the 11th Asia-Pacific Software Engineering Conference, 640-647.

The Open Group. (2009). The Open Group Architecture Framework: Version 9, Enterprise Edition.

Tichy, N.M. (1983). Managing Strategic Change: Technical, Political, and Cultural Dynamics. Wiley, New York.

Urbaczewski, L. & Mrdalj, S. (2006). A comparison of enterprise architecture frameworks. Issues in Information Systems 7 (2), 18-23.

Walentowitz, K., Beimborn, D., Schroiff, A. & Weitzel, T. (2011). The Social Network Structure of Alignment - A Literature Review. 44th Hawaii International Conference on System Sciences (HICSS), 4-7 Jan. 2011.

Whitman, L., Ramachandran, K. & Ketkar, V. (2001). A taxonomy of a living model of the enterprise. In Proceedings of the 33nd conference on Winter simulation, 848-855, IEEE Computer Society, Arlington.

Zachman, J. A. (1987). A Framework for Information Systems Architecture. IBM Systems Journal, 26 (3), 276-292.

# Requirements Elicitation for the Technology Conception of a Community Information System for the Indigenous Microenterprise: A Contextual Multi-Analysis Approach on Business and Community Requirements of Batik Making

**Nor Laila Md Noor and Ariza Nordin**
Universiti Teknologi MARA, Shah Alam, Malaysia
*Originally published in EJISE (2012) Volume 15, ISS 1*

### Editorial Commentary

It is now well-documented that the economic development of developing countries is highly dependent on the advancement of a robust small, medium and micro enterprise (SME) sector. So the untapped economic potential of the developing world is reliant on innovative approaches to develop this sector. The rapid advances of our Information Society are inextricably tied to the latter. Community-based enterprises are a critical cog in the wheel of the emerging economic sector driven by the Information Society. This paper advances our understanding of the methods related to the design and deployment of IS at a community level, highlighting cultural and other localised issues into future evaluation frameworks to provide an improved basis for the development of ex-ante evaluation frameworks during the IS design phase for community-based enterprises.

**Abstract:** Batik is a traditional art form whose charm lies in its power of storytelling. Batik making is practiced by various indigenous communities in Asia and Africa and has evolved into a socio-economic uplift existing as a cottage industry. The Malaysian batik industry was revived by the government intervention to emphasize batik as a cultural identity and also to improve the livelihood of batik producers where the majority operates as indigenous microenterprises. However, the batik making tasks and the management of batik microenterprises are currently not supported by the use of ICT. To facilitate batik microenterprises ICT adoption we proposed the development of ICT-based information systems that emphasize the cultural context of batik production. In our work we argued that the facilitation of batik microenterprises ICT adoption can happen by developing an ICT-based information system that emphasize the cultural context of batik production. We argued that a technology conception needs to consider the ecological aspect of batik production that comprises of resources, technology and geography to understand barriers and opportunities of technology. To support our argument, we conducted a batik microenterprise business requirements elicitation to formulate the technology conception for an ICT-based information system. We adopted the framework that considers a cultural diversified practice and focus on the cultural context as a business requirement for ICT adoption. We conducted a contextual inquiry using multi-activity inquiries that include site visits, face-to-face and focus group interviews with an informal batik making community of practice. Our participants are representatives of batik advocators, entrepreneurs, practitioners and apprentices. We strategize the focus group inquiry in a workshop setting using verbal and visual cues to navigate the chaotic and fragmented storytelling of group members. From the contextual multi-analysis conducted we discovered that the technological conception for batik microenterprise is incomplete if we only address the usual business productivity requirements. Our findings reveal that the concern for batik aesthetics and the fear of batik cultural erosion should not be overlooked as these concerns are equally imperative as business productivity. In addition we also discovered that a social structure dimension is an important input to understand the primary and secondary actors within a technological conception. This concept will be useful in defining roles within future socio-technical systems that will be created to support business and knowledge activities of indigenous microenterprise. We formulated this technology conception as core elements of the community information system requirement specification for the batik microenterprise. Our work will contribute to the literature on systems engineering of ICT-based information systems for indigenous or cultural influenced business.

**Keywords:** community informatics, requirements engineering, microenterprise, technology adoption, indigenous business, socio-technical system

# 1. Introduction

Batik is an indigenous cultural artefact that is influenced by the creativity of a single or collective human actions inspired by natural surroundings. Batik is predominant in various indigenous communities in South East Asia, Africa, India and China. The charm of batik lies in its power of pictorial storytelling where batik motifs depict nature as well as everyday lives and practices. Batik making has evolved into a socio-economic uplift within indigenous communities and has long existed as a cottage industry. In Malaysia, the batik industry has been revived by the government intervention in support of the industry. Besides emphasizing batik as a cultural identity, the Malaysian government is also interested in improving the livelihood of batik producers where the majority operates their trade as microenterprises. The Malaysian Ministry of International Trade and Industry has emphasized on the necessity of enhancing domestic capabilities and competitiveness of manufacturers of batik by facilitating the utilisation of ICT and new technologies in the design, production and marketing of batik. The interest to promote and increase the production of batik is currently hampered by use of traditional methods of batik making like hand painting and block printing. Currently the management of batik microenterprises is also not supported by the use of ICT. This situation prevails as batik makers are concerned with issues of the disruption of the craft's cultural heritage and acts of design theft when batik designs are published. The unique situation of batik making as an indigenous business is a strong motivating factor to explore on the ICT adoption of batik microenterprise to gain an insight on to improve their operational efficiencies and market positioning. Here, we present our technology conception approach for batik microenterprises practices from the framework of socio-technical systems. We scope our work on the elicitation of business requirements for batik microenterprise business management. Realizing that batik making involves a cultural heritage influence, we focus on the demand of rational and affective attitude towards batik making in the elicitation. We argue that the approach of contextual inquiry can help us gain better understanding of the batik making situation before attempting to look into possible socio-technical systems solutions. Our paper covers a broad literature review of microenterprise and batik making, technology adoption and socio-technical systems issues. We then report on the contextual inquiry work that we conducted to elicit business requirements of batik making and our findings highlighted pertinent issues in business and ICT strategy alignment.

## 2.  Literature review

This section covers a review on pertinent issues of the Malaysian batik industry, ICT adoption and microenterprise, ICT-based work systems and elicitation methods.

## 2.1    The batik making enterprise

The Malaysian batik industry is clustered under the creative industry and is divided into small and medium enterprises (SMEs) and the cottage industry which operates as microenterprises (Wan Teh 1997). However, based on Porter's industry cluster (Porter 1990) batik will be placed as a handicraft industry and categorized as a historic know-how-based cluster. Within this cluster, the batik business knowledge is based on the traditional activities that survived over the years through the inheritance phenomenon across generations spurned by a mentoring process knowledge transfer traditions. Batik microenterprise business model is about producing batik traditionally for the local market and batik microenterprise are known for the expertise in batik making technique and design creativity. In Malaysia there is no official differentiation between batik manufacturers and batik artist as they both belong to one nationwide community of batik makers. Batik has been endorsed as a cultural heritage entity by UNESCO in 2009. The knowledge asset is one of the preservation entities. Batik exists as the object of traditions that inherits traits of traditional knowledge and preservation, imperative to the community memory. As a handicraft product, batik reflects the cultural aspect of the batik making community and is subjected to the batik makers' prioritized agenda. The batik maker is comprehended to have both an artist and a designer attitude within the batik making task model. A batik maker is a person who assumes the role as an artist, a designer and a promoter to make batik for cultural and business endeavour. The versatility of the role playing is due to the craftsmen model of business as microenterprises and livelihood strategies. As the role of batik maker is to "make" batik, this demands both rational and affective attitude towards the artefact and its making. The attitude of an artist features of adhering to self-driven task model, having artistic sense and life enrichment objective. On the other hand the designer attitude emphasized on engineering process driven task model, having the technical sense and creative sensibility as attitude towards product development.

Our synthesized understanding of the Malaysian batik maker is illustrated in Figure 1 and is derived from formal sources of batik maker definitions from Jamal (1994), Ismail (1997) and Elamvazuthi and Morris (2000). An elaboration of the synthesized understanding refers to the duality of creative design which described designing as a rational and a non-rational process (Schön,1983) and between reflective practice and technical rationality (Schön, 1983). In addition the dual faceted attitudes in batik making can be described from the need perspectives which influence the cognitive reasoning of the batik maker. Maslow's (1943) hierarchy of needs is the theoretical basis of understanding levels of need. The artist as a romanticist need is to create for self-actualization. The satisfaction gained from the batik artefact is beyond economical purpose in contrary to the need to develop a product for market acceptance. The designer as a rationalist emphasized on the engineering process driven task model, having technical sense and creative sensibility as attitude towards product development. However the transcendental, proximity, aesthetics and serendipity characterizing elements of both attitudes are presence within the artist and designer task models to provide the philosophical component of the batik design artefact.

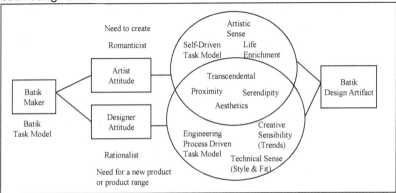

**Figure 1:** A synthesized understanding Malaysian Batik Maker

The synthesized understanding of the batik maker gives an important insight to their attitude towards ICT adoption.

## 2.2 ICT adoption, community informatics, socio-technical systems and knowledge systems

The adoption and diffusion of ICT throughout a productive system assumes a core position in the new economy and has spurred numerous ICT adoption research conducted from different approaches. Generally there are three approaches to ICT adoption: the diffusion approach, the adoption approach and the domestication process (Manueli, et al 2007).

### 2.2.1 The diffusion approach

In the diffusion approach, the Roger's Diffusion of Innovation (DOI) theory is used to explain the role of the media and interpersonal contact in providing information that influences a person's opinion and judgment of the technology that leads to the adoption of the technology. DOI theory is used to view the adoption stages and factors leading to adoption. From the DOI theory, the Rogers' Innovation-Decision Process model is used to gain further understanding of the adoption process related to issue of access. ICT adoption by SMEs is studied in many settings. In the Italian industries, Atzeni and Carboni (2006) revealed that weak ICT penetration is due to the size of industry, the lower reorganization of work practices and the sectoral specialization. For the Malaysian SMEs, Khong and Eze (2008) confirmed the factors of DOI theory and added two other factors which are ICT security and costs. For SMEs in Poland, Spain, Portugal and the United States, Arendt (2008) highlighted that the impact of the lack of access to ICT is less important when compared to the lack of proper knowledge, education and skilled owner-managers and employees within the enterprise. This indicates that the issue of ICT non-adoption cannot be solved simply by the provision of ICT access.

ICT adoption studies also scope into adoption by rural poor focusing on the barrier to ICT adoption from the digital divide perspective. Barriers often cited are factors of limited physical access, socio-economic and socio-personal factors and low education level of potential adopters (Foley et al 2002). However, when addressing ICT adoption in community development, issues of technology compatibility is more important than issues of access. Helmersen (2006) criticised the approach of ICT adoption that forces Western technologies on the poor in developing and third world nations and stressed the need to have a deep local insight that attempt to understand the cultural context that facilitates ICT adoption. Similarly, Kivunike, et al (2009) studied the facilitating and inhibiting factors of ICT adoption by the rural poor in Uganda from a demand-oriented perspective. They too highlighted the importance of understanding the contextual factors that influence ICT adoption. They then suggested that strategies of ICT adoption should move beyond the provision to facilitate adoption and the use of ICT by the rural poor by considering factors such as maintenance costs, quality of services, ICT skills and creating awareness of potential benefits in the rural communities.

Community ICT adoption has evolved into a new discipline known as community informatics (CI) and is related to the discipline known as development informatics or ICT4D. Led by Gurstein (2008), research on CI explored into various methods of research inquiry and practice. Moor (2009) conceived different aspects of community informatics research to consist of contexts/values, cases, process/methodology, and systems and is illustrated in Figure 2.

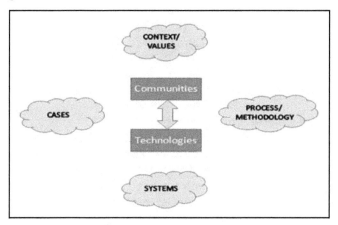

**Figure 2:** Pillars of community informatics research (sources: Moor 2009)

Moor (2009) also highlighted two important CI research contexts: community-centred development and community knowledge sharing through the development of socio-technical systems such as knowledge management systems (KMS).

### 2.2.2    The adoption approach

The adoption approach explains the adoption decision of users applying different individual and social decision making theories. The adoption literature began with the technology acceptance model (TAM) which was first presented by Davis in 1975. Since then TAM has been validated in numerous technology settings and is heavily cited in the literature. TAM is used to determine adoption influencing factors in IT systems both in the voluntary and mandatory used systems and adoption is reflected in the overall user acceptance. Key constructs of TAM are perceived usefulness and perceived ease of use of IT systems and have been used to determine the acceptance of the technology. However in TAM, personal control factors like behavioural accounts are not taken into consideration. TAM is also used with the Delone and McLean IS Success Model to determine the influence of systems quality and information quality of the IT systems on the success and failures of IT systems. Further extension of TAM will be the Information Technology Adoption Model (ITAM) by Dixon (1999) that seeks to refine the IT requirements of the information systems that influences IT adoption leading to the development of the IT adoption framework that includes the interaction between individuals, technology and tasks (FITT framework). The FITT framework focuses on the significance of the optimal interaction (fit) of individual user, technology, and task attributes. Now the fit between the attributes is seen to be more important than the individual attributes themselves. For example, IT skills of the users are not sufficient for the success of an introduction. The IT skills must match the requirements by the IT software.

### 2.2.3    The domestication process

Domestication is described as the process of technology adoption into everyday life and originates from other disciplines such as anthropology, consumption studies and media studies. Domesticating ICT involves a process of bringing new forms of ICT into the home (Chen and Zhang 2009) and involves the integration of technologies into social relationships and structures. The domestication framework has four concurrent phases: the appropriation, the objectification, the incorporation and the conversion. This approach of adoption considers the context in which ICT is experienced by the people using them. Conceptual context distinctions are applied to approach where three important distinct contexts are identified. The first is the work and leisure context, the second will be the end-users that belong or do not belong to a demographic group and the third is the private and the public.

## 2.3    Microenterprise, information systems and socio-technical systems

Researches on ICT adoption by SMEs attempt to determine whether ICT adopted throughout the production process can produced positive outcomes related to operational efficiencies, increased revenues and better market positioning. Alter (2002), defined an information systems framework that outline nine elements that can be used to analyze the professional context to address issues of productivity and sustainability. However, the challenge of microenterprise ICT adoption is multi-dimensional where human factor is a central issue (Duncombe and Molla 2009). Kamal, et al (2010) raises the issues of affordability, awareness, management capabilities and the lack of ICT infrastructure which are not addressed in the earlier information systems framework such as Alter's framework. Duncombe and Molla (2009) who presented four archetypes of information systems formalization amongst SMEs in Botswana, pointed out the importance of looking into the systemic approach when considering the adoption of information systems in SMEs. A firmer assertion was made by Hoffman, et al (2009) who argued that information systems can be viewed from the socio-technical systems perspective to include cultural phenomena approach that will help researchers comprehend the application of works systems outside the professional work context. They further elaborated on the macrocognition approach to help comprehend information systems robustness, resilience and adaptiveness.

A micro-perspective of microenterprise ICT adoption can be viewed from the theoretical lens of socio-technical systems (STS). STS is a social system sitting upon a technical base and comprises of the technology, the people and their personal communication and tasks, views, organizational structures, co-operation and others (Whitworth 2008). Here an STS perspective will shed some light on factors to work on promoting microenterprise ICT adoption. This view is aligned to earlier findings of Tschiersch and Schael (2003) who stated that as industry gets shaped by technology through the process of production automation, computer-supported information and co-operation networks, the reliance will no longer be on mere technical systems but rather on STS. Three technology related dimensions of STS are namely, the workplace, the group work and the network. In the workplace dimension, the concern will be on the actual use of technology within the working process. According to Tschiersch and Schael (2003), from the human centered perspective, the most complex aspect of human work takes into consideration the intrinsic need of people to develop themselves further and to experience through their work, challenges, motivation, success and satisfaction. They further added that the design of STS should try to fulfill meaningful and rewarding tasks which also take account of the individuality of the human operator. The approach to design a socio-technical system is to explicitly recognize the technology's symbiotic relationship with society, and so tries to involve end-users in the creation of the technical products that will affect their lives.

## 2.4 Business requirements elicitation

The traditional approach of requirements elicitation is mainly centered on hardware and software requirements and is often dominated by technical issues of functionality, connectivity, interoperability and security. Isabirye

(2009) highlighted the issue of design-reality gaps between ICT analysts and users which is due to the detachment from the context of a proposed system to be implemented. This follows Heeks (2002) beliefs of the gaps between the system design which is based on the analyst's perceptions and the reality which is often foreign to the analyst. According to Disse (2001) system requirements are best determined through merging the different viewpoints of the stakeholders involved. Whitworth (2009) presented a comprehensive view of socio-technical requirements that he hierarchically group into physical, information, personal and communal requirements. He suggested that STS which involves community influence and participation should consider personal and communal requirements that he prescribed in his Web Of System Performance (WOSP) model. We interpret this into the necessity of understanding the cultural context of the problem domain of batik making. This implies that the technological conception of an ICT-based information system for batik microenterprise demands a holistic understanding of the problem situation and the current resolution towards community empowerment with desirable cultural identity development. A contextual inquiry is therefore necessary for the requirements elicitation.

## 2.5    Contextual inquiry

The contextual inquiry is useful for examining and understanding users and their workplace, tasks, issues and preferences. Within the human computer interaction (HCI) literature, contextual inquiry is commonly-known as the user-centered approach. It is viewed as a synthesis of ethnographic, field research, and participatory design methods that provide designers with grounded and detailed knowledge of user work as a basis for their design (Hotzblatt and Jones 1993). Contextual inquiry studies on the users are made in the context of their work by observing how they perform tasks, the tools they used and the process involved in their work. In HCI, contextual inquiry can be conducted in a laboratory where participants in the inquiry are observed under a usability testing set-up or conducted in an ethnography study set-up or conducted as a focus group workshop (Summers, et al 2004).

Outside the context of HCI studies contextual inquiry is also used in information systems requirements elicitation that apply the soft systems methodology (SSM) as seen in the work of Bednar and Welch (2005a, 2005b, 2005c 2006) and Bednar (2009). Bednar's work view contextual inquiry as a technique for interpretive modelling of a problem situation in recognition of the importance of context for systemic analysis. In further refinement of the contextual analysis, Bednar (2009) introduced the Strategic Systemic Thinking (SST) framework consisting of three aspects of analysis: the intra-analysis, the inter-analysis and the value-analysis. SST is intended to be iterative, and therefore it is possible to move from one analysis to another repeatedly and in any direction and this is easily aligned with the grounded theory methodology. The researcher acts as the external analyst facilitating the research participants to articulate their worldviews using various methods such as rich pictures, brain-storming, mind-maps, diversity networks, drama transfers, role-playing all of which are supporting creation, visualization and communication of mental models and narratives. The purpose of intra-analysis is to enable the creation of an individual process for structuring a problem (through individual interviews and workshop observation). This analysis aims to create and capture a range of narratives from participating stakeholders by providing an enrichment and visualization process for them. Inter-analysis is the aspect of the inquiry which represents collective reflections of decision-making alternatives (through focus groups). The aim is to have a dialogue and to reflect upon ranges of narratives derived through intra-analysis. The purpose is not to achieve consensus or to establish common ground, but to produce a richer base upon which further inquiry and decision-making could proceed. Grouping of narratives takes place through consideration and discussion of individually produced narratives. Results of these inquiries might be considered to form a knowledge base relating to problem spaces under investigation.

The strength of conducting contextual inquiry in requirements elicitation is the ability to investigate the phenomenon of the processes that involves human interaction that gives an opportunity to recognize individual emergence. This will be useful if the information system is seen as a network of human actors, interacting and communicating using available means (including technological artifacts), and then complexity is recognized through the individual sense-making processes of each actor Bednar (2009).

## 3.  Methodology
We aim to formulate a technological conception of an ICT-based information system for batik microenterprise. We employed the contextual inquiry in accordance with the work of Bednar (2009) in the elicitation of business requirements of batik microenterprise to gain insight on batik

making operational efficiency and sustainability. Based on our literature work, our research took into account the importance of community and cultural context of the batik microenterprise. We described our approach in the next sub-section.

## 3.1 The overall method

The data collection is conducted over a period of six months through different data collecting activities consisting of personal interview with stakeholders, visits to actual business sites and focus group interview before attempting to produce the refinements of the business requirements (Figure 3).

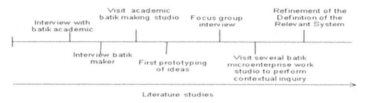

**Figure 3:** Overall method

Although the focus of this research is on batik microenterprise the contextual inquiry covers other batik making stakeholders to gain an understanding of the batik making ecosystem. The data collection was done sequentially to allow for re-adjustment and re-alignment of our understanding the batik making context.

## 3.2 Sampling

For the sampling process, an informal categorization of the batik community membership was made based on early discussion with batik academics with reference to the context of batik knowledge transfer mode (Figure 4).

**Figure 4:** Batik knowledge transfer mode

The informal categorization consists of the experts group (designers, advocators, advocating designers) and novice group (apprentices) and is used in this study as a duality strategy (individual – collective) is chosen for the unit of analysis and comprises of (1) individual microenterprise/SME and (2) the collective- component of informal batik community of practice made of advocators, designers and apprentice). The overall sampling for the contextual inquiry is done based these different stakeholders and the roles of the actors within these groups are illustrated in Table 1.

**Table 1:** Hierarchy of batik makers

| Actor | Role |
|---|---|
| Apprentice | A novice designer who have less than 5 years experience of practice. |
| Designers | A designer with experience more than 5 years in practice and still actively practicing. |
| Advocating Designers | A teacher for formal learning who is a textile designer by formal training and practice with more than 10 years practicing experience or teaching or mentoring |

## 3.3 Face-to-face interview

We conducted face-to-face interview with an advocating designer and a practising designer to familiarise with the research context. As we familiarised with the research phenomenon our ability of focusing into areas the respondents considered important is crucial. For example, one of the respondents introduced the conception design by accident/serendipity which means that knowledge is sometimes shared in ad hoc situations and this received further attention in the following interviews. The interviews were recorded and after transcription they were sent to the respondents to be verified.

## 3.4 Focus group interview

The focus group interview was conducted in a story-telling workshop that allows the participants to share their story and able to express their opinion. The participants consist of representatives from three actor groups shown in Table 1. A facilitator from the research team was involved in the story-telling session. Video recording of the workshop session was done and two assistant researchers transcribed the discussion in the session. The preparation and the conduct of the workshop were done in a careful manner to take great care that the participants' opinions are respected.

## 3.4.1 Instrumentations

Two types of instruments were used. The first is the visual cues which are digitized images of batik artefacts. Artefact digitization sessions were done during the early stage of the research before focus groups session. The visual cues are used similarly like technology probe to trigger stories and boundaries for the storytelling session. Verbal cues are used by the facilitator to align stories with the research questions formulated prior to the workshops. The verbal sues used are shown in Table 2.

**Table 2:** Verbal cues

| Objective | Cues |
|---|---|
| Domain Knowledge Acquisition | *Tell us your life story of making batik:* How you do learn to make batik? How do you get involve in batik making? What are your social network, social responsibility as a batik maker? How can we identify traditional and contemporary batik? |
| Applied Design Knowledge Visualization | *Describe your experience to produce a batik product from planning to finish product:* How do you know what to produce? |
| Aesthetic Knowledge Visualization | *Describe stages of idea development until sketches of design* How do you know your product has aesthetics value realized? How do you judge batik aesthetics? |

## 3.4.2 Procedures

The activities of the focus group interview are described in Table 3.

**Table 3:** Focus group activities

| Component | Description |
|---|---|
| Structure | Each focus group workshop was conducted with 12 selected participants who are group according to their actor's role. |
| Timeframe (150 minutes) | Introduction. (5 minutes): The facilitator explained the research-driven story to the group and provided everyone with paper and pens. The timing was controlled to avoid unnecessary delay. Case Story Session (5 – 10 minutes) The workshop participants spent time before the session writing their story based on their experience of a particular theme. As the story is being told, participants were told to note details of the story and ideas for questions and not to interrupt, and to respect confidentiality. The observer for each group took notes. Conversational & Informal Dialogue (25 – 30 minutes) The listeners write down their immediate reflections on the story: similarity/difference of the story with own story. Then they share their reflections within the group, one at a time with no interruptions. The observer for each group took notes. |

| Component | Description |
|---|---|
| Group Ethics & Protocol | *Promotes Emergence Not Forcing:* Critical, asking and answering probing questions about the subject matter in order to do it better not to force emergence. *Promotes Caring:* Ensure that our questions and our answers are generated in a climate of respect for the values. *Promotes Confidentiality:* Respecting the storytellers who are taking the risks to share their experiences. Video Recording is done with permission from participants |
| Provision of Visual Cues | Visual cues are used to trigger stories and boundaries for the storytelling session. Verbal cues are used by facilitator to align stories with the research questions formulated prior to the workshops. |
| Video Re-cording | Video Recording is done with permission from participants |

## 3.5 Actual site visit

We visit two batik microenterprise sites to make live observation of the batik making realities. We also conducted informal interview with the batik maker. The live observations verify processes of batik making for each technique to gain inside knowledge of actual practices and to gain real life experience in batik making for comparison with stories acquired from interviews and focus group sessions.

## 4. Analysis and findings

A micro analysis was conducted where content of the transcripts from the personal and focus group interview were coded to make sense of data to facilitate the emergence of open codes using the In Vivo Coding by Atlas TI. As the process is tedious, we took care to avoid the tendency of over-conceptualizing. The open codes for this study were derived from multiple sources of data allowing a precise differentiation among categories. The contextual analysis attempted to model the problem situation using text from data corpus using reflective coding matrix. The content analysis attempts to triangulate the empirical data with secondary data from literature. Observations made during the site visit also supported the contextual analysis and these observation forms evidence of multiple sources of data.

Two important discoveries emerged. The first is the business reliance on batik makers' tacit knowledge gained from personal experience, batik mentor storytelling and non-textual references such as photographs and images from books and other repositories of knowledge that includes batik collection.

The second is the concern for the business sustainability in the globalization era related to the concept of batik cultural erosion. This stems from batik makers resort for discontinuity of batik cultural rules in order to survive the socioeconomic impact of business globalization. The discontinuity of traditional aesthetics attributes category of concept is characterized by a number of properties, processes and dimensions reflecting individual and contextual causal themes which either singularly or in combination provided a foundation for cultural erosion situation. Themes emerged as singular definitional concepts and on a causally or implicationally linked. The discontinuity category of concepts has a relationship with the core categories modelling community-based information system as a requirement. We further enumerate three dimensions that cover competency deficit, isolated strategies and diverse level of need shown in Figure 5. The rest of this section presents the dimensions and related elements.

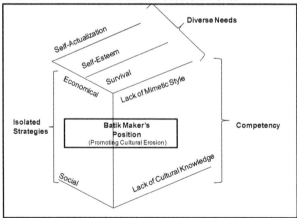

**Figure 5:** Dimensions of batik makers' position

# 4.1   Competency deficit

As illustrated in Figure 5, the lack of cultural knowledge and mimetic style is related to the batik maker's competency dimension. Competency refers to the set of skills related to cultural knowledge and attributes that allow an individual to make batik. There are two types of competency: (1) personal and mimetic. Personal competency relates to individual emotional intelligence while mimetic competency relates to mimetic styles capability and social semiotic.

Personal competency deficit comprised of cognitive and behavioural attributes causing dissenting conducts reflected by themes such as: "copycat syndrome"; "shortcut to market"; "compromised quality" and "shallow in feel", "forgoing tradition for material gained", "motif hallucination", "chaotic arrangement" and "technique disunity". These themes are resulting trajectories of personal competency deficit which have led to isolated strategies for batik making in addition to livelihood and business drivers: poverty alleviation, and mass production. To gain better understanding of the situation a sensitized interpretation has been done. Drawing from psychological theory of emotional intelligence by Goleman(1998) personal competency embodied a form of intelligence relating to the emotional side of life, such as the ability to recognize and manage one's own and others' emotions, to motivate oneself and restrain impulses, and to handle interpersonal relationships effectively. The theory denoted the cluster of abilities relating to the emotional side of life as components of emotional intelligence: knowing our own emotions, managing our own emotions, motivating ourselves, recognizing the emotions of others, and handling relationships. As for learning capability it is claimed that potentials for learning the practical skills are based on the five elements: self-awareness, motivation, self-regulation, empathy, and adeptness in relationships. Participants have pointed out that due to livelihood condition batik makers have adversities (hardship) to deal with. As a result personal competency development has been neglected to survive a better income and living conditions (fire fighting phenomenon). Table 4.2 below maps an array of adversities theme which interprets the state of personal competency deficit in batik making task associated with Golemans' traits of personal emotional competencies.

**Table 4:** Adversities theme Interpretations

| Themes – Adversities | EQ Traits for personal competency |
|---|---|
| Emotional but lack of awareness<br>Personal strength engulf by adversities<br>Self-worthiness low | LACK OF SELF-AWARENESS<br>Emotional Awareness: recognizing one's emotions and their effect<br>Accurate Self-assessment: knowing one's strengths and limits<br>Self-confidence: A strong sense of one's self-worth and capabilities |

| Themes – Adversities | EQ Traits for personal competency |
|---|---|
| Feel insecure , self-control dependent on others Honesty and integrity secondary, follow the flow to survive Personal performance determine by following market trend Innovation is secondary, livelihood is priority | LACK OF SELF-REGULATION Self-control: Keeping disruptive emotions and impulses in check Trustworthiness: Maintaining standards of honesty and integrity Conscientiousness: Taking responsibility for personal performance Adaptability: Flexibility in handling change Innovation: Being comfortable with novel ideas, approaches and new information |
| Lack of initiative to improve Not important to strive for quality Out-of-group perception towards quality Not willing to increase cost for design improvement | LACK OF MOTIVATION Achievement drive: Striving to improve or meet a standard of excellence Commitment: Aligning with the goals of the group or organization Initiative: Readiness to act on opportunities Optimism: Persistence in pursuing goals despite obstacles and setbacks. |

The argument lead by the emerging themes of both competency issues and adversities is the lack of cultural knowledge and mimetic style related to batik maker's competency dimension is a main concern for business sustainability of batik making. Mimetic as defined by Hofstadter (1976) is "the idea to describe a unit of information residing cognitively and is mutating in human cultural dynamics". Mimetic has been claimed to be an approach to evolutional model of cultural knowledge. The workshop participants have also pointed out due to livelihood condition batik makers have adversities to deal with. As a result personal competency development has been neglected as survival process strives for better income and living conditions. The process of survival demands low cost of production and product market availability.

## 4.2   Isolated strategies

Participants highlighted that isolated strategies results from the lack of understanding of the inherent culture and the overwhelming urge to improve livelihood. Isolated unwritten strategies that govern behaviours to meet those demands, places the batik maker in a difficult position to oblige to the cultural rules (indigenous nature) to fit in the business scenario. Four areas of concern related to these strategies are:

- Efficiency: the optimal method to accomplish batik making task;
- Calculability: quantifiable aesthetics values rather than subjective, establishing mass production, to match quantity with quality and to meet demand at lowest cost of production;

- Predictability: Standardized and uniformity;
- Control: Replacement of human and non-human technologies in batik making.

The isolated strategies dimension declares the plan of actions batik makers formulated for batik making. As identified from intra analysis and verified by inter analysis these isolated strategy themes are: (1) acting not part of community; (2) act to promote non-conformance to community memory and (3) act to promote non-conformance to cultural heritage requirement. Isolated strategies are closely related to individual motivational factors to make batik which can be clustered as creative expression, entrepreneurship and profit generation, cultural heritage preservation and economic and social survival. These motivational factors explain differences in intensity and direction of batik makers' attitude. The isolated strategies dimension of position in addition to competency was revealed by two factors: social and economic driven.

Social cultural factors include ideology; belief and language represent a perspective of solitary attitude contributing to the discontinuity of traditional aesthetics attributes. Social change emerged as a conceptualisation promoting risk or threat that exists with every batik tradition. There is, primarily, difference between the collective and individual culture. This differential illustrates how the cultural attributes of individual in terms of issues of cognition and dissenting behaviours provide impetus for out-of-group perception and the consequences of isolating strategies. This trajectory provides the understanding of motivations for discontinuing traditional aesthetics attributes. To illustrate this contention a number of cases are explored during the focus group sessions. The first case of exemplary analysis illustrates two batik designs produced from isolated strategies. Both designs shows traits of traditional discontinuity but fit the customer requirement while maintaining a structural fit with aesthetic need. It was revealed by the designs that both are business artefact made to satisfy modern taste of batik. The isolating strategy of making these designs for modern taste was instigated by the consumer requirements.

The economic motivational factor reveals in one of the batik design exemplary case during the focus group. Not knowing the aesthetics attributes for judging batik aesthetics was found to be the core of dissenting behaviour. Focus group participants voiced out that they know that some batik makers do not have the skill to make batik but are able to sell batik products in large scale. Knowingly bending the rules was identified with a few participants acknowledging that their practices were not in accordance to the standards but their motivations lay within the immediate needs of the customers and opportunities to make profit. The livelihood factor is dominant, isolated strategies can arise from not knowing the rule; just accepting the rules; and mentor-apprentice relationships. The isolated strategies contribute to the dissenting phenomenon that the participants voiced out. This isolated strategies revealed by not knowing the aesthetics values of the community, and if the aesthetics values were known, ignoring them can be part of their choice. Participants revealed many isolated batik designers experience the lack of understanding of cultural knowledge.

## 4.3   Diverse need

The need of a community system is unlikely to be singular. The batik makers have needs and their decisions to make batik depend highly on fulfilment of needs.  Batik makers were propelled by the need to address the acuity of the survival situation, either an issue of social, economical or an individualized issue. The diverse need dimension portraying the decision making position can be viewed as follows:

- Batik Artist: The experienced artist aims for self-actualization when designing batik to realize paintings or craft work for the collector's market. On the other hand the new artist aims for acceptance and recognition by the community and to be able to compete in the marketplace. Themes emerging related to need of batik artist are "uniqueness", "art" and "creation"  which are interpreted as Striving towards Self-Actualization;

- Batik Designer: The batik designers who have more than 10 years experience express needs of culture heritage preservation while the apprentices are striving to be recognised and accepted. Themes related to their needs are "exclusiveness", "taste", "storytelling, "drawn batik" which are deduced as Projecting Self-Esteem and Gaining Self-esteem; and

- Form Maker: The form maker needs are inclined to getting paid and realizing batik for consumer market. Themes related to their needs are "clothing need" which is interpreted as Act of Survival.

## 4.4 Community-based information system model for batik microenterprise

We synthesized our findings to depict a core concept for the technology conception for a community-based information system for a batik micro-enterprise. Sustainability of batik making is pointing towards batik maker's competency dimension and adversities. We propose that competency issue due to the lack of cultural knowledge and mimetic style may be addressed by the provision of information systems that provide access to batik documentary and learning system as a complement. In addition, a mentor-apprentice relationship community strategy can help overcome the discontinuity of traditional aesthetics attributes due to the lack of knowledge. From these findings we formulated the core concepts that need to be addressed and captured during requirements elicitation. They are the content requirement (the batik domain knowledge), the cultural requirement (batik community culture) and the context requirement (pertinent or critical issue that pose risk to the batik business survival). In our observation, we discovered that the batik domain knowledge is mainly captured in visual forms either as batik artefacts which are worn or displayed or as images in books or exhibited as museum or gallery exhibits. Batik making knowledge on the other hand is encapsulated in the batik making process and is shared through the mentoring process during batik making itself and/or through story-telling scenarios. Issues influencing the survival or the flourishing of batik can be a barrier to ICT adoption. The fear of cultural erosion of batik amongst batik advocators and batik makers is strengthen by their belief that ICT can propagate the erosion process. We strongly propose that the technology conception must try to remove this fear. Figure 6 illustrate the core concepts that we have discovered from our analysis and synthesized them as a technology conception for the community-based information system model for batik making.

A technology conception of a community-based information system model for batik microenterprise must not endanger the survival of batik making and must respect the different knowledge and role of the community members. For instance if a technology conception is achieved through a batik digital gallery, it becomes an important system's requirement that the gallery protects the intellectual right of the batik community member as well as the batik knowledge so that the gallery do not actually contribute towards the cultural erosion of batik.

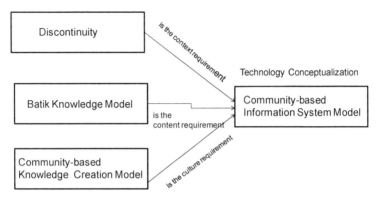

**Figure 6:** Core concepts of the technology conceptualization

The findings from this work have huge implication on the development of ICT-based information systems for batik microenterprise. Although batik makers were concern with efficiency, they are not willing to sacrifice the indigenous nature of their batik artefacts. An ICT-based information system that only increases their operational efficiency may not be able to help them retain the competency of batik making which is seen to be more crucial. A new set of requirements dictated by the batik domain knowledge cannot be ignored. A relevant ICT-based information system for batik microenterprise will be one that supports the knowledge creation of batik either for an individual or for a community of batik makers.

## 5. Conclusion

In this paper we have presented our concern for the technology conceptualization required for the development of an ICT-based information system for the batik microenterprise. We attempted a business requirement elicitation work for batik microenterprise by conducting a contextual inquiry aligning it with concern of batik community. We made two important discoveries of batik makers' concern which influences the batik making business requirements. The first is on the reliance of tacit knowledge of batik making and the second is on the fear of batik cultural erosion which cannot be overcome by the development of production-based information systems that only emphasize efficiency. From our findings, we are suggesting that any attempt to develop an ICT-based information system for batik microenterprise must not ignore these two concerns. Our future work will be on the exploration of future ICT-based information systems for batik microenterprise.

# Acknowledgements

This research is supported by the research grant (Grant No: 01-01-01-SF0068) awarded by the Ministry of Science, Technology and Innovation, Malaysia under the E-Science Grants Scheme.

# References

Arendt, L. (2008). Barriers to ICT adoption in SMEs: how to bridge the digital divide? Journal of Systems and Information Technology, 10(2):93-110

Atzani, G. E. and Carboni,O. A. (2006). North-South Disparity in ICT Adoption in Italy: An Empirical Evaluation of the Effects of Subsidies. Working Papers 2006/08, Centro Ricerche Economiche Nord Sud, Università di Cagliari and Università di Sassari

Bednar, P.M. and Welch, C. (2009). Contextual Inquiry and Requirements Shaping in Information Systems Development, Springer, pp:225-236

Bednar, P M, Welch, C and Graziano, A (2005a) 'Learning Objects and their implications on Learning: a case of developing the foundation for a new Knowledge Infrastructure,' Proceedings of Informing Science & IT Education Joint Conference (InSITE 2005), Northern Arizona University, Flagstaff, Arizona, USA.

Bednar, P and Welch, C (2005b). 'IS, Process and Organizational Change and their Relationships to Contextual Dependencies', ECIS 2005. Proceedings of 13th European Conference on Information Systems: Information Systems in a Rapidly Changing Economy, University of Regensburg, Germany.

Bednar, P and Welch, C (2005c). 'Critical Systemic Thinking – or The Standard Engineer in Paris'. ECRM 2005. Proceedings of the 4th European Conference on Research Methods in Business and Management, Université Paris-Dauphine, France.

Dixon DR (1999). The Behavioral Side of Information Technology. International Journal Medical Informatics, 56(1-3):117-123.

Duncombe, R. and Heeks, R. (2001) Information and Communication Technologies and Small Enterprise in Africa, Lessons from Botswana. IDPM, University of Manchester.

Duncombe, R. Molla, A. (2009). Formalisation of Information Systems in sub-Saharan African Small and Medium Enterprises: Case of Botswana. African Journal of Information Systems, 1(2):1-29.

Elamvazuthi , I. and Morris, A. (2000). "An investigation of the Colour of Reactive Dye on Woven Fabrics for the Batik Colouring Process", Proceedings of the Malaysian Science and Technology Congress, Kuala Lumpur, Malaysia, pp:680-700

Foley, P, Alfonso, X. and Ghani. F. (2002) The Digital Divide in a World City. Report Prepared by IECRC and Citizens Online for the Greater London Authority, London Connects and the London Development Agency.

Goleman, D. (1998). Working with emotional intelligence. New York: Bantam Books

Heeks, R. (2002). Failure, Success and Improvisation of Information Systems Projects in Developing Countries. Manchester: Manchester University.

Helmersen, P. (2006). Human Factors in Emerging Markets: First World Solutions Addressing Third World Needs. Proceedings of the 20th International Symposium on Human Factors in Telecommunication, France, 20-23 March

Hoffman, R.R., Norman, D.O. and Vagners, J. (2009). "Complex Sociotechnical Joint Cognitive Information systems"? IEEE Intelligent Systems, May-June 2009

Hofstadter, A. And Kuhns, R. (1976). Philosophies OF Art and Beauty: Selected Readings in Aesthetics from Plato to Heidegger. Chicago: University Of Chicago Press.

Ismail, S.Z. (1997). The Traditional Malay Handicraft Design. Kuala Lumpur: Dewan Bahasa dan Pustaka.

Jamal ,S.A. (1994). Form & Soul. Dewan Bahasa dan Pustaka: Ministry of Education Malaysia Kuala Lumpur

Khong, S.T. and Eze, U.C. (2008). An Empirical Study of Internet-Based ICT Adoption Among Malaysian Smes. Communications of the IBIMA, Vol 1.

Manueli, K., Latu, S., and Koh, D. (2007). ICT Adoption Models. Proceedings of the 20th Annual Conference of the National Advisory Committee on Computing Qualifications (NACCQ 2007), Nelson, New Zealand.

Maslow, A.H. (1943). A Theory of Human Motivation, Psychological Review 50(4):370-96.

Moor, A. (2009). Collaboration Patterns as Building Blocks for Community Informatics. Keynote Address, Prato Community CIRN Conference 2009, Prato, Italy.

Porter, M. (1990). The New Competitive Advantage of Nations. Free Press: New York.

Schon, D. A. (1983). The Reflective Practitioner: How Professionals Think in Action, London: Temple Smith.

Stillman, L. and Linger, H. (2009). Community Informatics and Information Systems: Can They Be Better Connected? The Information Society: An International Journal, 25(4): 225-264

Summers,K., Knudtzon, K., Weeks, H.,, Kaplan, N., Chisik, Y., Kulkarni, R., Moulthrop, S (2004). Supporting Sociable Literacy in the International Children's Digital Library. Proceedings of the 2004 Conference on Interaction Design and Children: Building a Community.

Tschiersch, I. and Schael, T. (2003). Concepts of Human Centered Systems

W.H. Wan Teh (1996) Malay Handicraft Industries. Kuala Lumpur: Dewan Bahasa dan Pustaka,

Yusof, A.,Y. and Lim, Y.P. (2003). ICT For development (ICT4D) - Understanding ICT Thematics for Malaysia: a sourcebook, UNDP.

# Research on IT/IS Evaluation: A 25 Year Review

**Xingchen Song and Nick Letch**
**UWA Business School, The University of Western Australia, Perth, Australia**
*Originally published in EJISE (2012) Volume 15, ISS 3*

**Editorial Commentary**
This paper provides a comprehensive assessment of 176 papers relating to IS evaluation published in five journals viz. European Journal of Information Systems (EJIS), Information Systems Research (ISR), Journal of Information Technology (JIT), MIS Quarterly (MISQ) and Journal of Management Information Systems (JMIS). The outcomes of this intensive review, based on the Content Context and Process (CCP) Model (Symons, 1991), identifies critical gaps in the extant literature and thus points the way forward for leading issues in the field. The authors found that nearly a third of all articles examined ignored the purpose of evaluation, while nearly half neglected to even identify stakeholders. A key proposition in this paper is that the classification of IS evaluation should be re-specified as an evolving continuum of efficiency-driven evaluation, effectiveness-driven evaluation, and understanding-driven evaluation. Consequently, this paper, in settings solid foundation for future work, is a worthy candidate as a leading issue. This reclassification should provide the IS evaluation fraternity with a common framework for IS evaluation, improving the goal of achieving better comparative research in the field.

**Abstract:** The conduct of IT/IS evaluation and its associated approaches, techniques and methods have been the subject of IS research for many years, particularly in the last two decades. This paper reflects on the body of knowledge which has emerged over the past twenty-five years in order to identify where research efforts are focussed, what are the important issues in IT/IS evaluation research, and where future research efforts should be placed. This study presents a descriptive analysis of research on IT/IS evaluation over the last 25 five years, from 1986 to 2010, in five leading IS journals In total, 176 papers related to IT/IS evaluation are identified and reviewed in this study. Based on the Context, Content and Process model, IT/IS evaluation can be broken down to five interrelated elements: *why* evaluation is carried out, what is evaluated,*whenwhen* evaluation takes place, *how* evaluation is performed and *who* is involved in evaluation. Each of these elements are identified and classified in the sample research articles and based on this analysis, we propose a new perspective for classifying IT/IS evaluation approaches.

**Keywords:** IT/IS evaluation, literature review; Content, Context and Process (CCP) model, evaluation streams

# 1. Introduction

It is widely accepted that the application of information and communications technology has become critical to the success of business (Willcocks & Lester 1996). While there has been worldwide increasing expenditure on IT/IS over the past few decades (Ballantine & Stray 1999, Serafeimidis & Smithson 1999, Willcocks & Lester 1996), it is recognised that the successful deployment of IT/IS does not occur by default. On the contrary, it has been widely noted that a mismatch exists between the outcomes delivered and the benefits that are promised. This is often cited as the "productivity paradox" (Irani & Love 2008, Farbey et al. 1999c, Willcocks & Lester 1996). A perennial managerial task for organisations is therefore to be able to effectively evaluate the contribution of investments in information and communications technology. Given the importance of effective evaluation to managers, this paper reviews the research literature on IT/IS evaluation has developed over the past twenty-five years.

Evaluation is a process used to identify, measure, and assess the value of an object in a given context. Evaluation processes play a critical role in organisations' efforts to assess the success and payoffs of their investments in IT/IS. Consequently, in the research literature there have been extensive efforts to understand the nature of IT/IS evaluation and to develop improved approaches and techniques. Given that IT/IS evaluation has been an important and ongoing of domain of research interest, it is worth reflecting on how research in the area has evolved. Peer reviewed journals in the information systems discipline are, in theory, representations of current thinking and theoretical development. In order to understand the changes in development in thinking with respect to IIT/IS evaluation, this study conducts a rigorous, quantitative review of IT/IS evaluation literature in five leading IS journals over the last 25 years. As a starting point for our analysis we adopt the approach taken by Serafeimidis (2002) who briefly reviewed research on IS evaluation based on the concepts embodied in the Content, Context and Process (CCP) model. His analysis elaboratedthree different streams of IT/IS evaluation: the technical/functional stream, the economic/financial stream and the interpretive stream. Our aim is to updateSerafeimidis' study and further enhance the understanding of the three evaluation streams.

In the remaining sections of this paper, the framework that we use for analysis – the Content, Context and Process model – is first described followed by an outline of the research methodology and the analytical approach adopted. The data representing the published IT/IS research on evaluation is then analysed in accordance with the CCP model. The final sections of the paper discuss the findings of the analysis and show how the comprehensive analysis over 25 years provides an alternative classification to Serfieimidis' categories of research. Through a discussion of the critical features of relationships between each stream of IT/IS evaluation research identified, we then suggest directions for future research in the domain.

## 2. Understanding IT/IS Evaluation Research– The Content, Contextand Process (CCP) Model

IT/IS evaluation is a multifaceted and complicated phenomenon which can be examined from multiple perspectives. As a domain of study it can be considered to be an interactive social system that is interwoven with different stakeholders, various resources and multiple decision-making processes (Irani & Love 2008, Farbey et al. 1999b). It is possible for example to examine the variety of techniques that can be applied during evaluation, the activities and processes involved in evaluation, as well as the layers of political motivations that drive the conduct of evaluations. In order to capture the breadth of research conducted in IT/IS evaluation we use a recognised and well-structured framework,(Irani & Love 2008, Farbey et al. 1999b), namely, the Content Context and Process (CCP) model. This model was first introduced to IT/IS evaluation research to investigate and analyse important elements in an IT/IS evaluation by Symons (1991). Subsequently, theCCP model has been successfully applied in several IT/IS evaluation studies (Huerta & Sanchez 1999, Avgerou 1995, Serafeimidis 2002, Stockdale & Standing 2000, Serafeimidis & Smithson 1999). In one such study, Serafeimidis (2002) conducted a brief review of research on IT/IS evaluation based on the concepts of CCP in order to draw out the themes of study in IT/IS evaluation. This work was valuable in orienting the focus of research at that time and the study described in this paper aims to extend this work with a further application of the CCP model as the framework for analysis.

In the CCP model, the Context dimension aims to capture why evaluation is carried out and who is involved in the evaluation. Context refers to both the internal and external environment of an organization (Avgerou 1995). Internally, it includes aspects such as the structure, business strategies, management procedures, and culture of an organization. Externally, it includes factors like technologies, market structures, and government policies. In each specific context, IT systems are designed and implemented to serve different purposes, to fulfil various requirements and deliver diverse benefits. The context dimension of the CCP model captures the internal and external context by assessing the underlying motivations for conducting evaluations and an exploration of the various stakeholders involved.

The Content dimension of the model is concerned with the subject/object of evaluation, the criteria that are used to assess the IT/IS, and any changes caused by the IS (Avgerou 1995). That is, this dimension addresses questions of what is being evaluated? Serafeimidis' study suggested that efficiency and effectiveness measures have been the most frequently applied criteria (Serafeimidis 2002) to evaluating the content dimension and in addition, this dimension is closely related to the context in which evaluation is carried out.

The third dimension of the CCP framework - the process dimension focuses on questions of when evaluation takes place, and how evaluation isperformed. In the framework, process refers to the actions, reactions, and interactions of the interested parties involved in the IT/IS evaluation. Again there is a strong relationship between this dimension and the content dimension of evaluation (Serafeimidis & Smithson 2000). In addition to the method of evaluation, the timeframe in which the evaluation occurs is also a critical issue.  For instance Farbey (1992) suggests that evaluation can take place either at a point in time or it may be conducted continuously across the lifecycle of an IT/IS implementation.

Other frameworks or models are found in the literature for understanding IT/IS evaluation or implementation (Özkan et al. 2007, Farbey et al. 1999a), but the CCP model is applied in this research for understanding and discussion of evaluation for two reasons. First, there is a wide acceptance of the CCP model among leading contributors to IT/IS evaluation theory. Efforts of conducting or promoting CCP can not only be found in IT/IS research (Huerta & Sanchez 1999, Symons 1991, Avgerou 1995, Serafeimidis 2002, Stockdale & Standing 2006, Serafeimidis & Smithson 1999), but also other topics, such as organizational performance (Ketchen et al. 1996), openness to organizational change (Devos et al. 2007), and marketing strategies (Baines & Lynch 2005).

Secondly, the concepts contained within CCP are broad enough to accommodate the myriad ideas and arguments in this well-documented field, while still providing parameters for reviewing them (Stockdale & Standing 2006). The CCP model breaks evaluation into a number of elements: purpose (why), the subject and criteria (what), timeframe (when), methodologies (how) and people (who). By doing so, the CCP model allows for the recognition of a wide scope of interrelated factors that need to be taken into account in an effective evaluation (Stockdale & Standing 2006, Serafeimidis 2002).

# 3. Research Method and Data Collection

In order to investigate the evolution of research in IT/IS evaluation, we examine research published in five premier IS journals spanning the period 1986-2010. Journal papers were selected as the source of data because by nature of their review and editorial processes they exhibit a higher reliability than other resources such as working papers, dissertations and conference proceedings. In total, 176 studies published in European Journal of Information Systems (EJIS), Information Systems Research (ISR), Journal of Information Technology (JIT), MIS Quarterly (MISQ) and Journal of Management Information Systems (JMIS) related to IT/IS evaluation were identified and included in this study. The five particular journals were selected because of their consistently high reputation and ranking across a range of indicators. Each of these journals for example are ranked as A* publications in the Australian Business Deans Council journal rankings as well as the Association of Information Systems Senior Scholars basket of journals.

In selecting papers from the journals, IT/IS evaluation papers were chosen according to keywords identified in the title and abstract. This approach therefore focussed analysis on those papers that included IT/IS evaluation as a primary subject of the article. For each paper reviewed, the purpose of the study, the organization sector in which the study was conducted, the unit of analysis and the research methodology were identified. This general analysis provided an overall perspective of the trajectory that IT/IS evaluation research has taken over the last 25 years.

For a more detailed analysis of IT/IS evaluation, concepts related to IT/IS evaluation in each paper were identified and categorized according to the underlying questions of the dimensions defined by the CCP model. Previous research has yet to identify a clear and comprehensive analysis of the purpose of evaluation. Therefore our analysis of understanding the question of why evaluation is conducted uses a grounded approach and relevant concepts are abstracted from each article and then categorised. To assess the content dimension of evaluation where the focus is on questions of what is being evaluated, our analysis was guided by the measures inherent in the DeLone and McLean IS success model (Delone and McLean 1992, 2003) because of its wide acceptance and recognition in the IS research field. To assess the important temporal dimension of evaluation we draw on Farbey's (1992) definition of IT/IS evaluation and abstract the evaluation timeframes identified and discussed in each of the papers. The classification used by Serafeimidis' (2002) study in identifying the methodologies, tools and approaches to evaluation, was used to assess how evaluation is performed.For questions of who was involved in evaluation which is important in assessing the context dimension of the CCP model, major players were identified directly from each paper and then categorised.

## 4. Data Analysis

An overview of the IT/IS evaluation research articles examined are provided in table 11 below. As can be seen, there was an increase in the number of published evaluation studies from late 1980s to early 2000s with a sharp decrease in the period 2006-2010. One possible reason for this decline is that IT/IS evaluation has more recently been seen as being embedded with broader managerial issues in IT/IS implementation (Irani & Love 2008, Huerta & Sanchez 1999). From our analysis of articles published in our journal sample, a large number of studies discussed concepts of IT/IS evaluation, but were not primarily focussed on evaluation per se. Therefore, these studies were not included in this review.

There was an almost even distribution of the number of papers across all journals. moredueMISQ and JMIS had relatively moredue to their longer publication history relative to the other journals. Most papers in the period 1986 to 1990 were published in these two journals whereas EJIS and ISR were first published in early 1990s. It was found that JIT had less focused on IT/IS evaluation compared to the other journals sampled.

**Table 1:** Papers Distribution by Journals and Years

|  | EJIS | ISR | JIT | MISQ | JMIS | Total |
|---|---|---|---|---|---|---|
| **1986-1990** | 0 | 1 | 5 | 6 | 8 | 20 (11.4%) |
| **1991-1995** | 4 | 3 | 9 | 14 | 9 | 39 (22.2%) |
| **1996-2000** | 5 | 6 | 9 | 11 | 14 | 45 (25.6%) |
| **2001-2005** | 10 | 14 | 5 | 6 | 14 | 49 (27.8%) |
| **2006-2010** | 10 | 4 | 1 | 3 | 5 | 23 (13.1%) |
| **Total** | 29 (16.5%) | 28 (15.9%) | 29 (16.5%) | 40 (22.7%) | 50 (28.4%) | 176 (100%) |

Table 1 depicts the research purpose, context, unit of analysis and research methods of paper reviewed by different journals and periods. For each of the papers analysed we aimed to identify the underlying research purpose in order to understand the objectives of each article. Six purposes were identified in this study:

*Instrument/method development:* these studies consider that evaluation tools or methods in use are either problematic or unable to fit into a specific context. Therefore, researchers attempted to develop new or modify current evaluation instrument or methods, either practically or theoretically.

*Instrument/method validation:* these studies examine the validity and reliability of the instruments and methods proposed in previous studies (not limited to 176 papers reviewed), and serves as an external validation.

*Construct/measurement development:* these studies attempt to develop evaluation criteria in a certain context or environment. About 22.2% papers studied serve this purpose.

*Construct/measurement validation:* these studies can be considered as external validation of constructs or measurements proposed by other studies and further examine their validity and reliability.

*Study of evaluation practice:* these studies analyze actual evaluation practices and report important finding(s) from them.

**Carrying out an evaluation:** in this group of studies, the authors are the ones who actually conduct the evaluation. They then report their evaluation process, outcomes and findings.

In general, a large portion of the studies focused on the development of evaluation instruments/methods (43.2%) and construct/measurement (22.2%) (see Table 2). However, relatively fewer studies further examined the reliability and validity of the instruments/methods developed (11.9%) or the constructs/measurement (5.1%) as an external validation. In addition, a number of articles examined completed evaluations in practice (12.5%), but only a few carried out an actual in-situ evaluation and reported on that process and the findings (5.1%). This finding was reflected in each journal separately. Most papers focused on instrument and construct development, but only a few efforts were put into other aspects. Nevertheless, JIT showed a special interest in study of evaluation practice. Moreover, the general trend did not change much over the years (see Table 3).

**Table 2:** Features of the Papers by Journals

| | | EJIS | ISR | JIT | MISQ | JMIS | Total |
|---|---|---|---|---|---|---|---|
| Research Purpose | Instrument/method development | 12 (41%) | 12 (43%) | 9 (31%) | 18 (45%) | 25 (50%) | 76 (43.2%) |
| | Instrument/method validation | 3 (10%) | 2 (7%) | 0 (0%) | 9 (23%) | 7 (14%) | 21 (11.9%) |
| | Construct/measurement development | 6 (21%) | 12 (43%) | 6 (21%) | 5 (13%) | 10 (20%) | 39 (22.2%) |
| | Construct/measurement validation | 1 (3%) | 0 (0%) | 1 (3%) | 4 (10%) | 3 (6%) | 9 (5.1%) |
| | Study of evaluation practice | 5 (17%) | 0 (0%) | 11 (38%) | 3 (8%) | 3 (6%) | 22 (12.5%) |
| | Carrying out an evaluation | 2 (7%) | 2 (7%) | 2 (7%) | 1 (3%) | 2 (4%) | 9 (5.1%) |
| Context | General | 13 (45%) | 13 (46%) | 10 (34%) | 17 (43%) | 27 (54%) | 80 (45.5%) |
| | Private | 11 (38%) | 14 (50%) | 17 (59%) | 23 (57%) | 18 (36%) | 83 (47.2%) |
| | Public | 5 (17%) | 1 (4%) | 2 (7%) | 0 (0%) | 5 (10%) | 13 (7.4%) |

|  |  | EJIS | ISR | JIT | MISQ | JMIS | Total |
|---|---|---|---|---|---|---|---|
| Unit of Analysis | IT | 9 (31%) | 11 (39%) | 5 (17%) | 12 (30%) | 22 (44%) | 59 (33.5%) |
| | IS | 11 (38%) | 11 (39%) | 9 (31%) | 17 (43%) | 15 (30%) | 63 (35.8%) |
| | Both | 3 (10%) | 1 (4%) | 2 (7%) | 7 (18%) | 2 (4%) | 15 (8.5%) |
| | IT/IS investment | 6 (21%) | 5 (18%) | 13 (45%) | 4 (10%) | 11 (22%) | 39 (22.2%) |
| Research Methods | Survey | 5 (17%) | 7 (25%) | 7 (24%) | 18 (45%) | 15 (30%) | 52 (29.5%) |
| | Case study and qualitative | 12 (41%) | 2 (7%) | 12 (41%) | 11 (28%) | 16 (32%) | 53 (30.1%) |
| | Concept description | 8 (28%) | 3 (11%) | 5 (17%) | 2 (5%) | 9 (18%) | 27 (15.3%) |
| | Secondary data (literature review) | 1 (3%) | 10 (36%) | 4 (14%) | 4 (10%) | 8 (16%) | 27 (15.3%) |
| | Experiments | 1 (3%) | 3 (11%) | 0 (0%) | 2 (5%) | 2 (4%) | 8 (4.5%) |
| | Combined methods | 2 (7%) | 3 (11%) | 1 (3%) | 3 (8%) | 0 (0%) | 9 (5.1%) |

According to the CCP model, context determines the reason for an evaluation which then further influences the evaluation content and process (Stockdale & Standing, 2006). Therefore, evaluation cannot be understood in isolation from its context (Symons, 1991). A large proportion of the research reviewed was focussed on the general context (45.5%), in which researchers did not or were unable to distinguish the differences between public and private organisations. About 47.2% of the studies conducted in a private context. Very few of them specifically targeted at the IT/IS evaluation in the public sector (7.4%). One important change over the last 25 years was anan increasing proportion of papers related to the public sector, as shown in Table 3. This implies an increasing interest in IT/IS evaluation in public organizations including hospitals and government agencies in which management need to be accountable to the taxpaying public.

**Table 3:** Features of the Papers by Years

|  |  | 1986-1990 | 1991-1995 | 1996-2000 | 2001-2005 | 2006-2010 | Total |
|---|---|---|---|---|---|---|---|
| Research Purpose | Instrument/method development | 10 (50%) | 18 (46%) | 16 (36%) | 22 (45%) | 10 (43%) | 76 (43.2%) |
| | Instrument/method validation | 2 (10%) | 3 (8%) | 8 (18%) | 5 (10%) | 3 (13%) | 21 (11.9%) |

| | | 1986-1990 | 1991-1995 | 1996-2000 | 2001-2005 | 2006-2010 | Total |
|---|---|---|---|---|---|---|---|
| | Construct/measurement development | 4 (20%) | 5 (13%) | 11 (24%) | 13 (27%) | 6 (26%) | 39 (22.2%) |
| | Construct/measurement validation | 0 (0%) | 6 (15%) | 1 (2%) | 1 (2%) | 1 (4%) | 9 (5.1%) |
| | Study of evaluation practice | 4 (20%) | 4 (10%) | 8 (18%) | 6 (12%) | 0 (0%) | 22 (12.5%) |
| | Carrying out an evaluation | 0 (0%) | 3 (8%) | 1 (2%) | 2 (4%) | 3 (13%) | 9 (5.1%) |
| **Context** | General | 7 (35%) | 21 (54%) | 21 (47%) | 22 (45%) | 9 (39%) | 80 (45.5%) |
| | Private | 13 (65%) | 17 (44%) | 21 (47%) | 23 (47%) | 9 (39%) | 83 (47.2%) |
| | Public | 0 (0%) | 1 (3%) | 3 (7%) | 4 (8%) | 5 (22%) | 13 (7.4%) |
| **Unit of Analysis** | IT | 4 (20%) | 8 (21%) | 15 (33%) | 21 (43%) | 11 (48%) | 59 (33.5%) |
| | IS | 9 (45%) | 18 (46%) | 15 (33%) | 14 (29%) | 7 (30%) | 63 (35.8%) |
| | Both | 2 (10%) | 5 (13%) | 2 (4%) | 5 (10%) | 1 (4%) | 15 (8.5%) |
| | IT/IS investment | 5 (25%) | 8 (21%) | 13 (29%) | 9 (18%) | 4 (17%) | 39 (22.2%) |
| **Research Methods** | Survey | 5 (25%) | 11 (28%) | 9 (20%) | 20 (41%) | 7 (30%) | 52 (29.5%) |
| | Case study and qualitative | 8 (40%) | 13 (33%) | 16 (36%) | 8 (16%) | 8 (35%) | 53 (30.1%) |
| | Concept description | 2 (10%) | 10 (26%) | 4 (9%) | 7 (14%) | 4 (17%) | 27 (15.3%) |
| | Secondary data (literature review) | 2 (10%) | 2 (5%) | 11 (24%) | 20 (20%) | 2 (9%) | 27 (15.3%) |
| | Experiments | 2 (10%) | 3 (8%) | 1 (2%) | 1 (2%) | 1 (4%) | 8 (4.5%) |
| | Combined methods | 1 (5%) | 0 (0%) | 4 (9%) | 3 (6%) | 1 (4%) | 9 (5.1%) |

We make a distinction between the concepts of IT and IS as the unit of analysis in evaluation, with the emphasis of IT evaluation being focussed on the objective characteristics of hardware and software deployment

(Nagm 2008) as opposed to evaluation of IS in which the technologies are evaluated in the context of the wider business processes and activities in which they are embedded (Ammenwerth et al. 2003). Some research also discussed both IT and IS evaluation or did not make a distinction between the concepts. Moreover, some research focused on the evaluation of IT/IS investment rather than the IT/IS projects themselves. In total, 33.5% of the studies clearly stated their units of analysis to be the evaluation of IT and 35.8% focused on IS. In addition, a noticeable number of studies (22.2%) focused on the evaluation of investment in IT/IS rather than the IT/IS projects themselves, and fewer discussed IT or IS evaluation in general without a distinction. .In terms of different journals, EJIS and MISQ were slightly more oriented to IS, and JMIS seemed to be more focused on IT. JIT on the other hand published a greater proportion of articles related to IT/IS investment. In term of the changes over time, it was interesting to notice that the evaluation of IT increased in the last 25 years, whereas papers investigating IS evaluation decreased. One possible reason for this is that when considering IT/IS evaluation, the concepts of IT, IS and IT/IS investment were often mixed and it was not possible to clearly differentiate an emphasis on IT, IS or IT/IS investment.

In relation to the research methods that were used in the analysed studies, surveys (29.5%) and case studies (30.1%) were the most frequently used approaches. The theoretical or logical development of concepts (15.3%) and secondary data (15.3%)%) including analyses literatures were also widely employed methods in IT/IS evaluation research. Only a few studies used experiments (4.5%) or combined methods (5.1%). Different journals tended to have  preferred research methods. For instance, EJIS had more papers using concept description than average, ISR preferred using secondary data, JIT used case studies and other qualitative methods more often and MISQ used more surveys. No specific findings were found when considering research methods in different years.

## 4.1   Conceptualization of Evaluation Research using Content, Context and Process Dimensions

As noted previously, the CCP model lends itself to addressing a series of questions in relation to IT/IS evaluation. That is, by asking "why, what, how, when and who" in relation to IT/IS evaluation, the three dimensions of content, context and process can be assessed. The following analysis addresses each of these questions in relation to the sample research articles examined.

### 4.1.1   Why evaluation is carried out

Evaluation can serve a number of purposes. Serafeimidis (2002) addressed the usefulness of evaluation in his review of IT/IS evaluation literature, and found the major purposes or reasons for an evaluation were related to efficiency in terms of technical performance and control of resources; a desire to achieve predetermined outcomes. Our research however finds that the reasons for evaluation go beyond Serafeimidis' findings. Furthermore, previous research provides only a limited perspective of the underlying purpose of evaluation. Our findings suggest that evaluation purpose can be delineated into three categories: conceptual purpose, instrumental purpose, and political purpose. Conceptual purpose (21.0%) refers to evaluations that are carried out to discover and understand issues related to IT/IS implementation. This purpose for evaluation primarily enables understanding of IT/IS value (14.2%) to the organisation to be identified. This includes not only the identification of the benefits, costs or risks of IT/IS (10.8%), but also the appraisal of such value (3.4%). Evaluation can also improve the understanding of the performance or problems related to IT/IS projects (3.4%), as well as the use of such projects (2.8%). In addition, a few researchers also suggested that evaluation could improve the understanding of other issues (1.7%), such as stakeholders' interests. Instrumental purpose (38.6%) refers to the decisions made or actions that are taken based on evaluation. Information generated from evaluation can be used for IT/IS project planning (13.64%), including resource control, alternative prioritization, IT/IS investment decisions and system deployment. Further, effective using evaluation findings is believed to be able to improve IT/IS usage (4.55%) and organizations' business/management process (7.39%). Political purpose (1.1%) refers to the political impacts of evaluation on people involved, including user acceptance/resistance of the project, empowerment of stakeholders, gaining commitment and improved communication or discourse among stakeholders. However, there was little evidence of such a purpose found in this study. A number of articles were found with mixed purposes to conduct an evaluation (8.0%). Despite the various roles evaluation played in an organisation, a noticeable portion of research did not specify the purpose to carry out an evaluation (31.3%).

## 4.1.2 What is evaluated

DeLone and McLean's IS Success Model (1992, 2003) identifies definitions of IS success and their corresponding measures, and classifies them into six major categories: Information Quality, System Quality, Service Quality, System Use, User Satisfaction and Net Benefits. IT/IS business value (35.8%) is the most frequently cited consideration in evaluation, including strategic (2.3%), tactical (1.1%) and operational (20.5%) values. A specific classification of those values is provided by Irani et al (2005). Comparing to system (7.4%) and service (7.4%) quality, information or system outputs (3.0%) receives a lower attention. Large efforts has also been put into the examination of IT/IS use (9.1%) and user satisfaction (8.0%). Moreover, some research has mixed focuses (11.9%), while a number of researchers argued that the content of evaluation should be context based (9.1%).

**Table 4:** WHY evaluation is carried out?

| WHY evaluation is carried out? | | | Number (%) | |
|---|---|---|---|---|
| **Conceptual Purpose\*** | IT/IS Value | | 25 | (14.2%) |
| | | Identification of the value | 19 | (10.8%) |
| | | Appraisal of the value | 6 | (3.4%) | In total 37 (21.0%) |
| | IT/IS Project | | 6 | (3.4%) |
| | IT/IS Use | | 5 | (2.8%) |
| | Other | | 3 | (1.7%) |
| **Instrumental Purpose\*** | -IT/IS planning and implementation | | 24 | (13.6%) |
| | -Decision making | | 17 | (9.7%) |
| | -Improved IT/IS Usage | | 8 | (4.6%) |
| | -Improved management & business | | 13 | (7.4%) | In total 68 (38.6%) |
| | -Other | | 8 | (4.6%) |
| | | Benefits realisation | 4 | (2.3%) |
| | | Improved IT/IS service | 2 | (1.1%) |
| | | Benchmarking | 2 | (1.7%) |
| **Political Purpose** | | | 2 | (1.1%) |
| **mixed** | | | 14 | (8.0%) |
| **Not discussed and specified** | | | 55 | (31.3%) |

\* indicates an overlap

**Table 5:** WHAT is evaluated?

| WHAT is evaluated? | | Number (%) | |
|---|---|---|---|
| IT/IS value | | **63** | **(35.8%)** |
| | Strategic Value | 4 | (2.3%) |
| | Tactical Value | 2 | (1.1%) |
| | Operational Value | 36 | (20.5%) |
| | Mixed | 21 | (11.9%) |
| **System quality** | | **13** | **(7.4%)** |
| **Outputs quality** | | **7** | **(3.0%)** |

| Service quality | 13 | (7.4%) |
|---|---|---|
| IT/IS use | 16 | (9.1%) |
| User satisfaction | 14 | (8.0%) |
| Context based | 16 | (9.1%) |
| Mixed | 21 | (11.9%) |
| Not discussed or specified | 13 | (7.9%) |

### 4.1.3    When is evaluation carried out

According to Farbey et al. (1992), evaluation can take place either at the specific point of time or continuously through the system development life cycle. The former includes both evaluation conducted before the implementation or ex-ante (18.8%), and after the implementation or ex-post (59.7%). The later suggested evaluation is an ongoing process, and it can be carried out at various stages (8.5%) in the IT/IS development and implementation. In our sample, 11.4% of articles do not specify when evaluation should take place.

**Table 6:** WHEN evaluation takes place?

| WHEN evaluation takes place? | Number (%) | |
|---|---|---|
| ex-ante | 33 | (18.8%) |
| ex-post | 105 | (59.7%) |
| ongoing/various stages | 15 | (8.5%) |
| Not discussed or specified | 20 | (11.4%) |

### 4.1.4    How evaluation is performed

Serafeimidis (2002) identified and categorised a number of evaluation methods and tools in his study. In assessing the IT/IS value to business, finance (11.4%) and economic (19.9%) based techniques, such as Net Present Value (NPV), Return on Investment (ROI) and Cost-Benefits Analysis (CBA) are the most frequently reported or studied methods in the articles reviewed. Behaviour driven (21.0%) methods, such as SERVQUAL (Van Dyke et al. 1997), are the major method carried out to understand IT/IS use and user satisfaction. A number of survey instruments (10.2%) are developed for understanding IT impacts. Technical standards (6.8%) are used to assess IT/IS system quality, including software metrics and outcome comparison methods. A few studies discussed mixed methods in evaluation (4.5%), and other 6.3% of authors argued the method selected should depend on the context. A significant number of the articles did not specify the evaluation methods (19.9%).

### 4.1.5 Who is involved in evaluation

Evaluation is a process that different people involved to either provide or analyse information related to IT/IS. Almost half of the papers reviewed (47.7%) does not specify clearly who should be responsible for the evaluation. For the ones specified people, evaluation is majorly carried out at the senior management level, where IT staff (18.2%) and financial department (28.4%) are the major evaluators. Top management (9.7%) support is believed to be critical to an effective IT/IS evaluation. Users (36.4%) are reported to be the major stakeholders who provided information for evaluation. Only 8.0% of the research states that multiple stakeholders should be involved in evaluation rather than solely IT or finance department.

**Table 7:** HOW is evaluation performed?

| HOW evaluation is conducted? | Number (%) | |
|---|---|---|
| Technical standards | 12 | (6.8%) |
| Finance based | 20 | (11.4%) |
| Economic based | 35 | (19.9%) |
| Behaviour driven | 37 | (21.0%) |
| Survey method | 18 | (10.2%) |
| Mixed | 8 | (4.5%) |
| Context based | 11 | (6.3%) |
| Not discussed or specified | 35 | (19.9%) |

**Table 8:** WHO is involved in evaluation?

| WHO is involved in evaluation? | | Number (%) |
|---|---|---|
| Senior Managers* | | |
| IT* | | 32 (18.2%) |
| | Finance* | 50 (28.4%) |
| Top Manager | | 17 (9.7%) |
| User* | | 64 (36.4%) |
| Other | | 4 (2.3%) |
| Multiple stakeholders | | 14 (8.0%) |
| Not discussed or specified | | 84 (47.7%) |

\* indicates an overlap

# 5. Discussion

## 5.1 A Respecifiction of Evaluation Streams

From this review, we have found that current IT/IS evaluation research still places excessive emphasis on the technological (e.g. software standards) and financial (e.g. discounted cash flow techniques) aspects of evaluation at the expense of the organisational and social dimensions. However, the role of IT/IS in organisations can be seen as a movement from automating to supporting decision-making, and more recently to transformation (Ballantine et al. 1996). The traditional technical/financial evaluation techniques are widely reported to be problematic and unable to cope with these changes (Serafeimidis & Smithson 1999, Irani & Love 2008, Symons 1991, Avgerou 1995). Therefore, research focusing on traditional evaluation streams contributes to one piece of the picture but is not comprehensive enough to describe the complexity of IT/IS evaluation. To overcome this problem, many researchers (e.g. Smithson & Hirschheim 1998, Symons 1991, Farbey 1999) suggest that IT/IS evaluation would be improved by "interpretive" alternatives, which take perceptions of multiple stakeholders into consideration.

The aforementioned "technical", "financial" and "interpretive" approaches are accepted classification of IT/IS evaluation streams in IS research. . These classifications reflectededdifferent evaluation strategies and were significant in identifying and understanding issues related to IT/IS.. Serafeimidis (2002) briefly reviewed literature and investigated the important features of each stream based on the concept of CCP model. Our current study extends Serifeimidis' work and reinforces  his findings with enhancements to the current classification of IT/IS evaluation.

The technical, financial and interpretive evaluation classification streams that Serafeimidis identified indicate a clear separation between three discrete evaluation categories. However, our analysis found that "technical" factors are always embedded to some degree within a "financial" evaluation context. In addition, because it aims to understand different interests of various stakeholders, "interpretive" evaluation tends to include both "technical" and "financial" considerations to some extent. Evaluation strategies have evolved with the development of IT. The evolution of IT/IS in organizations can be seen as a movement from automating to informing, and more recently to transformation (Ballantine et al. 1996) and as the role of IT/IS has changed from one of support to one of strategic importance, the focus of evaluation has also evolved from efficiency to effectiveness, and further to understanding (Irani & Love 2008, Huerta & Sanchez 1999). Therefore, while Serafeimdis' classification is a useful starting point for orienting understanding of approaches to IT/IS evaluation, the delineation between his categories is not as defined as these classifications suggest.

In addition, the terminology Serafeimidis used for different approaches implies its underlying evaluation content and method. For instance, "technical" evaluation indicatess a focus on IT/IS system quality, and technical

standards might be the major evaluation methods. However, in Serafeimidis' (2002) discussion, technical evaluation also includes other criteria such as cost reduction and manpower savings. His financial evaluation
not only focussesfocusses on IT/IS business value, but also examinesIT/IS
use and user satisfaction. A number of behaviour driven techniques are
also included and discussed in addition to financial or economic techniques.

Based on our analysis of the literature, we believe that Serafeimidis' classification should be revised  so that classification is based on the context of
the evaluation being performed.  From this perspective evaluation can be
viewed as efficiency-driven evaluation, effectiveness-driven evaluation, or
understanding-driven evaluation. The terminology was derived from the
underlying assumptions of evaluation identified in Serafeimidis' (2002)
review. Detail of each approach is summarized in Table 9.

Using this revised classification scheme, only 10.2% of the articles reviewed are in the efficiency-driven evaluation category and the majority of
these were published prior  to 1995.In contrast, most understanding-
driven evaluation articles were published after 2000, representing only
11.4% of the 176 papers reviewed. Effectiveness-driven evaluation drew
the most attention in the literature with 68.2% of the papers can categorised in this group fairly evenly distributed over the 25 year periodpeiod of
the sampled research. A small number of articles (10.2%) provided a general discussion on issues related to IT/IS evaluation and  were not classified
into any of  the revised streams.
This revised classification scheme overcomes the aforementioned problems of previous studies. Firstly, the terminology used clearly implies the
focus of each evaluation stream. Secondly, rather than being treated as
discrete categories, the relationship between the three evaluation streams
is evolutionary. To be more specific, efficiency-driven evaluation implies
that its focus is on the quality of the system under analysis and its direct
outputs. From this perspective when managers are confident of the efficiency of evaluation of IT/IS quality, they can shift their focus to effectiveness considerations of IT/IS outcomes, impacts and IT/IS-human interactions. The effectiveness of IT/IS is the primary concern for any organization. However, various interpretations of effectiveness might be held by
different stakeholders. Thus, based on the assessment of different stakeholders' interpretation of IT/IS effectiveness, understanding-driven evalua-

tion includes both efficiency-driven and effectiveness-driven evaluation. This evolutionary approach to understanding IT/IS evaluation overcomes three problems faced by managers as identified in the literature. Firstly, it amelioratestheir neglect of intangible, qualitative and in-direct objectives, and their inability to measure them (Serafeimidis & Smithson 1999). Secondly, It accounts for the IT/IS effects which organizations are most interested in assessing but are subject to change and traditional techniques are unable to cope with (Avgerou 1995). Thirdly, it accounts for multiple stakeholders involved within the IT/IS investment process, with their own set of objectives and expectations, a fact neglected by thattraditional techniques with a limited financial or technical (Irani & Love 2008, Huerta & Sanchez 1999).

**Table 9:** Streams of IT/IS Evaluation

| Type | CCP elements and details | | Number (%) |
|---|---|---|---|
| Efficiency driven | Why | To understand and improve IT/IS efficiency | 18 (10.2%) |
| | What | IT/IS quality, outcomes quality, cost reduction, etc. | |
| | When | ex-ante or ex-post | |
| | How | Technical standards, Software metrics, Outcome comparison | |
| | Who | IT Department, Senior Managers, Data collected from Users | |
| Effectiveness driven | Why | To understand and improve IT/IS effectiveness | 120 (68.2%) |
| | What | IT value, IT use, User satisfaction, Service quality, etc. | |
| | When | ex-ante or ex-post, some ongoing | |
| | How | Finance-based, economic-based, behaviour driven | |
| | Who | Top management support, Senior managers, IT and Finance department, data collected from users | |
| Understanding driven | Why | To improve understanding of different interests and perceptions | 20 (11.4%) |
| | What | Stakeholder interests, mixed focuses, often dependent on the context | |
| | When | On-going process | |
| | How | Interpretive methods, often context-based | |
| | Who | Multiple stakeholders needed to be involved | |
| General | General discussion on issues related to IT/IS evaluation, e.g. the ethical issues | | 18 (10.2%) |

## 5.2    Gaps in IT/IS Evaluation Research

There has been a significant amount of research on IT/IS evaluation in the last 25 years. Our review of the sample literature based on the CCP model identifies several gaps in the published literature in relation to IT/IS evaluation.

Firstly, nearly a third of all articles examined ignore the  purpose of evaluation (31.3%) and nearly half did not identify stakeholders (47.7%) whereas the other dimensions were usually accounted for and rarely left out of the discussion of evaluation - only 7.9% of studies neglected content, 11.4%% neglected timeframe and 19.9% neglected methods.Given that only 10.2% of papers are classified as "general discussion", the neglect of evaluation purpose and people involved is considerable. This  underestimation of the importance of purpose of evaluation suggests that evaluation is frequently being used in a ritualistic manner (Nijland & Willcocks 2008). For instance, ex-ante evaluation usually is used as a means to gain project approval (Nijland & Willcocks 2008), and ex-post evaluation has been used to formally complete or sign-off the task and disengage the IT/IS department from a project (Jones 2008). Also, the neglect of people involved in evaluation suggests that researchers often fail to take into consideration the impacts that different stakeholders have on evaluation, or alternatively, the impact of evaluation on stakeholders.

Secondly, there is an unbalanced focus in each element of evaluation in research. In terms of evaluation purpose, there appears to be little published research which reflects the political aspects of evaluation.When evaluating the value an IT/IS project, most research focuses on the operational level but underestimates its strategic and tactical value. More attention has been paid to ex-post evaluation than either ex-ante or ongoing evaluation. Traditional finance/economic based techniques and user satisfaction survey methods remain predominant approaches to evaluation. Hence, IT and finance departments tend to be the major players in evaluation and IT/IS users are the primary source of data. As a consequence, not all interested stakeholders are involved in evaluation and therefore they have little opportunity to shape further development.

Thirdly, this study indicates a mismatch between IT/IS evaluation research and practice. For instance, regarding the timeframe of IT/IS evaluation, more research pays attention to ex-post than ex-ante. Nevertheless, ex-ante evaluation is found to be more prevalent than ex-post evaluation in practice (Avgerou 1995, Nijland & Willcocks 2008, Al-Yaseen et al. 2008). Also, a large number of evaluation methods have been developed in research, but very few of them have been seen in practice. Moreover, while evaluation research is currently shifting from the efficiency and effectiveness-driven approaches to understanding-driven (Serafeimidis, 2002) and comprises various interpretive or informal evaluation methods (Avgerou 1995, Irani & Love 2008, Symons 1991),IT/IS evaluation in practice still focuses on the assessment of the efficiency and effectiveness of the system (Serafeimidis 2002, Nijland & Willcocks 2008).

# 6. Conclusion

This study reviewed 176 papers in five leading IT/IS research journals over the last 25 years. Concepts of evaluation in all papers were analysed based on the CCP model. Based on findings from this research, we propose that the classification of IT/IS evaluation should be respecified as an evolving continuum of efficiency-driven evaluation, effectiveness-driven evaluation ,and and understanding driven evaluation. we suggest that According to CCP model, people are the core of any evaluation. It is people who make decisions on what is evaluated, when evaluation takes place and how evaluation is done. Thus, the stakeholders involved in evaluation are critical to an effective evaluation. The study of human factors in evaluation also consists with the shift from traditional evaluation to understanding-driven stream. Further research can be carried out to investigate different stakeholders involvement strategies and their impacts on the evaluation process and outcomes.

This study also suggests that the evaluation can serve a number of conceptual, instrumental or political purposes. However, in practice evaluation is often carried out in an ad hoc or ritualistic manner. The potential usefulness of evaluation outcomes and processes is underestimated. Therefore, further research can focus on how to make the evaluation outcomes and processes effectively used.

Lastly, the mismatch between research and practice indicates a long distance from developing evaluation methods to put them in actual use. Particularly, the calls for interpretive methods seem rarely being heard by practitioners. Researchers therefore need to address the obstacles between research and practice, communicate the problems or risks of using those methods and to identify ways to promote the evaluation methods we have developed to decision makers in practice.

# References

Al-Yaseen, H., Eldabi, T., Pual, J. & El-Haddadeh, R. (2008). "Post-Implementation Evaluation Of IT Systems: A Close Review Of Practice". In: Z, I. & Love, P. E. D. (Eds.) Evaluating Information Systems: Public And Private Sector. Butterworth-Heinemann, Burlington

Ammenwerth, E., Graber, S., Herrmann, G., Burkle, T. & Konig, J. (2003). "Evaluation of health information systems--problems and challenges", International journal of medical informatics, Vol 71, Iss 2/3, pp 125-135.

Avgerou, C. (1995). "Evaluating Information Systems By Consultation And Negotiation", International Journal Of Information Management, December, Vol 15, Iss 6, pp 427-436.

Baines, P. & Lynch, R. (2005). "The context, content and process of political marketing strategy", Journal of Political Marketing, Vol 4, Iss 2, pp 1-18.

Ballantine, J. A., Galliers, R. D. & Stray, S. J. (1996). "Information Systems/Technology Evaluation Practices: Evidence From Uk Organizations", Journal Of Information Technology, June, Vol 11, Iss 2, pp 129-141.

Ballantine, J. A. & Stray, S. (1999). "Information Systems And Other Capital Investments: Evaluation Practices Compared", Logistics Information Management, Vol 12, Iss 1/2, pp 78-93.

Delone, W. H. & Mclean, E. R. (1992). "Information Systems Success: The Quest For The Dependent Variable", Information Systems Research, March, Vol 3, Iss 1, pp 60-95.

Delone, W. H. & Mclean, E. R. (2003). "The Delone And Mclean Model Of Information Systems Success: A Ten-Year Update", Journal Of Management Information Systems, Spring, Vol 19, Iss 4, pp 9-30.

Devos, G., Buelens, M. & Bouckenooghe, D. (2007). "Contribution of Content, Context, and Process to Understanding Openness to Organizational Change: Two Experimental Simulation Studies", The Journal of Social Psychology, Vol 147, Iss 6, pp 607-630.

Farbey, B. (1992). "Evaluating investments in IT", Journal of Information Technology, Vol 7, Iss 2, pp 109-122.

Farbey, B. (1999). "The moving staircase problems of appraisal and evaluation in a turbulent environment", Information Technology & People, Vol 12, Iss 3, pp 238-252.

Farbey, B., Land, F. & Targett, D. (1999a). "Evaluating Investments in IT: Findings and a Framework". In: WILLCOCKS, L. P. & LESTER, S. (eds.) Beyond the IT Praductivity Paradox. John Wiley & Sons Ltd,

Farbey, B., Land, F. & Targett, D. (1999b). "IS evaluation: a process for bringing together benefits, costs and risks". In: CURRIE, W. & GALLIERS, B. (eds.) Rethinking Management Information Systems: An Interdisciplinary Perspective., Oxford University Press, Oxford, UK

Farbey, B., Land, F. & Targett, D. (1999c). "Moving IS evaluation forward: learning themes and research issues", The Journal of Strategic Information Systems, Vol 8, Iss 2, pp 189-207.

Huerta, E. & Sanchez, P. (1999). "Evaluation Of Information Technology: Strategies In Spanish Firms", European Journal Of Information Systems, December, Vol 8, Iss 4, pp 273-283.

Irani, Z. & Love, P. E. D. (2008). "Informaiton Systems Evaluation: A Crisis Of Understanding". In: Irani, Z. & Love, P. E. D. (Eds.) Evaluating Information Systems: Public And Private Sector. Butterworth-Heinemann, Burlinton

Irani, Z., Sharif, M. & Love, P. E. D. (2005). "Linking Knowledge Transformation To Information Systems Evaluation", European Journal Of Information Systems, September, Vol 14, Iss 3, pp 213-228.

Jones, S. (2008). "Social Dimension Of It/Is Evaluation: Views From The Public Sector". In: Z, I. & Love, P. E. D. (Eds.) Evaluating Information Systems: Public And Private Sector. Butterworth-Heinemann, Burlington

Ketchen, D. J., Thomas, J. B. & McDaniel, R. R. (1996). "Process, content and context: synergistic effects on organizational performance", Journal of Management, Vol 22, Iss 2, pp 231-257.

Nagm, F. (2008). IS project Evaluation in Practice: An Actor-Network Theory Account. Doctor of Philosophy PhD Thesis, University of New South Wales.

Nijland, M. & Willcocks, L. P. (2008). "How It Evaluation Methods Are Used: Examining Case Research From An Ant Perspective". In: Z, I. & Love, P. E. D. (Eds.) Evaluating Information Systems: Publich And Private Sector. Butterworth-Heinemann, Burlington

Özkan, S., Hackney, R. & Bilgen, S. (2007). "Process based information systems evaluation: towards the attributes of "PRISE"", Journal of Enterprise Information Management, Vol 20, Iss 6, pp 700-725.

Serafeimidis, V. (2002). "A Review Of Research Issues In Evaluation Of Information Systems". In: Grembergen, W. V. (Ed.) Information Systems Evaluation Management. IRM Press, London.

Serafeimidis, V. & Smithson, S. (1999). "Rethinking The Approaches To Information Systems Investment Evaluation", Journal Of Enterprise Information Management, Vol 12, Iss 1/2, pp 94-107.

Serafeimidis, V. & Smithson, S. (2000). "Information Systems Evaluation In Practice: A Case Study Of Organizational Change", Journal Of Information Technology, June, Vol 15, Iss 2, pp 93-105.

Smithson, S. & Hirschheim, R. (1998). "Analysing information systems evaluation: Another look at an old problem", European Journal of Information Systems, Vol 7, Iss 3, pp 158-174.

Stockdale, R. & Standing, C. (2006). "An Interpretive Approach To Evaluating Information Systems: A Content, Context, Process Framework", European Journal of Operational Research, September, Vol 173, Iss 3, pp 1090-1102.

Symons, V. J. (1991). "A Review Of Information Systems Evaluation: Content, Context And Process", European Journal of Information Systems, August, Vol 1, Iss 3, pp 205-112.

Van Dyke, T., Kappelman, L. & Prybutok, V. (1997). "Measuring Information Systems Service Quality: Concerns On The Use Of The Servqual Questionnaire", MIS Quarterly, June, Vol 21, Iss 2, pp 195-208.

Willcocks, L. & Lester, S. (1996). "Beyond the IT productivity paradox". European Management Journal, 14, pp 279.

# Information System Evaluation through an Emergence Lens

**Olgerta Tona and Sven A. Carlsson**
**Informatics, Lund University School of Economics and Management,**
**Lund, Sweden**
*Originally published in EJISE (2013) Volume 16, ISS 1*

**Editorial Commentary**

Tona and Carlsson make a significant contribution to the advancement of theoretical perspectives in IS evaluation. Their point of departure is that from three views of IS – connection, immersion and fusion – fusion is the least dominant, but given new imperatives in modern organisations from an IS-business alignment perspective, it is actually of increasing importance. This forms the basis for the development of theory to inform this perspective of IS evaluation. The fusion view, they posit, is a perspective in which business and IS are indistinguishable to standard time-space perception, forming a unified fabric in which IT-enabled work and processes are treated as one. The value of the paper is the operationalisation of the fusion view through the use of a critical-realist lens using relational emergence theory. As a leading issue, the paper provides the groundwork for further interrogation of a fusion perspective to IS evaluation. Moreover, this is an important demonstration of the application of emergence theory, encouraging further IS evaluation research to be framed within this particular theoretical lens.

**Abstract:** The development and expansion of evaluation theory and practice is at the core of several different disciplines. There exist different traditional Information System (IS) evaluation approaches, like experimental, pragmatic, constructivist, pluralist and realist IS evaluation. IS evaluation approaches are influenced by the way they address to technology. Recently actor network theory (ANT) and sociomateriality are two influential information systems (IS) entanglement perspectives. Additionally, El Sawy identified three faces of IS views: connection, immersion, and fusion. In terms of IS evaluation approaches, connection and immersion view are the dominant views in which these approaches are positioned. We believe the IS fusion view calls for IS evaluation approaches to be revised. This paper uses the relational emergence theory, based on the philosophy of critical realism to

*Olgerta Tona and Sven A. Carlsson*

theorize and operationalize the fusion view, as it lacks a theoretical grounding and as well to push forward the traditional IS evaluation research approaches. At the core of relational emergence theory is the emergence concept, in which parts are structured by the relations among each other to create an entity as a 'whole'. Based on this, we present and discuss the implications for IS evaluation in terms of how to evaluate a process as well as the output of the process. The discussion on IS evaluation is illustrated through an empirical example, drawn on a longitudinal research study within a police organization. This paper concludes that in the fusion view, the evaluation process shall embrace a holistic perspective. The focus of the evaluation process shall be the emergent entity consisting of IS, users, task and processes structured by means of relationships among each other. The properties exhibited by this emergent entity shall be evaluated.

**Keywords:** Information System evaluation, IS evaluation approaches, fusion view, IS views, relational emergence theory

# 1. Introduction

The development and expansion of evaluation theory and practice is at the core of several different disciplines. It is important to scrutinize theories, approaches, and models used in evaluation (research) as well as evaluation research approaches' philosophical underpinnings (Carlsson 2003).

Information Systems (IS) evaluation and IS evaluation research have been stressed as critical means in advancing the IS field (Bjørn-Andersen & Davis 1988). Generally, IS evaluation is concerned with the evaluation of different aspects of real-life interventions in the social life where IS are critical means in achieving the interventions' anticipated goals. Different evaluation approaches such as: the experimental approach, the pragmatic approach, the constructivist approach, the pluralist approach and the realistic approach (Carlsson 2003) have been researched and applied.

Driving the development and use of IS evaluation are IS theories and how IS are perceived (viewed). Recently, in the IS field, different theories have changed the way we address to technology and we believe that these theories drive the type of approaches evaluators embrace. This type of research can be characterized with the label 'entanglement in practice' and the main influential entanglement perspectives are Actor Network Theory (ANT) and the notion of sociomateriality (Orlikowski 2010). ANT's main focus is the construction of a network of actors, humans and non-humans. In the network the users divide their roles and may invite other actors in the network. The main mechanism by which this network is created is by means of the translations, which invite the actors and create links among them. The associations which keep these actors together are important for the continuation of the network. Both human and non-human actors are aligned together, so there is no discrimination among them in terms of emphasis (Elbanna 2012). Stability of the network is reached when all the actors within the network are aligned and they have reached one common interest (Callon 1991). Sociomateriality is another perspective which is related to the constitutive entangling of the material and social. It refers to the blurring of boundaries between technical and social matters and the importance of materiality in activities and relations. Said Orlikowski and Scott (2008: 455–456): 'In other words, entities (whether humans or technologies) have no inherent properties, but acquire form, attributes, and capabilities through their interpretation . . . Any distinction of humans and technologies is analytical only, and done with the recognition that these entities necessarily entail each other in practice'. In sociomateriality, both the social and the technical are intertwined and they cannot be separated, but instead conceptualised as such during their entanglement in practice.

Additionally, El Sawy (2003) presented three different views on IS: connection, immersion, and fusion. He contends that it may be time for a natural shift of emphasis from the connection view to the immersion view to the fusion view as IT continues to morph and augment its capabilities. In the connection view, IT and IS are viewed as separable artefacts and artificial systems that are used by people as tools. They are separable from work, processes, and people. In the immersion view, IT and IS are immersed as part of the business environment and cannot be separated from work, processes, and the systemic properties of intra- and inter-organizational processes and relationships. This view stresses work context and systemic relationships and mutual interdependencies. In the fusion view, IT and IS are fused within the business environment, such that business and IT and IS are indistinguishable to standard time-space perception and form a unified fabric. Hence, IT-enabled work and processes are treated as one.

Most, if not all, of the existing IS evaluation approaches have been developed based on the IS connection and immersion views. The fusion view will influence the way IS is evaluated and the already existing approaches have drawbacks if used in fusion view. IS evaluation based on the principles and philosophy of critical realism can be used to develop an IS evaluation approach well linked with the fusion view (Carlsson 2003). Critical realism

(CR) sees structure as *"...the constituent components [of structure and agency]"* and *"cannot be examined separately....In the absence of any degree of autonomy it becomes impossible to examine their interplay"* (Archer 1988). The relational emergence theory, based on the philosophy of critical realism (Elder – Vass 2010), presents a perspective which overcomes the critique of ANT for treating all actors, human and non-human in the same way and the critique towards sociomateriality as pointed out by Leonardi and Barley (2010: 35) 'Whereas Orlikowski urges us to weave the social and the material together conceptually, we argue for unravelling them empirically in order to study how each contributes to the whole. At the very least, this means that, in addition to studying social processes, researchers need to pay attention to what a technology lets users do, to what it does not let them do, and to the workarounds that users develop to address the latter'.

Therefore we propose another IS evaluation approach based on the emergence concept. Emergence refers to an entity (system) created by different parts, which exhibits different behaviour as a result of interactions between its composite parts (Elder-Vass 2010). An emergent entity is characterised by the dependency upon interactive parts; fundamental changes to the parts will lead to fundamental changes in the whole; its effects cannot be broken down to the part level (Morgan 2007). The parts are organised such that the sum of the whole is greater than its parts (Odell 2002). Emergence is a way to address fusion based on a specific philosophy and a way to "operationalize" the fusion concept. Both fusion and emergence refer to different parts coming together by interacting and acting as one identity. If the parts are split up, the same entity with the same properties will no longer be obtained.

This paper has two main contributions. The first is theoretical, in which fusion view introduced by El Sawy (2003) will be discussed and elaborated from a CR and emergence perspective. The second contribution will be a discussion on the implications of IS evaluation in the fusion view, in terms of how to evaluate a process as well as the output of the process. The discussion will be illustrated by means of an empirical example.

The remainder of the paper is organized as follows. The next section presents a brief summary of the main IS evaluation approaches and their corresponding views. Section 3 discusses the emergence concept and its properties which are adopted. This is followed by an empirical example. Conclusions are presented in the final section.

## 2. IS evaluation approaches

This section reviews the major IS evaluation (research) approaches and points out their major strengths and weaknesses. The approaches are the experimental approach, the pragmatic approach, the constructivist approach, the pluralist approach, and the realistic approach (Carlsson 2003). Next, the approaches are positioned to the IS view(s) they can be applied to.

### 2.1 Experimental IS evaluation

The experimental IS evaluation approach is the oldest IS evaluation approach and it builds on the logic of experimentation: take two more or less matched groups (situations) and treat one group and not the other. By measuring both groups before and after the treatment of the one, an evaluator can get a "clear" measure of the impact of the treatment.

Evaluators and evaluation researchers have recognized the practical difficulties in doing pure experimental evaluation, and thus the idea of quasi-experimental evaluation was developed (Campbell & Stanley 1963). Quasi-experimental evaluation research does not meet the experiment requirements and therefore does not exhibit complete internal validity. According to Carlsson (2003) there are two major problems with experimental IS evaluation. First, the studies are to a large extent a-theoretical and non-theoretical. In discussing DSS evaluation—especially presentation formats in DSS—Carlsson and Stabell conclude: "As we see it, part of the problem is research without a suitable theory, at time without any theory. Typically such work does not present a coherent theoretical argument for how alternative presentation formats might make a difference in the decision context considered." (Carlsson & Stabell 1986). Second, to meet the experiment requirements an experimenter (evaluator) must in most cases create an unrealistic situation and reduce intermediary variables that might affect the outcome. In other words, experimental IS evaluation tries to minimize all the differences, except one, between the experimental and the control groups. This means stripping away the context and yielding results that are only valid in other contextless situations.

## 2.2    Pragmatic IS evaluation

Pragmatic IS evaluation research was developed, in part, as a response to the problems associated with the experimental IS evaluation approach. The pragmatic evaluation approach represents a use-led model of evaluation research, stressing utilization: the basic aim of IS evaluation is to develop IS initiatives (implementation of IS) which solve "problems"— problems can be organizational problems like reduced competitiveness or far from good customer services. The problems addressed in an intervention and the intervention's goals are not given, but are politically colored and defined by stakeholders. Following Patton's (1982, 2002) view on evaluation, this approach stresses that the test bed is whether the practical cause of IS intervention is forwarded or not. It is not a question of following certain epistemological axioms. The pragmatic IS evaluation approach has a toolbox view on evaluation methods. Pragmatic evaluation is comprised of standard research tasks. Evaluation research success is depending on a researcher's sheer craft and this craft is primarily learned through exemplars. In doing evaluation an evaluator or a researcher selects the appropriate tools and measures from the available toolbox. The rule of thumb is that the evaluation mandate comes from the stakeholder(s) responsible for the development, implementation, and use of the information systems. The more explicit the mandate is the more compressed and technical is the evaluator's role. Since the evaluation mandate is coming from stakeholders this can lead to "evaluation (evaluator) for hire" which is one of the major problems with pragmatic IS evaluation.

## 2.3    Constructivist IS evaluation

In line with the general development in many social sciences during the 1970's, phenomenology, hermeneutic, and interpretative approaches influenced IS evaluation. This meant that focus came to be on social processes. The constructivist evaluation approach argues that IS initiatives should not be treated "…as 'independent variables', as 'things', as 'treatments', as 'dosages'." (Pawson & Tilley 1997). Instead all IS initiatives are "…constituted in complex processes of understanding and interaction" and an IS initiative (IS implementation) will work "through a process of reasoning, change, influence, negotiation, battle of wills, persuasion, choice increase (or decrease), arbitration or some such like." (Pawson & Tilley 1997). Following Guba and Lincoln (1989) it can be argued that the social world is fundamentally a process of negotiation and so are IS initiatives. Hence, evaluation is a process of negotiation and evaluators are the "or-

chestrators" of negotiation processes. The major problem with the constructivist IS evaluation approach is its inability to grasp those structural
and institutional features of society and social organization which are in
some respects independent of the agents' reasoning and desires but influence (affect) an IS initiative and the negotiation process. To develop theories of why an IS initiative (IS implementation) works for whom and in what
circumstances requires an evaluator or a researcher to generate some
means of making independent judgments about the institutional structure
and power relations present in an IS initiative. This is something not possible in constructivist IS evaluation, but institutional structure and power
relations affect—working as constrainers and enablers—an IS initiative and
the negotiation process.

## 2.4 Pluralist IS evaluation

Having presented three "traditional" IS evaluation approaches and noted
their strengths and weaknesses, one can imagine the attractiveness of developing an approach combining the strengths of the three approaches: an
approach combining the rigor of experimentation with the practice of
pragmatism, and with the constructivist's empathy for the voices of the
stakeholders. The pluralist IS evaluation approach was developed more or
less on these premises. The major problem of the approach is that it does
not address what it is with an IS initiative which makes it work. It also lacks
an ontological position.

## 2.5 Realistic IS evaluation

Driving realistic IS evaluation is the aim to produce ever more detailed answers to the question of why an IS initiative—IS, types of IS, or IS implementation—works for whom and in what circumstances. This means that
evaluators and evaluation researchers attend to how and why an IS initiative has the potential to cause (desired) changes. Realistic IS evaluation is
applied research, but theory is essential in every aspects of IS evaluation
and IS evaluation research research design and analysis. The goal is not to
develop theory per se, but to develop theories for practitioners, stakeholders, and participants.

## 2.6 IS evaluation approaches in relation to IS views

The previous sections presented a short description of the four major IS
evaluation approaches and an alternative IS evaluation approach (realistic

evaluation). **Table 1** shows the approaches' primary target(s) in relation to El Sawy's IS views.

**Table 1:** IS evaluation approaches

| IS evaluation approach | Short description | Views |
|---|---|---|
| Experimental | By measuring the treated and untreated groups before and after the treatment of the one, an evaluator can get a "clear" measure of the impact of the treatment. | Connection |
| Pragmatic | Represents a use-led model of evaluation research, stressing utilization: the basic aim of IS evaluation research is to develop IS initiatives (implementation of IS) which solve problems | Connection |
| Constructivist | All IS initiatives are "…constituted in complex processes of understanding and interaction" and an IS initiative (IS implementation) will work "through a process of reasoning, change, influence, negotiation, battle of wills, persuasion, choice increase (or decrease), arbitration or some such like." (Pawson and Tilley 1997). | Connection, Immersion |
| Pluralist | Combines the strengths of the three approaches: an approach combining the rigor of experimentation with the practice of pragmatism, and with the constructivist's empathy for the voices of the stakeholders. | Connection, Immersion |
| Realistic | Its aim to produce ever more detailed answers to the question of *why* an IS initiative—IS, types of IS, or IS implementation—works for *whom* and in *what* circumstances. | Connection, Immersion (potentially Fusion) |

In general, the IS evaluation approaches described are positioned mainly in two IS views: the connection and immersion view. The approaches consider IS either as a tool, separated from the work and process (in the case of the connection view), or as immersed in the work and process (in the case of the immersion view). None of them consider the evaluation of IS, when it is fused in the organization and as such IS is not treated as one together with tasks, processes and people. The CR-based concept emergence could be an alternative for developing an IS evaluation approach for the fusion view. The realistic approach with its idea of mechanism-based explanations

(Hedström and Ylikoski, 2010) and its emergence perspective (Elder-Vass 2010) has the potential for being used in the fusion view.

Taking into consideration the emergence of IS towards fusion view, there is a need for the evaluation approaches to be revised. IS can no longer be separated from its environment (context), as it is already fused into it. During the evaluation process, IS has to be considered as a whole, together with users, tasks, processes, etc.

## 3. Emergence in critical realism

Critical realism has become an important perspective in modern philosophy and social science (Archer et al. 1998; Robson 2002), but critical realism has to a large extent been absent in IS research. We argue that IS evaluation and IS evaluation research based on the principles and philosophy of critical realism overcomes some of the problems associated with "traditional" IS evaluation (research) approaches.

CR's manifesto is to recognize the reality of the natural order and the events and discourses of the social world. It holds that "we will only be able to understand—and so change—the social world if we identify the structures at work that generate those events and discourses ... These structures are not spontaneously apparent in the observable pattern of events; they can only be identified through the practical and theoretical work of the social sciences." (Bhaskar 1989).

Emergence is a cornerstone in critical realism. Smith (2010: 25–26) writes that emergence refers to the process of constituting a new entity with its own particular characteristics through the interactive combination of other, different entities that are necessary to create the new entity but that do not contain the characteristics present in the new entity. Emergence involves the following: First, two or more entities that exist at a "lower" level interact or combine. Second, that interaction or combination serves as the basis of some new, real entity that has existence at a "higher" level. Third, the existence of the new higher-level entity is fully dependent upon the two or more lower-level entities interacting or combining, as they could not exist without doing so. Fourth, the new, higher-level entity nevertheless possesses characteristic qualities (e.g., structures, qualities, capacities, textures, mechanisms) that cannot be reduced to those of the lower-level entities that gave rise to the new entity possessing them. When these four things happen, emergence has happened. The whole is more than the sum of its parts.

Elder–Vass (2010) introduced the relational emergence theory based on the philosophy of critical realism. He provides a general ontological framework to discuss the social structures and human individuals as entities with emergent properties which determine the social events. An entity is a 'whole', which consists of parts structured by means of the relations among each-other. Emergent entities possess some properties produced by mechanisms which depend on the properties of individual parts and the way the parts are structured in order to form the entity (whole). The properties which derive from the entity are not possessed by its individual parts. The way the parts are related at a certain point in time will depict the joint effect they will have. Therefore the relation between the entity and its parts is not of causation, but of composition (Elder-Vass 2010).

The importance of the interactions between the parts is expressed by Holland (1998:121-122) as:

Emergence is above all a product of coupled, context-dependent interactions. Technically these interactions, and the resulting system, are nonlinear: The behavior of the overall system cannot be obtained by summing the behaviors of its constituent parts... the whole is indeed more than the sum of its parts. However, we can reduce the behavior of the whole to the lawful behavior of its parts, if we take the nonlinear interactions into account.

There are some elements which an emergent entity should have (Elder-Vass 2010). First of all, the different parts which an emergent entity consists of should be recognized. The relationships between the parts which cause this type of entity should be identified. The emergent entity should be explained in terms of morphogenetic and morphostatic causes. Morphogenetic refers to "those processes which tend to elaborate or change a system's given form, structure or state" (Buckley, 1967: 58-59). Morphostasis refers to the causes which maintain an entity either internal (the causes which maintain the parts in a certain relationship) or external (the causes coming from the environment). The latter, Buckley (1967: 58-59) defines as "those processes in complex system-environment exchanges that tend to preserve or maintain a system's given form, organization or state".

Additionally, De Wolf and Holvoet (2005), based on a literature review, have listed different properties possessed by an emergent entity:

- *Interactive Parts.* The interaction between the parts is responsible for the emergent system (Odell 2002; Heylighen 2002).
- *Micro-Macro level effect.* An emergent properties that an emergent system shows as the results of the interaction between its components (Holland 1998).
- *Novelty.* Emergent properties cannot be understood by the properties of the components. Anyhow, they still can be studied via the components and their relations in the context of the whole system (Holland 1998; Elder-Vass 2010).
- *Coherence.* An emergent property tends to maintain its own identity during the time, by converting the interactive parts into a 'whole' (Heylighen 2002).
- *Dynamical.* Emergent properties of a system are related to the time dimension, meaning that they can arise or change over time (Holland 1998).
- *Decentralised Control.* No parts alone can direct or control the emergent properties of a system (Odell 2002).
- *Two-Way Link.* The interaction between the parts influences the emergent system, which on the other hand can influence its individual parts (Odell 2002).
- *Flexibility.* As no single part is fully responsible for the emergent properties of a system, its substitution or non-functionality will not lead to a total failure of the emergent entity (Odell 2002).

# 4. IS evaluation in the fusion view

As previously discussed, different approaches have been used to address 'entanglement in practice', including sociomateriality and ANT. Additionally, the fusion concept introduced by El Sawy (2003) tries to explain how the advances in technology are fusing IS/IT in organisations. To address the technology fused we take a holistic perspective grounded in the relational emergence theory. The parts which constitute the whole and their relations should be recognised in order to understand the generation of events and impacts.

In the fusion view, IT and IS are fused within the business environment and are indistinguishable. They can no longer be separated from work, processes and users, but instead they should be treated as one. Both IS fusion and the emergent entity refers to different elements merging together by interacting and acting as one identity. If the parts are split up, no longer will the same entity with the same properties be obtained. Using emergence as a conceptual lens we argue that, in the fusion view, different parts such as IS, tasks, users, etc., structured by relations among each other, give rise to an emerging entity showing different emerging properties. In this sense we try to operationalize and theorise fusion.

IS fusion view calls for IS evaluation approaches to be revised. The traditional IS approaches described in Section 2 do not meet the challenges of the fusion view. IS evaluation based on the emergence theory will move IS evaluation from the connection and immersion view, towards the fusion view. The result of an IS evaluation is a concept of interest which represent an emergent property. We need to identify the entity which produces this property and the relations between its parts. It is also important to explain the mechanisms of how they interact to produce these events. IS can no longer be evaluated separated from its users, processes and tasks. The evaluation process should take a holistic perspective. The parts which constitute the whole and their relations shall be recognized in order to understand the generation of the impacts and events. Hence, the impacts of the entity as a whole shall be evaluated—since the result of IS evaluation is produced by the entity—shifting the focus from the evaluation of IS per se to the entity in which IS is part of. When evaluating the impacts and benefits of IS the macro – level impacts should be considered. It means that the emergent properties need to be evaluated instead and the mechanisms which bring the emergent properties should be described. In this way, based on the evaluation results, changes in different parts can be undertaken if necessary to maintain the whole as such and keep IS fused in the organization.

To illustrate the emergence concept in an evaluation process we will in the next section use an empirical example. Possible emergent entities will be observed and evaluated by means of the emergent properties, and based on the theoretical framework discussed above.

## 4.1   Empirical example
In this section we will illustrate via an empirical example how to begin an IS evaluation based on the emergence theory. The empirical example is

based on a longitudinal research study we have been performing in a police organization since 2009. For more details about the case, see Carlsson et al. (2010).

Skåne is the third largest police authority in Sweden and it has approximately 3240 employees, where approximately 2340 are police officers and 900 civil servants. The Business Intelligence (BI) system, created with the software QlikView, started as a single application based on the system RAR (a system for crime statistics, where all reported crimes are registered). (QlikView is a BI/DSS software company, see: http://www.qlikview.com). The system was used by crime analysts to forecast when and where crime could occur. The main objective of the system was to support decision-making processes in order to increase efficiency and effectiveness. The system creates associations on the processed data which makes it easy to distinguish relationships between them. The information can be visualized by diagrams, tables or dashboards. The BI applications existed primarily in two categories: 'view' and 'analyse'. The view applications were available to all employees through the police intranet. The analysts had the same access as the viewers, but also the option to do more detailed analyses.

The police organizations' BI system is slowly emerging to the fusion view. We will evaluate the societal impact of an entity consisting of: BI system users and other policemen, BI system, and the specific tasks to be solved with two different examples. The first example is a single-shot analysis for solving a crime. The second example is an on-going analysis of crimes for improving crime prevention.

Case 1: *Finding the serial shooter.* BI usage in the police organization in Skåne proved to be successful in the solution of a crime which was scaring the citizens of Malmö (a city in Skåne). During the last years, a serial shooter in Malmö shot many people (emigrants, second generation emigrants, and refugees) in the streets, at bus stops, and in the victims' cars. Many were seriously wounded and one was killed. For this case, after finding a suspect, the police in Skåne gathered all the reports dating back to 1998 and found that there were about 58 reports connected to the shooter. The police used a BI application, which can read about 1.5 million reports in less than 10 minutes. According to one of our interviewees the specific application took about "four hours to build—because we knew how to do it". During the analysis 6–7 key words were used in the free-text search application. The analysis produced *"27000–32000 rows [of information] in Excel with 11–13 words in each row"*. This information identified the reports that should be read and evaluated. Reading and evaluating had to be done the old way (manually).

Case 2: *Crime prevention*. One example of 'car theft' prevention in Malmö shows how "hot spot" analyses can be both effective and efficient in terms of crime prevention. According to Weisburd and Telep (2010), crime hot spot strategies for fighting crime have been embraced recently by some police forces. The idea underpinning the crime hot spot strategy is that crime is better prevented by focusing on areas (hot spots), for example, specific streets, buildings, blocks, and areas within a community or zone, rather than by focusing on individuals. The process started by using the BI system to point out some areas with the highest number of car thefts. Further analyses, by means of other systems, proceeded to identify the parking lots and streets of those hot zones. Action was taken to allocate the patrol forces to the hot spots. This strategy revealed to be effective in relation to reducing crime not only in the hot spot areas but also in most zones of the city. Thus, the BI system enabled the police to implement the hot spot strategy.

The successful Malmö-cases show BI usage in crime solutions. The case against the shooter was stronger in court (the shooter was sentenced to life in prison). In this case the interaction between at least four parts—BI system, BI system users and other policemen, and the task to be solved—led to *macro-level effects*. Based on the specific type of organization, we refer to these effects as societal benefits. The users constructed the necessary application within BI to read the reports, saving months of work. In this case, time is critical as the police have to handle a serial shooter and the sooner he is caught, the better. Hence, we deduce that the interaction between the parts resulted in time reduction (enhanced efficiency) and strongly supported the crime solution.

The same type of analyses can be applied to the 'car theft' example. As a result of the interactions between BI system, the BI system users and other policemen, and the task to be solved, societal benefits in terms of crime prevention are produced. The entity—the parts and the interactions—has brought novel ways of dealing with crime prevention, hot spot, which cannot be achieved by the parts operating on their own. Although hot spot analyses have been criticized for moving the crime to the "next corner", many other studies and experiments have concluded that hot spot analyses are followed by the diffusion of crime prevention benefits (Weisburd and Telep 2010). This study supports the arguments of Weisburd and Telep (2010) because the benefits of crime prevention were not limited to the hot spots but also extended to the nearby areas. Now the police can identify hot spots and better allocate their resources with the main intention of preventing crime. The parts and their interactions have improved efficiency in terms of reducing the number of target spots and allocating resources better, leading to improved crime prevention. Hence, we observe some sort of emerging entity giving rise to macro effects by means of the interacting parts, which cannot produce these results on their own in isolation. Considering this process in terms of *morphogenic* causes, the interaction between BI and the users for a specific task, the capabilities of the BI system to analyse data very fast, and the ability of the employees to interpret the data are the main contributory causes which give rise to the exhibition, by the emerging entity, of macro-level effects which cannot be reached on a micro-level.

It is worth considering that in both examples the interaction between BI and users existed only during the first phases of the crime analyses, where all the data needed are collected. Afterwards, the users had to carry out manual work: for instance in the Malmö case they had to analyse the reports manually and in the case of 'car theft' they had to use other sources to obtain more details regarding the specific 'hot' streets and blocks. However, we believe that extra BI capabilities to support all of the phases of analytical work will drive BI even more towards the total fusion view. This study support the arguments of El Sawy (2003) that more technological advances in BI will shift it to fusion view and at the same time we will observe more solid emergent structures.

In coherence terms, in the case of the serial shooter some identity properties are shown. The news headline "Swedish Police Arrest Man over Malmö Racist Shootings" (Associated Press in Malmo 2010) demonstrates how neither the analyst group nor the BI system whose interaction saved so many months of work were mentioned, but the entity was given another name: the Swedish police. The entity is recognized by the organization's name, as the interaction between the BI and users to solve the crime takes place within the context of the police organization. One question in this case is: will the macro-level effects drive micro-level behaviour in leading to a *two-way link*? Basically, the success of this interaction between the users and the BI in crime solution and prevention may lead the users to a more extensive usage of the system in other cases, where their needs will also drive updating of the BI system or inclusion of other technological capabilities in it. For instance, during the 'hot spot' analysis, the users realized that the integration of a map in their BI system would further improve hot spot analyses, and would, as stated by a respondent, "take our work very, very far". In its current state BI displays the hot crime zones by means of zone numbers, but it is unable to direct the police to specific streets or buildings referred to as spots. Additionally, we can observe the *characteristic of flexibility*. If we substitute the users with others, nearly the same effects and benefits will be obtained, and also if the BI system is down some of the work can be done manually, but that would result in a waste of time, and in some cases time can be critical, for instance in crime prevention or solution. For example in the case of the Malmo serial shooter, if the BI system went down, the users could still manage but the work would take about nine months, which could even lead to the release of the suspect until the evidence was ready. To summarize, this was an empirical example where the evaluation of societal impact was focused on the emergent properties of the entity (the pars and their interactions).

## 5. Conclusions

This paper has discussed the implication of IS evaluation in the fusion view (El Sawy 2003). We presented a short description of the main IS evaluation approaches which all target the IS connection view or the immersion view. The fusion view, calls for the IS evaluation approaches to be revised. This paper uses the relational emergence theory based on critical realism to theorize and operationalize the fusion view and discuss its impact on IS evaluation. Based on the emergence concept, within IS fusion view an emerging entity rise, where IS is a part constituting this entity. We discussed the implications of the evaluation process when IS are positioned in the fusion view. We suggested that the evaluation process should embrace a 'holistic' perspective, where IS, users, task processes, etc. should be considered as one entity. The relationship between the parts and the entities' properties should be evaluated. Therefore emergence is used as a conceptual lens and we illustrated the idea by evaluating the organizational and societal impact of a BI system in a police organization in a holistic perspective. The arguments of El Sawy (2003) that with more technological advances fusion view will be reached are supported in the example. Once more capabilities will be implemented in the BI system, it will be extensively used and other emergent properties may emerge.

# References

Archer, M. (1988) Culture and Agency: The Place of Culture in Social Theory, Cambridge University Press, Cambridge, UK.

Archer, M., Bhaskar, R., Collier, A., Lawson, T. and Norrie, A. (ed.) (1998) Critical Realism: Essential Readings, Routledge, London.

Associated Press in Malmo (2010) 'Swedish police arrest man over Malmö racist shootings', The Guardian, Available At : < http://www.guardian.co.uk/world/2010/nov/07/malmo-race-shooting-arrest>, Accessed 10 January 2013.

Bhaskar, R. (1989) Reclaiming Reality, Verso, London.

Bjørn-Andersen, N. and Davis G. B. (ed.) (1988) Information Systems Assessment: Issues and Challenges. North-Holland, Amsterdam.

Buckley. W. (1967) Sociology and modern systems theory, Englewood Cliffs, NJ: Prentice Hall.

Callon, M. (1991) 'Techno-economic networks and irreversibility', in: Law J. (ed.) A Sociology of Monsters: Essays on Power, Technology and Domination, Routledge, London, UK.

Campbell, D. and Stanley, J. (1963) Experimental and Quasi-Experimental Evaluations in Social Research, Rand McNally, Chicago, IL.

Carlsson, S.A. (2003) 'Advancing Information Systems Evaluation (Research): A Critical Realist Approach', Electronic Journal of Information Systems Evaluation, Vol. 6, No. 2, pp. 11-20.

Carlsson, S., Skog, L.-M. and Tona, O. (2010) 'An IS success evaluation of a DSS in a police organization', in Respício, A., Adam, F., Phillips-Wren, G., Teixeira, C. and Telhada, J. (eds.) Bridging the socio-technical gap in decision support systems, IOS Press, Amsterdam, pp. 443–454.

Carlsson, S. and C.B. Stabell (1986) 'Spreadsheet programs and decision support: a keystroke-level model of system use', in McLean, E.R. and Sol H.G. (ed.) Decision Support Systems: A Decade in Perspective, North-Holland, Amsterdam, pp.113-128.

De Wolf, T. and Holvoet, T. (2005) 'Emergence versus self-organisation: Different concepts but promising when combined', in Brueckner, S., Di Marzo Serugendo, G., Karageorgos, A., Nagpal, R. (ed.) Engineering Self Organising Systems: Methodologies and Applications. Lecture Notes in Computer Science, Springer Verlag: Berlin, pp. 1–15.

Elbanna, A. (2012) 'Applying actor network theory and managing controversy', in Dwivedi, Y.K., Wade M.R. and Schneberger S.L. (ed) Information Systems Theory, Springer, New York, pp. 117–129.

Elder-Vass D. (2010) The Causal Power of Social Structures: Emergence, Structure and Agency, Cambridge University Press, New York.

El Sawy, O. A. (2003) 'The IS Core IX: The 3 Faces of IS Identity: Connection, Immersion, and Fusion', Communications of the AIS, Vol. 12, pp. 588-598.

Guba, Y. and E. Lincoln (1989) Fourth Generation Evaluation. Sage, London

Hedstrom, P. and Ylikoski, P. (2010) 'Causal mechanisms in the social science', The Annual Review of Sociology, Vol. 36, pp 49-67.

Heyligen, F. (2002)'The science of self-organisation and adaptivity', in The Encyclopedia of Life Support Systems, UNESCO Publishing-Eolss Publishers.

Holland J.H. (1998) Emergence: From chaos to order, Oxford: Oxford University Press.

Leonardi, P.M. and Barley, S.R. (2010) 'What's under construction here? Social action, materiality, and power in constructivist studies of technology and organizing', The Academy of

Management Annals, Vol. 4, Nr.1, pp. 1–51.                                    Morgan, J. (2007) 'Emergence', in Hartwing M. (ed.) Dictionary of Critical Realism, Routledge, London, UK, pp. 166

Odell, J. (2002) 'Agents and complex systems', JOT, Vol. 1, pp. 35–45.

Orlikowski, W.J. (2010) 'The sociomateriality of organisational life: considering technology in management research', Cambridge Journal of Economics, Vol. 34, pp. 125-141.

Orlikowski, Wanda J. and Scott, Susan V. (2008) The entanglement of technology and work in Organization, LSE Working paper series, 168, Information Systems and Innovation Group, London School of Economics and Political Science, London, UK

Pawson, R. and N. Tilley (1997) Realistic Evaluation, Sage, London.

Patton, M.Q. (1982) Practical Evaluation.Sage, Beverly Hills, CA.

Patton, M.Q. (2002) Qualitative Research and Evaluation Methods. Third edition,Sage, London

Robson, C. (2002) Real World Research, Second edition, Blackwell, Oxford.

Smith, C. (2010) What is a Person? Rethinking Humanity, Social Life, and the Moral Good from the Person up, University Of Chicago Press, Chicago..

Weisburd, D. and Telep, C. (2010) 'The efficiency of place based policing', Journal of Police Studies, Vol. 17, pp. 247-262.

# Identifying Multiple Dimensions of a Business Case: A Systematic Literature Review

**Kim Maes, Wim Van Grembergen and Steven De Haes**
University of Antwerp, Antwerp Management School, Antwerp Belgium
*Originally published in EJISE (2014) Volume 17, ISS 1*

**Editorial Commentary**
Business cases factor as fundamental input in justifying IT investment. Regardless of the size or type of organisation, business cases are a compulsory aspect in justifying either build or buy IS decisions. However, the extant literature has neglected this important basis for evaluating the value of IS projects. This paper therefore makes an important contribution from a leading issue perspective by proposing a framework for developing and managing business cases throughout the life cycle of the IS project. This framework, determined from an analysis of 169 papers, brings coherence to that which is considered a fragmented body of knowledge, thereby providing a pragmatic structure for the field. The six key findings in the paper provide a vital foundation for future work in respect of IS business case-related research. Amongst the issues relating to the non-financial components of business cases, the lack of attention in the finance stream of research and the optimal use of stakeholders are two critical future issues.

**Abstract:** A business case is in many organisations perceived as a valuable instrument for the justification and evaluation of information technology (IT) investments. This attention from practice has been ascertained by academic scholars, resulting in a growing number of publications in both top academic and practitioner journals since 1999. However, much knowledge on business case research is scattered throughout literature and a clear definition of what actually constitutes a business case is still missing. Therefore, the present paper aims to understand and integrate the current state of research on business cases in an attempt to realise two objectives with clear contributions. First, we tackle the problem of scattered knowledge by organising fragmented knowledge into a newly developed Business Case Research Framework that clearly structures the study field into six dimensions. Second, we identify what constitutes a business case and provide a clear definition to resolve the misunderstanding among scholars. A systematic literature review methodology is performed in a selection of top academic and practitioner journals. Based on the literature findings, we observe that the application of business cases is useful in a broad range of investment contexts. We also find sufficient argumentation that using a business case continuously throughout an entire investment life cycle can increase the investment success rate, that a richer set of information (rather than only financial numbers) should be included in a business case and that stakeholder inclusion is important when developing and using business cases.

**Keywords:** Business Case, Business Case Process, IS/IT Investments, Framework Development, Systematic Literature Review, Concept Definition, Future Research

# 1. Introduction

Literature defines a business case as a formal document that summarises the costs, benefits and impact of an investment (Hsiao 2008; Krell and Matook 2009). It gathers the available useful information and defines possible alternative solutions to realise the investment scope (Frisch 2008; Kettinger et al. 1997). Per alternative, the necessary changes, associated costs and risks, and potential benefits should be defined in an objective way (Ashurst et al. 2008; Ward et al. 2008). Such a business case can help to evaluate an investment endeavour before significant resources are invested (Erat and Kavadias 2008; Kohli and Devaraj 2004). More and more, a business case is being used in contemporary organisations. In a survey by AMR Research, ASUG and SAP, organisations argued that in order to realise the potential value from such investments, a detailed business case is perceived as crucial and should therefore always be developed (Swanton and Draper 2010). Likewise, two-third of the European organisations surveyed by Ward et al. (2008, p2) are convinced that a business case is a very important instrument in order to gain value out of investments, and consequently 96 per cent of them were required "to produce some form of business case when justifying IT investments."

Since the turn of the century, the interest in *business* cases is also growing among academic scholars. Figure 1 provides a year-by-year overview of the number of articles mentioning business case, which are published in a selection of top academic and practitioner journals. Since 1999, a noticeable increase can be ascertained in both journal types. Some of these publications have *business* case within the scope of their research or address considerable attention to the subject (e.g. Franken et al. 2009; Krell and Matook 2009; Ward et al. 2008). Most mention however a limited aspect of a business case in the course of their article without further elaboration, such as the relevance of developing a business case, the information one needs to include in a business case or who is involved in the development (Hsiao 2008; Lin and Pervan 2003). Hence, much knowledge on business case research is scattered throughout literature. Only a handful of scholars provide some definition on what constitutes a business case, but a clear definition is still missing. Post (1992) was among the first calling for additional research on business cases in order to develop a deeper understanding of their impact. Yet, so far few have answered this call to focus on business cases within their research. The lack of a clear definition and the fragmentation of knowledge may stimulate misunderstanding and consequently discourage further research.

The present paper addresses the call for additional research, as business cases are an important instrument in value creation through (IT) investments. As a result, we want to understand, accumulate and integrate the current state of research on business cases. This fragmented knowledge is organised into a newly developed Business Case Research Framework that clearly structures the study field. An improved definition on what constitutes a business case is proposed. Interesting observations suggesting promising future research opportunities are shared as well. By doing so, the systematic literature review contributes in two ways (Webster and Watson 2002). First, it shows that little research has substantially addressed the topic of business cases so far. Second, it provides a new theoretical understanding on a research topic in which the current knowledge is dispersed over numerous academic and practitioner publications.

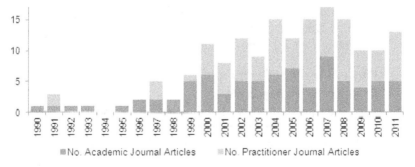

**Figure 1:** Distribution of articles by year over the past twenty-one years

## 2. Methodology

A comprehensive description of the literature review process is desirable according to Vom Brocke et al. (2009). The objective of the systematic literature review is to understand and accumulate the current state of research on business cases with the aim to organise the fragmented knowledge into a newly developed framework. It focuses on publications dealing with business case as a management practice only in passing or in a considerable manner. An exhaustive search is performed in top academic and practitioner journals which have been selected based on journal ranking publications (Vom Brocke et al. 2009; Mylonopoulos and Theoharakis 2001) and the ISI web of knowledge 5-year impact factor in the business and finance category (only for finance journal selection). The search is executed in multiple e-databases (EBSCO, JSTOR, ScienceDirect, Swetwise, WILEY) and on journal websites with "business case" in full text and a time frame between 1990 and 2011. Unfortunately, for some journals the time frame was not entirely available. Yielding 495 initial results, each paper was thoroughly analysed to understand the context in which the term 'business case' is being employed. All irrelevant papers only mentioning 'business case' in the reference list, journal advertising or as in "proving the business case of..." have been omitted. This step has led to a final list of 169 relevant papers including one paper (Sarkis and Liles 1995) that has been added through backward searching. All relevant publications were then analysed through qualitative content analysis to structure and interpret individual text fragments (Mingers 2003). Based on these findings, we identified six dimensions that characterise an aspect of the business case concept (Bryman 2001). Each dimension is a way to perceive the business case from a certain angle: its application area, goals, content, stakeholders, as a process or the risk factors if a business case is not employed in a adequate manner. Together, these dimensions constitute the Business Case Research Framework displayed in Figure 2.

## 3. Dimensions defining a holistic Business Case Research Framework

The Business Case Research Framework reflects the versatility of the business case concept as a research topic. To accumulate and structure the study field, the content of each dimension is discussed hereafter. In line with Elo and Kyngäs (2008), sub dimensions were created to structure text fragments within each dimension. Alternatively, some of them have been directly linked to three stages of an investment life cycle: before, during and after implementation Hitt et al. (2002). During implementation begins when the investment decision has been made and the organisation starts to invest resources in the investment, and ends when the investment has officially been launched. The official launch implicates that all planned applications have been implemented, all anticipated organisational changes have been produced and the organisation can now start using the product of the investment. Consequently, all process phases with regard to feasibility that precede the investment approval belong to the *before implementation phase and the post-implementation review is considered to be part of the after implementation phase.*

**Figure 2:** Business Case Research Framework

## 3.1  Business case application area

The literature findings show a wide variety of investments in which a business case can be employed. This insight has led to a first business case dimension titled the business case application area, defined as the specific type of investment for which the development of a business case can be beneficial to achieve one or more of its goals. As portrayed in Table 1, this dimension is further divided into two major sub dimensions. First, a business case is developed for investments with a technological orientation incorporating both software applications (e.g. e-business, data warehousing system) and infrastructure (e.g. broadband development, RFID) (Weill and Vitale 2002). Second, a diverse set of investments with an organisational focus can benefit from a business case as well (Balaji et al. 2011). These investments can range from a strategic alliance to corporate social responsibility and gender diversity. For instance, the latter provides an argumentation to get more women into leadership roles (Wellington et al. 2003).

**Table 1:** Business case application area

| | Business case application area | |
|---|---|---|
| | Broadband development | Material requirements planning |
| | Data warehousing system | Offshore sourcing |
| | E-business | Point-of-sale debit services |
| Technological orientation | E-government | RFID |
| | E-health records | Software product line adoption |
| | Global data synchronization network | Software repositories |
| | Group decision support systems | Software reuse |
| | Business processes | IT and service-oriented architecture |
| | Business rules | New product development |
| | Collaborative innovation | Project management office |
| Organisational orientation | Corporate social responsibility | Quality management |
| | Effective global business teams | Strategic alliances |
| | Executing strategic change | Strategic vision for IT |
| | Gender diversity | Supply chain integration |
| | Global shared service centres | |

## 3.2    Business case content

A business case document is considered to be a structured overview of specific elements that characterise an investment, such as objectives, costs and benefits (Hsiao 2008). During the literature review, multiple of these elements have been identified in various publications. To integrate this fragmented representation of what should be included in a business case, we have clustered all elements into one business case dimension that is defined as the business case content. The content is further structured through sub dimensions clarifying content elements that are related to each other as presented in Table 2.

Most scholars agree that a business case must include information on the investment's vision and objectives, the changes required to realise the scope, the anticipated benefits and costs, and associated risks (Krell and Matook 2009; Ward and Daniel 2006). Others also include information that might be more related to project management. For instance, an investment planning or roadmap specifies when the required changes should be implemented and which actions should be undertaken in parallel (LeFave et al. 2008; Mirvis and Googins 2006). Franken et al. (2009) and Reimus (1997) argue that the assignment of responsibilities and accountabilities is essential in a business case in order to increase individuals their commit-ment. Examples include a business sponsor (Weill and Vitale 2002), a change owner and a benefit owner (Peppard et al. 2007; Ward et al. 2008). According to Luna-Reyes et al. (2005), a business case may incorporate best practices on how to approach something, such as business processes, technology or other organisational aspects.

**Table 2:** Business case content

| | Business case content | |
|---|---|---|
| Investment description | Project planning and roadmaps (tables, figures) Project description | Drivers for change |
| Investment objectives | Explicit project objectives Performance goals Business goals | Align and link objectives of: - business and IS - investment and organisation |
| Investment requirements | Requirements Resource requirements Customer needs Organisational needs | Technical needs Market needs Strategic requirements |
| Investment impact | Benefits and costs (business and technological) over con-secutive years: - tangible and intangible - monetary and non-monetary - quantifiable, measurable and observable - certain and uncertain - direct and indirect - realistic  Clear benefit definition | Cost-benefit analysis  Financial investment justifica-tion  Financial plan / benefits plan  Feasibility study  Organisational changes  Link investment metrics to business performance Business variables and measures are targeted against baselines prior to investing |
| Investment risks | Investment risk factors (tech-nical and business-change risks) | Risk management plan |
| Investment assumptions considera-tions and scenarios | Realistic assumptions Organisational, strategic, op-erational, technological issues Time / organisational con-straints Qualitative considerations | Intervening variables Best practices research Investment options Realistic technology scenarios |
| Investment governance | Roles and responsibilities Accountability | Compliance |

Over the years new insights have been put forward in this dimension. Gregor et al. (2006) and McAfee (2009) identified the need to determine intangible or qualitative benefits next to financial and quantitative benefits. DellaVechia et al. (2007) found that a simple enumeration of the investment objectives and which tangible and intangible benefits can be expected does not suffice anymore.

## 3.3 Business case process

While most scholars approach a business case as a document, some have built a process to guide its development. Sarkis and Liles (1995) are first to develop a high-level process that includes five interrelated steps, which are closely related to business case development: identify system impact, identify transition impact, estimate costs and benefits, perform decision analysis, and audit decision. Ward et al. (2008) extended this seminal work. They have designed a process for the development of a business case consisting of six steps with multiple individual tasks. The business case development process is executed through the following six steps. In the first step, one identifies issues and challenges for the organisation in its internal and external environment (i.e. business drivers), and what the investment will try to achieve in order to tackle one or more of the business drivers (i.e. investment objectives). Second, anticipated benefits should be identified in line with the objectives, with clearly defined benefit measures and owners. In this step, one identifies benefit owners who are responsible to provide a correct value for each benefit, to ensure the development of a benefits realisation plan and to ultimately get the benefits realised. The third step requires one to develop a framework in which benefits and changes are categorised and linked to each other. Step four specifies that organisational changes that will enable the anticipated benefits, should be identified and added to the framework from step three. Change owners are assigned to ensure their commitment that each identified change will also be implemented. In the fifth step, one needs to determine an explicit value for each benefit based on valid evidence. In step six, all costs that will result from the investment should be identified as well as the risks that might jeopardise a successful outcome of the investment.

In addition, various scholars mention the use of a business case casually during some stage of an investment life cycle. De Haes et al. (2011) stipulate that the development of a detailed business case can be preceded by a high-level business case in which a first rough outline of the investment purpose and implications is delineated. According to Franken et al. (2009), a business case can assist in performance monitoring during investment implementation. Once the investment has been finalised, the business case helps to independently evaluate the investment outcome during the post-implementation review (Jeffrey and Leliveld 2004; Shang and Seddon 2002). We identified various tasks in literature with regard to a business case and linked them with the investment stages as presented in Table 3. Executing these practices during the three consecutive phases of the in-vestment life cycle, creates interesting insights to develop an initial busi-ness case process that runs in parallel.

**Table 3:** Business case process tasks

| | Business case tasks |
|---|---|
| | Understand investment relevance |
| | Split business case: <br> - into high-level and detailed business cases <br> - per sub investment |
| | Assess investment: <br> - feasibility (organisational, financial, technical) <br> - viability (economic, marketability, strategic) |
| | Identify, structure and determine explicit metrics and values of: <br> - benefits, costs and risks (if successful and in case of failure) <br> - resource requirements (financial, timing, staff) <br> - user requirements <br> - critical success factors |
| **BEFORE implementation** | Link benefits and changes explicitly |
| | Develop a: <br> - work plan, action plan, roadmaps <br> - benefits-delivery plan |
| | Develop and validate: <br> - proof-of-concept, prototype |
| | Perform and determine: <br> - what-if analyses and failure analysis <br> - preferred solutions <br> - investment alternatives |
| | Assign responsibilities and accountabilities: <br> - investment team <br> - investment sponsor <br> - benefit owners <br> in relation to investment objectives and benefits |
| | Identify and assure: <br> - stakeholder opinion (via workshop, …) |

| Business case tasks |
|---|
| - stakeholder ability to achieve investment change<br>- stakeholder confirmation of business case<br>- stakeholder commitment (e.g. top management) |
| Evaluate the business case |
| Communicate business case (stress investment vision, objectives, stakeholder commitment) |
| Approve the business case or stop the investment |

| | Business case tasks |
|---|---|
| | Audit investment decision |
| | Allocate investment resources |
| | Establish evaluation team |
| | Monitor, evaluate and report on:<br>- investment progress, budget and performance<br>- investment changes |
| **DURING**<br>**implementation** | Review and update business case based on:<br>- investment progress and performance<br>- new insights from stakeholders<br>- organisational, technical and, market changes |
| | Identify and assure:<br>- stakeholder opinion (via workshop, …)<br>- stakeholder ability to achieve investment change<br>- stakeholder confirmation of business case<br>- stakeholder commitment (e.g. top management) |
| | In case of investment failure, reassess business case, assumptions and feasibility |
| **AFTER**<br>**implementation** | Evaluate investment performance against stated investment objectives, industry benchmarks or an ideal performance level |
| | Understand failure reasons |
| | Acquire lessons learned |
| | Audit investment performance |
| | Determine further investment opportunities and business cases |
| | Reward in relation to performance |

## 3.4  Business case goals

The development and use of business cases can help to achieve multiple objectives. For instance, it facilitates the collection of basic information and clear responsibility assignment (Smith et al. 2010). It can also be utilised as a communication instrument to convince people and to get top management commitment (Peppard and Ward 2005; Davenport et al. 2001). Investments can be compared and prioritised through a business case to identify high-priority and quick winning investments (LeFave et al. 2008; Smith et al. 2010) It can be an objective instrument to evaluate the investment outcome and to demonstrate its impact (Raymond et al. 1995; Ward et al. 2008). During the literature analysis, this wide variety of objectives has been integrated into a business case goals dimension, which is defined as any particular reason why a business case should be developed and which tangible and intangible contributions it can bring to the organisation. The business case goals are organised through the investment stages and presented in Table 4.

**Table 4:** Business case goals

| | Business case goals | |
|---|---|---|
| BEFORE implementation | to ensure an investment owner is assigned<br>to ensure basic investment information is<br>  collected<br><br>to identify how IT and business changes will<br>  deliver the identified benefits<br>to increase the investment success rate<br>to link benefits to organisational changes<br>  and to investment objectives<br>to convince people<br><br>to ensure involvement, support and get<br>  commitment<br>to increase motivation and stimulate action<br>to obtain investment resources (funding, staff, time…) | to improve the relationship and develop trust<br>to communicate an investment's concept,<br>  status and results among its stakeholders<br>to transfer knowledge<br>to compare investments<br><br>to balance risks between investments<br>to filter out unattractive investment ideas<br>to identify "low-hanging fruits"<br>to identify high-priority investments<br><br>to prioritise investments<br>to get investment approval<br>to make well-founded investment decisions<br>to successfully launch an investment |
| DURING implementation | to obtain additional investment resources<br>  (funding, staff, time…)<br>to remove unattractive investments | to disallow additional resources for an<br>  unattractive investment |
| AFTER implementation | to execute a post evaluation<br>to objectively evaluate investment outcome | to demonstrate an investment's impact |

## 3.5    Business case stakeholders

Literature findings indicate that a diversity of people are involved with a business case. Some of these people are responsible for its development or to give approval and provide funding to the investment while others are only consulted (Avison et al. 1999; Smith and McKeen 2008). This multitude of people has been categorised into a dimension focusing on business case stakeholders, which is defined as those people that can affect or are affected by the business case and have a stake in one or more business case tasks and in the achievement of the business case goals. Most stakeholders can be found in business and not in IT. Business people are responsible for the development and communication of the business case through their business unit executives or the investment sponsor (Beatty and Williams 2006; Teubner 2007) whether or not assisted by a business architect (Fonstad and Robertson 2006). Ross (2003) states that this responsibility should be shared with IT. Stakeholders from business and IT are put together to assess investment feasibility and its potential to add value to the organisation, as this requires in-depth knowledge on social, economic and technological implications (Charette 2006). A devil's advocate is added to the evaluation team to objectively critique the business case and depersonalise the discussion (Frisch 2008). Literature demonstrates that the business case is primarily a business responsibility. Although IT people are explicitly involved before implementation as portrayed in Table 5, they seem to be no longer involved after the investment decision has been made. Literature only mentions the finance organisation and post-implementation review team in these phases.

**Table 5:** Business case stakeholders

| | Business case stakeholders | |
|---|---|---|
| BEFORE implementation | Board of directors | Finance organisation / staff |
| | Executive committee | Capital control group |
| | CEO / CFO / CPO / CIO | IT steering committee |
| | Strategy management group | IT management team |
| | Senior management | Business demand office on IT side |
| | Business executives / managers together with  IT managers and business architects | Internal/external end users from  business and IT |
| | Business unit manager | Division information managers |
| | Business / investment sponsor | Designers |
| | Business planning board | Operation managers |

| | Business case stakeholders | |
|---|---|---|
| | Portfolio management team | Uninvolved project leaders and auditors |
| | Project investment department | Human resources/organisation department |
| | Capital IT project management board | A devil's advocate |
| | Project centre of excellence | |
| | Project manager | |
| DURING implementation | Finance organisation | |
| AFTER implementation | Post-implementation review team | Finance organisation |

## 3.6   Business case risk factors

Based on the previous five business case dimensions, an organisation should be able to understand how to build a sound business case (content, process, goals and stakeholders) and in which investment types such a business case can be applied. However, if an organisation does not adequately employ these guidelines impending unidentified risks may negatively impact the investment outcome. Therefore, the literature analysis has led to the identification of a last dimension focusing on the risk factors in relation to the business case and which potential results this might deliver, as presented in Table 6. Some risk factors are linked to investment stages such as lack of financial knowledge among IT staff, growing complexity due to inter-organisational investments and weak partnership between business and IT (Jeffrey and Leliveld 2004). Other risk factors give insight into important aspects that are worth attention during the business case process. For instance, organisational culture, personal characteristics of a manager or top management turnover can negatively impact the business case quality and the resource availability during the investment (Earl and Feeny 2000).

**Table 6:** Business case risk factors and impact

| | Business case risk factors | Potential impact |
|---|---|---|
| BEFORE implementation | Difficulties to formulate and position a business case because:<br>- IT staff lack working knowledge of financial concepts<br>- a weak partnership exists between business and IT<br>- it is hard to calculate strategic and tactical benefits | - not developing a business case<br>- developing a weak business case<br>- an ad hoc approach to execute investments<br>- benefits cannot be managed effectively<br>- systems development for the |

| Business case risk factors | Potential impact |
|---|---|
| - inter-organisational investments increase complexity<br>- investment is perceived as IT and not as business<br>- stakeholders are not included from the beginning | sake of technology<br>- progress is difficult to measure<br>- evangelists set their own targets<br>- investment approved by elbow grease (based on effort to convince people instead of on quality) |
| Business case not presented:<br>- in appropriate language<br>- with realistic, neutral, complete and valid arguments<br>- with investment alternatives or options<br>- with strong leadership to convince decision-makers<br>- with clear accountabilities and according rewards | - stakeholders do not understand investment objectives<br>- risks are described to persuade rather than to inform<br>- creating a narrow yes-or-no framework<br>- too much focus on financial arguments<br>- an 'IT-doesn't-matter' management attitude |
| The business case evaluation and approval:<br>- is based on technical instead of business criteria<br>- focus on short term benefits instead of long term needs<br>- is not executed thoroughly and quickly<br>- target the business case presenter and not the investment | - overspend of time and money<br>- under-delivery of benefits<br>- slow down or annulment of an investment<br>- less initiative will be taken to build and present a business case |

| | Business case risk factors | Potential impact |
|---|---|---|
| DURING and AFTER implementation | A business case is not:<br>- not further employed after its development<br>- regularly reviewed | - investment not adjusted to market changes and needs<br>- lessons learned cannot be collected and understood |
| Environmental influences to business case | A business case can be influenced by:<br>- organisational culture<br>- decision-makers<br>- personal characteristics (e.g. CIO role / influence behaviour)<br>- top management turnover | - inconsistent business case quality<br>- changing sponsorship<br>- changing resource availability |
| Business case limitations | A business case's project framing diminishes flexibility<br>Investment justification based only on a business case | - enabling project escalation<br>- additional approaches should be employed including executive level allocation and annual CIO allocation |

## 4.  Discussion and future research

Based on the systematic literature review, we observe that literature focusing specifically on business cases is scarce within academic literature. As a result, a holistic definition on what constitutes a business case is difficult to find. Benaroch et al. (2006, p835) defines it as "a comprehensive document that includes the project description, resources required, benefits and financial plans, and a risk management plan." Hsiao (2008) perceives a business case as a structured overview of benefits and costs associated with an investment. According to Ward and Daniel (2006), a business case is a document that supports the decision-making to make the investment or not, and therefore needs to include the required changes, their anticipated benefits and costs together with the associated risks. Krell and Matook (2009, p37) state that a business case "is a formal summary of benefits from an IS investment (...) and determines necessary actions to put anticipated benefits into practice." The document is often presented as a combination of figures, tables and texts to reduce complexity. A recent definition was provided by Nielsen and Persson (2012), who define a business case as "an artefact in the form of a document specifying the main rationale behind the expected value and cost of an IT investment for the adopting organisation." In practitioner literature, a business case is defined as "documentation of the rationale for making a business investment, used to support a business decision on whether to proceed or not with the investment" (ITGI 2008, p113). PRINCE2 argues that a business case describes "the justification for the project based on estimated costs, benefits and risks" (Office of Government Commerce 2009, p. 255).

Based on both academic and practitioner literature, there seems to be a consensus that a business case is a formal document that provides a structured overview of information about a potential investment. This information is in most cases limited to the investment benefits, costs and risks together with the information that is necessary to define them. For instance, the project description and scope is defined to specify what will be included in the investment and what not (Abraham and Junglas 2011; De Haes et al. 2011). This information can be further substantiated into a list of technology requirements and business changes that are required to be implemented in order to achieve the scope and the anticipated benefits. These aspects are equally important to determine the investment costs (Ward and Daniel 2006). Based on our literature findings, we observe that information like responsibilities and accountabilities, best practices and the investment planning is also included in a business case. LeFave et al. (2008) and Mirvis and Googins (2006) integrate an investment planning in the business case to specify when required changes should be implemented.

Franken et al. (2009) and Reimus (1997) argue that responsibilities and accountabilities should be assigned in the business case in order to increase the commitment of individuals.

All useful information is bundled in the business case and relevant calculations are described to provide a rationale and justification for the potential investment. The overall goal of a business case is consistently described as to enable business decisions to make, let proceed or stop the investment (ITGI 2008). In the words of Post (1992), "a business case can help management to make well-founded technology investment decisions". As a result, we propose the following definition of a business case:

*A business case is a formal investment document with a structured overview of relevant information that provides a rationale and justification of an investment with the intent to enable well-founded investment decision-making.*

The systematic literature review reveals multiple observations on upcoming research evolutions and interests in business case research. In this discussion we will focus on the most interesting suggesting promising opportunities for future research.

## 4.1 Observation 1: Business cases are applicable in variety of investments, organisations and industries

The business case application area is wide and diverse indicating that its use is not only beneficial in the implementation of IT investments but also in organisational investments or social changes throughout the organisation. Moreover, business cases can be used in different types of industries such as the insurance industry or the fashion industry (Nelson et al. 2010), as well as in different types of organisations ranging from SMEs to multinationals and governments (Ballantine et al. 1998). However, the literature does not describe whether a business case should be developed or managed differently in relation to the type of investment, industry or organisation. Hence, it could be interesting to investigate whether the implementation of other business case dimensions should be adjusted accordingly.

## 4.2 Observation 2: A business case is more than financial numbers

The content of a business case document is no longer limited to financial numbers. Today, both quantitative and qualitative benefits should be identified and defined. Smithson and Hirschheim (1998) argue that an organisation taking only quantifiable benefits into account will have no strategic alignment between investment and organisational objectives whereas business cases built with only monetary impacts are questionable (Urbach et al. 2010). Ward et al. (2008) found that qualitative benefits provide a more complete image of the potential business value of an investment. These benefits are frequently omitted due to their political sensitivity, difficulties in handling them and their potential to hinder in the approval procedures (Farbey et al. 1999). Furthermore, researchers call (i) for a link between the investment objectives and organisational goals (Bruch and Ghoshal 2002), and (ii) for a link between the impact of anticipated changes and their respective benefits (Avison et al. 1999)). Ward et al. (2008) address both issues. They argue that business case development should start with the identification of the business drivers for the organisation. "The business case then clearly states what the proposed investment seeks to achieve for the organization—the *investment objectives*—in a way that shows it can clearly address some or all of the business drivers" (Ward et al. 2008, p3). Their business case development process prescribes in addition that "benefits are explicitly linked to both the IT and the business changes that are required to deliver them" (Ward et al. 2008, p3). Only these linkages can consider a clear understanding of the investment impact during evaluation and decision-making. As many of these new insights have not yet been integrated and explicitly linked in the business case literature, we ask for future research to develop an innovative business case template.

## 5. Observation 3: It is not just about developing a business case

Many scholars present a business case as a useful and valuable instrument at the beginning of an investment to get a thorough understanding of the investment application (Balaji et al. 2011; Davenport et al. 2001). This has been perfectly captured by the multi-step approach for business case development by Ward et al. (2008). Nevertheless, the steps to develop a business case do not equal the business case process as a whole. A business case can be purposefully employed in case of major changes affecting the investment or project escalation, which might require a review of the business case to be in line with the prevailing reality or to justify the continuation of the investment (Brown and Lockett 2004; Flynn et al. 2009; Iacovou and Dexter 2004). After implementation, a business case can help to evaluate the investment outcome, and to understand failure reasons and lessons learned for future business case developments and investment implementations (Fonstad and Robertson 2006)). Until today, these additional tasks surpassing business case development have not been integrated. As Al-Mudimigh et al. (2001) argue that a business case is a useful and effective instrument throughout all investment stages, such integration should lead to a full business case process in parallel with the investment life cycle.

We identified that a continuous usage seems to facilitate eventually a higher success rate of the investment (Altinkemer et al. 2011). It is seen as a critical instrument during investment implementation, and increases the use and adoption of the information system as part of an investment (Gattiker and Goodhue 2005; Law and Ngai 2007). (Curley 2006) states that a disciplined business case approach is fundamental to benefits realisation while Al-Mudimigh et al. (2001) and Krell and Matook (2009) found that frequently developing and using a business case is one of the major success factors for an investment and a source of a competitive advantage.

## 5.1    Observation 4: Business case knowledge is scarce and limited to case development

Current knowledge on business cases is largely concentrated on the development of a business case (Ward et al. 2008), thus before the investment decision is made. This applies to the business case process tasks, its goals, the stakeholders and the identified risk factors. For instance, only six goals and four stakeholders are identified during and after the investment implementation. Hence, we can conclude that research on these dimensions of a business case during and after the implementation of an investment is still in its infancy. Although many scholars mention its usefulness during these investment stages (e.g. Al-Mudimigh et al. 2001; Franken et al. 2009), none have specifically drawn attention to this during their research. We argue that future research is necessary to build new theoretical knowledge that can further enhance our understanding in order to help practitioners willing to apply this knowledge. Future research can focus for instance on understanding how a business case can be used throughout the entire investment life cycle, i.e. a process approach. Such a business case approach can be initiated through a 'business case process' that will include supplementary tasks, which may include but are not limited to the evaluation and monitoring of the investment progress and risks, and the post-implementation review of the investment success (Franken et al. 2009; Jeffrey and Leliveld 2004; Luftman and McLean 2004).

## 5.2 Observation 5: Finance scholars have yet to discover business case research

Next to senior management, people of the finance organisation are closely involved in many tasks of the business case process. For instance, they execute the financial analysis, provide business case templates and train people on how to employ these, fund the investment idea, monitor the investment budget and business case, and facilitate the post-implementation review (Smith et al. 2010; Westerman and Curley 2008). Consequently, one could argue that the study field of business cases might be of great interest to finance scholars yet no relevant article mentioning 'business case' has been found in finance journals. This might imply that business case research is still not on the radar of finance scholars publishing in top finance journals, so we would like to invite them to enrich this emerging study field.

## 5.3 Observation 6: Stakeholders are an integral part of business case usage

Various publications identify multiple stakeholders that can be involved with a business case (e.g. De Haes et al. 2011; Fonstad and Robertson 2006)), yet none provides a complete list of who should really be involved. Hence, we are interested to know how many stakeholders should be involved in the business case process to achieve an optimal result. Including too many stakeholders will become difficult to organise and the new information provided by each additional stakeholder diminishes gradually due to information saturation. Future research could also investigate the implications of positioning particular stakeholder responsibilities in another hierarchical level or business area. For instance, with regard to a customer relationship management investment, what might be the impact of changing the business unit executive by the marketing manager as an investment sponsor (i.e. changing seniority for relevant domain expertise)?

# 6. Conclusion

Although the interest in business case research is growing, the study field is still in its infancy: business case knowledge is scattered and a clear definition is missing. Therefore, the present paper integrated the current state of research on business cases into a newly developed Business Case Research Framework and developed a new definition of the business case concept. We have also found multiple interesting observations based on literature findings that suggest promising opportunities for future research. The applicability of a business case is broader than just IT investments. Researchers tend to shift from document to process thinking on business cases as it may contribute to the investment success. They urge to enrich the content of a business case with qualitative information in addition to the more financially oriented arguments that are mainly included nowadays. Stakeholders are key in business case usage as they enrich the amount of information with their different view points, yet further research could investigate their role and impact from new angles. In addition, the knowledge base on business cases is scarce especially in the finance field and in their use beyond the development phase.

# Acknowledgments

Our research has been funded by a Ph.D. grant of the Belgian Agency for Innovation by Science and Technology.

# References

Abraham, C. and Junglas, I. (2011) "From cacophony to harmony: A case study about the IS implementation process as an opportunity for organizational transformation at Sentara Healthcare", The Journal of Strategic Information Systems, Vol. 20, No. 2, pp177–197.

Altinkemer, K., Ozcelik, Y. and Ozdemir, Z. (2011) "Productivity and Performance Effects of Business Process Reengineering: A Firm-Level Analysis", Journal of Management Information Systems, Vol. 27, No. 4, pp129–162.

Ashurst, C., Doherty, N. and Peppard, J. (2008) "Improving the impact of IT development projects: the benefits realization capability model", European Journal of Information Systems, Vol. 17, No. 4, pp352–370.

Avison, D., Cuthbertson, C. and Powell, P. (1999) "The paradox of information systems: strategic value and low status", The Journal of Strategic Information Systems, Vol. 8, No. 4, pp419–445.

Balaji, S., Ranganathan, C. and Coleman, T. (2011) "IT-Led Process Reengineering: How Sloan Valve Redesigned its New Product Development Process", MIS Quarterly Executive, Vol. 10, No. 2, pp81–92.

Ballantine, J., Levy, M. and Powell, P. (1998) "Evaluating information systems in small and medium-sized enterprises: issues and evidence", European Journal of Information Systems, Vol. 7, No. 4, pp241–251.

Beatty, R. and Williams, C. (2006) "ERP II: best practices for successfully implementing an ERP upgrade", Communications of the ACM, Vol. 49, No. 3, pp105–109.

Benaroch, M., Lichtenstein, Y. and Robinson, K. (2006) "Real Options in Information Technology Risk Management: An Empirical Validation of Risk-Option Relationships", MIS Quarterly, Vol. 30, No. 4, pp827–864.

Vom Brocke, J., Simons, A., Niehaves, B., Riemer, K., Plattfaut, R. and Cleven, A. (2009) "Reconstructing the Giant: On the Importance of Rigour in Documenting the Literature
Search Process", Presented at the European Conference on Information Systems, pp1–13.

Brown, D. and Lockett, N. (2004) "Potential of critical e-applications for engaging SMEs in e-
business: a provider perspective", European Journal of Information Systems, Vol. 13, No.
1, pp21–34.

Bruch, H. and Ghoshal, S. (2002) "Beware the Busy Manager", Harvard Business Review, Vol.
80, No. 2, pp62–69.

Bryman, A. (2001) Social Research Methods., Oxford University Press, Oxford, UK.

Charette, R. (2006) "EHRs: Electronic Health Records or Exceptional Hidden Risks?", Communications of the ACM, Vol. 49, No. 6, pp120–120.

Curley, M. (2006) "The IT transformation at Intel", MIS Quarterly Executive, Vol. 5, No. 4,
pp155–168.

Davenport, T., Harris, J.G., De Long, D.W. and Jacobson, A.L. (2001) "Data to Knowledge to
Results: Building an Analytic Capability", California Management Review, Vol. 43, No. 2,
pp117–138.

DellaVechia, T., Scantlebury, S. and Stevenson, J. (2007) "Three CIO advisory board responses
to managing the realization of business benefits from IT investments", MIS Quarterly Executive, pp13–16.

Earl, M. and Feeny, D. (2000) "How to be a CEO for the information age", Sloan Management
Review, Vol. 41, No. 2, pp11–23.

Elo, S. and Kyngäs, H. (2008) "The qualitative content analysis process", Journal of Advanced
Nursing, Vol. 62, No. 1, pp107–115.

Erat, S. and Kavadias, S. (2008) "Sequential testing of Product designs: Implications for Learning", Management Science, Vol. 54, No. 5, pp956–968.

Farbey, B., Land, F. and Targett, D. (1999) "Moving IS evaluation forward: learning themes and
research issues", The Journal of Strategic Information Systems, Vol. 8, No. 2, pp189–207.

Flynn, D., Pan, G., Keil, M. and Mähring, M. (2009) "De-escalating IT projects: the DMM model", Communications of the ACM, Vol. 52, No. 10, pp131–134.

Fonstad, N. and Robertson, D. (2006) "Transforming a company, project by project: The IT
engagement model", MIS Quarterly Executive, Vol. 5, No. 1, pp1–14.

Franken, A., Edwards, C. and Lambert, R. (2009) "Executing Strategic Change: Understanding
the Critical Management Elements That Lead to Success.", California Management Review, Vol. 51, No. 3, pp49–73.

Frisch, B. (2008) "When Teams Can't Decide", Harvard Business Review, Vol. 86, No. 11,
pp121–126.

Gattiker, T. and Goodhue, D. (2005) "What Happens after ERP Implementation: Understanding the Impact of Interdependence and Differentiation on Plant-Level Outcomes", MIS
Quarterly, Vol. 29, No. 3, pp559–585.

Gregor, S., Martin, M., Fernandez, W., Stern, S. and Vitale, M. (2006) "The transformational
dimension in the realization of business value from information technology", The Journal
of Strategic Information Systems, Vol. 15, No. 3, pp249–270.

De Haes, S., Gemke, D., Thorp, J. and van Grembergen, W. (2011) "KLM's Enterprise Governance of IT Journey: From Managing IT Costs to Managing Business Value", MIS Quarterly
Executive, Vol. 10, No. 3, pp109–120.

Hitt, L., Wu, D. and Zhou, X. (2002) "Investment in enterprise resource planning: Business
impact and productivity measures", Journal of Management Information Systems, Vol.
19, No. 1, pp71–98.

Hsiao, R. (2008) "Knowledge sharing in a global professional service firm", MIS Quarterly Executive, Vol. 7, No. 3, pp399–412.

Iacovou, C. and Dexter, A. (2004) "Turning Around Runaway Information Technology Projects", California Management Review, Vol. 46, No. 4, pp68–88.

ITGI. (2008) Enterprise Value: Governance of IT Investments: The Business Case, IT Governance Institute, p. 28.

Jeffrey, M. and Leliveld, I. (2004) "Best practices in IT portfolio", MIT Sloan Management Review, Vol. 45, No. 3, pp41–49.

Kettinger, W., Teng, J. and Guha, S. (1997) "Business Process Change: A Study of Methodologies, Techniques, and Tools", MIS Quarterly, Vol. 21, No. 1, pp55–80.

Kohli, R. and Devaraj, S. (2004) "Realizing the business value of information technology investments: an organizational process", MIS Quarterly Executive, Vol. 3, No. 1, pp53–68.

Krell, K. and Matook, S. (2009) "Competitive advantage from mandatory investments: An empirical study of Australian firms", The Journal of Strategic Information Systems, Vol. 18, No. 1, pp31–45.

Law, C. and Ngai, E. (2007) "ERP systems adoption: An exploratory study of the organizational factors and impacts of ERP success", Information & Management, Vol. 44, No. 4, pp418–432.

LeFave, R., Branch, B., Brown, C. and Wixom, B. (2008) "How Sprint Nextel reconfigured IT resources for results", MIS Quarterly Executive, Vol. 7, No. 4, pp171–179.

Lin, C. and Pervan, G. (2003) "The practice of IS/IT benefits management in large Australian organizations", Information & Management, Vol. 41, No. 1, pp13–24.

Luftman, J. and McLean, E. (2004) "Key issues for IT executives", MIS Quarterly Executive, Vol. 3, No. 2, pp89–104.

Luna-Reyes, L., Zhang, J., Gil-García, J. and Cresswell, A. (2005) "Information systems development as emergent socio-technical change: a practice approach", European Journal of Information Systems, Vol. 14, No. 1, pp93–105.

McAfee, A. (2009) "Shattering the Myths About Enterprise 2.0", Harvard Business Review, Vol. 87, No. 11, pp1–6.

Mingers, J. (2003) "The paucity of multimethod research: a review of the information systems literature.", Information Systems Journal, Vol. 13, pp233–249.

Mirvis, P. and Googins, B. (2006) "Stages of Corporate Citizenship", California Management Review, Vol. 48, No. 2, pp104–126.

Al-Mudimigh, A., Zairi, M., Al-Mashari, M. and others. (2001) "ERP software implementation: an integrative framework", European Journal of Information Systems, Vol. 10, No. 4, pp216–226.

Mylonopoulos, N. and Theoharakis, V. (2001) "On site: global perceptions of IS journals", Communications of the ACM, Vol. 44, No. 9, pp29–33.

Nelson, M., Peterson, J., Rariden, R. and Sen, R. (2010) "Transitioning to a business rule management service model: Case studies from the property and casualty insurance industry", Information & management, Vol. 47, No. 1, pp30–41.

Nielsen, P. and Persson, J. (2012) "IT Business Cases in Local Government: An Action Research Study", Proceedings of the Hawaii International Conference on System Science, pp2208–2217.

Office of Government Commerce. (2009) Managing successful projects with PRINCE2, The Stationery Office, 2009 Edition.

Peppard, J. and Ward, J. (2005) "Unlocking Sustained Business Value from IT Investments", California Management Review, Vol. 48, No. 1, pp52–70.

Peppard, J., Ward, J. and Daniel, E. (2007) "Managing the realization of business benefits from IT investments", MIS Quarterly Executive, Vol. 6, No. 1, pp1–11.

Post, B. (1992) "A Business Case Framework for Group Support Technology", Journal of Management Information Systems, Vol. 9, No. 3, pp7–26.

Raymond, L., Pare, G. and Bergeron, F. (1995) "Matching information technology and organizational structure: an empirical study with implications for performance", European Journal of Information Systems, Vol. 4, No. 1, pp3–16.

Reimus, B. (1997) "The IT system that couldn't deliver", Harvard Business Review, Vol. 75, No. 3, pp22–26.

Ross, J.W. (2003) "Creating a Strategic IT Architecture Competency: Learning in Stages.", MIS Quarterly Executive, Vol. 2, No. 1, pp31–43.

Sarkis, J. and Liles, D. (1995) "Using IDEF and QFD to develop an organizational decision support methodology for the strategic justification of computer-integrated technologies", International Journal of Project Management, Vol. 13, No. 3, pp177–185.

Shang, S. and Seddon, P. (2002) "Assessing and managing the benefits of enterprise systems: the business manager's perspective", Information Systems Journal, Vol. 12, No. 4, pp271–299.

Smith, H. and McKeen, J. (2008) "Creating a process-centric organization at FCC: SOA from the top down", MIS Quarterly Executive, Vol. 7, No. 2, pp71–84.

Smith, H., McKeen, J., Cranston, C. and Benson, M. (2010) "Investment Spend Optimization: A New Approach to IT Investment at BMO Financial Group", MIS Quarterly Executive, Vol. 9, No. 2, pp65–81.

Smithson, S. and Hirschheim, R. (1998) "Analysing information systems evaluation: another look at an old problem", European Journal of Information Systems, Vol. 7, No. 3, pp158–174.

Swanton, B. and Draper, L. (2010) How do you expect to get value from ERP if you don't measure it?, AMR Research.

Teubner, R. (2007) "Strategic information systems planning: A case study from the financial services industry", The Journal of Strategic Information Systems, Vol. 16, No. 1, pp105–125.

Urbach, N., Smolnik, S. and Riempp, G. (2010) "An empirical investigation of employee portal success", The Journal of Strategic Information Systems, Vol. 19, No. 3, pp184–206.

Ward, J. and Daniel, E. (2006) Benefits management: delivering value from IS and IT investments, Wiley, available at: (accessed 26 April 2013).

Ward, J., Daniel, E. and Peppard, J. (2008) "Building better business cases for IT investments", MIS Quarterly Executive, Vol. 7, No. 1, pp1–15.

Webster, J. and Watson, R. (2002) "Analyzing the Past to Prepare for the Future: Writing a Literature Review", MIS Quarterly, Vol. 26, No. 2.

Weill, P. and Vitale, M. (2002) "What IT infrastructure capabilities are needed to implement e-business models", MIS Quarterly Executive, Vol. 1, No. 1, pp17–34.

Wellington, S., Kropf, M. and Gerkovich, P. (2003) "What's holding women back", Harvard Business Review, Vol. 81, No. 6, pp18–19.

Westerman, G. and Curley, M. (2008) "Building IT-Enabled Innovation Capabilities at Intel", MIS Quarterly Executive, Vol. 7, No. 1, pp33–48.

# Critical Organizational Challenges in Delivering Business Value from IT: In Search of Hybrid IT Value Models

Nazareth Nicolian[1], Christine Welch[2], Martin Read[2] and Martyn Roberts[2]

[1]Faculty of Business and Economics, Department of MIS, American University of Science and Technology, Beirut, Lebanon

[2]Portsmouth Business School, Operations and Systems Management Group, University of Portsmouth, UK

*Originally published in EJISE (2015) Volume 18, ISS 2*

---

**Editorial Commentary**

Nicolian, Welch, Read and Roberts provide classic input into the IS evaluation literature. Their paper deals with the age-old conundrum of the 'dependent variable'. A key aspect of the paper's discussion hones in on an oft confused interpretation of IS evaluation models in respect of the difference between process and variance theories. This paper provides an important discussion in this regard, the primary reason for consideration of this paper as a leading issue. The extant literature is replete with studies which ignore this critical distinction between IS evaluation model subsets. In positing a hybrid model for IS value, the authors make a strong case for a complementary approach which juxtaposes process and variance competencies into a proposed dependent variable of 'business value'. In light of this, this paper provides future direction by honing in on an integrated perspective regarding 'how' to create value from IS against organisational conditions relating to the ideal conditions which derive value from organisational IS.

---

**Abstract:** This study forms part of a larger research project to explore and analyze the perceived value of IT and the organizational competencies needed to deliver that value. By identifying and evaluating the challenges faced by Lebanese organizations, this paper provides empirical evidence in support of hybrid models of IT value. While process-based IT value models provide an explanation for "how" IT value is created, and what steps occur to create that outcome, they lack the contingency theory found in variance models, which explain "why" IT value is realized, and what variable moderate that outcome. On the other hand, variance models alone are also ill-equipped to explain the greater scope and impacts of IT investments. Hybrid models combine both process and variance perspectives to provide a more comprehensive theory of IT value realization. Structured interviews are conducted with the Chief Information Officers (CIO) of 36 medium and large size Lebanese organizations to discover the challenges faced in delivering value from IT investments. Of the 14 challenges discovered, seven point to the need for process orientated competencies and these include "Change Management", "Organizational Readiness", "Relationship Management", "Benefits Management", "IT Governance", "IT Architecture Management", and "IT Talent Management". The other seven challenges are variance oriented and point to the factors that inhibit or enable deriving IT value, and these include internal factors, such as: "Family Business Ownership", and "Budgetary Constraints", and other external factors, such as: "Political/Social/Economic Instability, "Telecommunications/ Bandwidth Issues", "Lack of Governmental IT Laws", "Local Cultural Issues", and "Immature Local Suppliers/Vendors".

Rather than continuing an already-saturated research conversation about the dependent variable, "IT Value" and whether IT creates business value, this study contributes to the independent variable research stream - the investigation of "how to derive value from IT, and "when and under which conditions" value is realized, and for conceiving a Hybrid model explaining the IT value proposition.

**Keywords:** IT value Models; Organizational IT competencies and IT challenges; ERP CSFs; CIO

# 1. Introduction

While the predominant source of Information Systems (IS) research comes from the West, there is emerging IS research in developing countries and in the Middle East region. Although the IS literature coming out of Europe and the USA is relevant to the global community of academics and practitioners, valuable insights could be gained from the experiences of companies in other countries and continents. This paper reports the first part of a larger research project to explore and develop theories explaining how organizations derive business value from their investments in IS, and what competencies are critical to sustain that value, within the context of Lebanon. The aim of this paper is to develop a general baseline of the IS landscape in Lebanon, and to explore and assess the key challenges Lebanese organizations face in delivering business value from Information Technology (IT) and to suggest how these challenges point to the need for conceptualizing "hybrid" models of IT value which better inform the IT value proposition. It is important to note that the terms IT and IS are not necessarily synonymous. The former is commonly regarded as a wider term, encompassing human and procedural, as well as technical elements. However, these terms are used interchangeably throughout the literature of value creation, and that is how they are used in this paper also.

## 2.  Literature review

### 2.1    The dependent variable "IT Value"

Although the focus of this paper is to identify and assess the key factors, and the "independent variables" that affect an organization's ability to derive business value from IT, it is imperative to begin that quest with a brief review of the "dependent variable" literature. To understand the factors that enable or inhibit getting business value from IT investments, one must understand the value being sought. Although well over 1000 journal articles, conference papers, books, technical notes have been written on the subject of IT evaluation (Bannister and Remenyi 2000), only a relatively small subset of this literature has been concerned with the core issues of what precisely is meant by the term "value". Bannister and Remeny, (2000) argued that a weakness in much of the current research is the fact that the definition of value is usually unclear, frequently inadequate, often partisan and sometimes completely absent from the discussion.

In answering Keen's (1980) call for defining the IS dependent variable, and in seeing so much diversity and inconsistency in the definition of that variable, Delone and McLean (1992) (DandM) developed a comprehensive model of that dependent variable, which they called, "IS success". The authors evaluated over 180 references to one or more aspect of IS success to develop a taxonomy which involved the following categories of IS success – System Quality, Information Quality, Use, User Satisfaction, Individual Impact, and Organizational Impact. The significance of the DandM model is twofold: by abstracting the various attributes of IS success, the model confirms the complexity and elusiveness of IS success; and by grouping the various attributes of success, the model facilitates definition, measurement, and ultimate attainment of IS success. The model also implies that IS success is a multi-dimensional construct and that it should be measured as such.

In their updated paper, DandM (2003) evaluated over 300 IS success research efforts that applied, validated, challenged, and proposed enhancements to their original model. One of their key findings is that IS researchers are confused between the independent and dependent variables. They used as examples, "User Involvement" and "Top Management Support" as independent variables affecting the outcome of the dependent variable, "*IS success*". Based on their evaluation of those contributions, they proposed a minor refinement to the original model, adding the concept of service quality and net benefits. Service quality was added to measure the quality of the service provided by the IT function, or the IT provider. Individual and Organizational Impact were replaced by the concept of net benefits which reflected the positive or negative impact of IS on customers, suppliers, employees, organizations, markets, industries, economies or even society.

Additionally, the term IT business value has been commonly used to refer to the organizational performance impacts of IT, including productivity enhancement, profitability improvement, cost reduction, competitive advantage, inventory reduction, and other measures of performance (Devaraj and Kohli, 2003; Hitt and Brynjolfsson, 1996). General expectations are that IT provides services with better quality at a low cost and low business risk with increased agility (Govekar and Adams, 2010). Kohli and Grover (2008) have defined value as the ability to improve access to information, and the ability to generate value from information, and improving the quality and abundance of information.

The extant "dependent variable" literature alludes to the fact that there isn't a single agreed upon measure of the impact and value of IT, and there are many stakeholders involved in the IT value proposition, each having different and often competing needs. The business executive's view of IT value may be different than the view of the corporate IT function, and this in turn, may be different than the view of the actual users of IT, and the view of the other organizational stakeholders, such as customers, partners, and suppliers. While there's general agreement on the overall expectations, benefits, and resulting business value from IT, there continues to be challenges in delivering that value.

## 2.2    The Independent Variables

The difficulty in defining the business value of IT, and the multiplicity of meanings associated with the concept of IT value are not the only challenges in the IT value proposition. Agreement on the various factors that impact deriving that value is just as problematic. In order to understand and improve IT value derivation, many authors have developed theoretical models that trace the path from IT investments to business value (Lucas 1993; Sambamurthy and Zmud 1999; Markus and Soh, 1995; Peppard and Ward 2004; Melville *et al.*, 2004; Marshall *et al.*, 2007; Ashurst *et al.*, 2008; Ward and Daniel, 2012). These models provide an explanation of the IT value proposition, in terms of how IT value is created, and what factors contribute to maximizing that value.

The majority of such theories fall under one of three possible categories:

### 2.2.1   Process theories

These theories provide an explanation for 'how' something happens, and what steps occur to create that outcome. In a seminal research paper, Markus and Soh (1995) developed a pure process theory of how IT creates business value. The authors move away from earlier research focused on whether IT creates business value, to the question of how, when and why benefits in IT investments occur or fail to do so. The authors conduct a comprehensive literature review of IT value, and synthesize five previously-developed process models to derive at their own process model. The authors claim that IT value, the dependent variable, is delivered in increments, and that each phase of the IT value proposition creates an intermediate outcome. As depicted in Figure 1, the IT value journey is comprised of 3 major processes, and it begins with the "*IT Conversion process*", converting "IT Expenditures" to "IT Assets", and is followed by the "IT Use Process", where "IT Assets" are turned into "IT Impacts", and finally to "*Competitive Forces Process*", where "IT Impacts" result in "Organizational Performance".

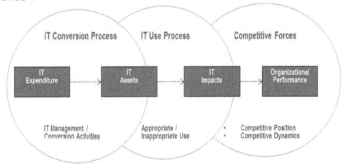

**Figure 1:** Markus and Soh (1995) – IT Value Model

Marshall *et al.*, (2007) analyzed the process model developed by Markus and Soh (1995) and proposed revisions to make the model more compre-hensive. The authors added a key process in the beginning of the lifecycle which they called *"IT Alignment Process"*, arguing that *"IT expenditure"* alone cannot give rise to business benefits, and that expenditures need to be linked back to business strategy and business requirements. Therefore, to ensure that the business focus of IT expenditures is both explicitly-recognized and featured in the model, they add the "Alignment Process". The new model is depicted in Figure 2.

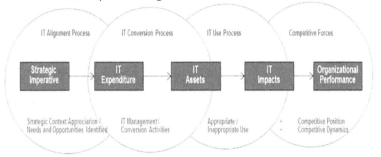

**Figure 2:** Marshall et al., (2007) – IT Value Model

In search for competencies that explicitly contribute to the realization of benefits from IT projects, and heeding the call to develop benefits man-agement practices from Peppard and Ward, (2000), Ashurst *et al.* (2008) developed a benefits realization competence framework that conceptual-izes the lifecycle of IT projects as comprising the following key phases: "Benefits planning", where the planned outcomes of an IT project are iden-tified, and the means of means of by which they will be achieved are stipulat-ed; benefits delivery, where the actual design and execution of what they called *"program of organizational change necessary to realize all of the benefits specified in the benefits realization plan"* takes place. "Benefits review", where the assessment of the success of an IT project takes place, and where the identification of the ways and means by which further ben-efits might be realized takes place. "Benefits exploitation", where what they called *'the adoption of the portfolio of practices required to realize the potential benefits from information, applications and IT services, over their operational life'* take place. Their model is depicted in Figure 3.

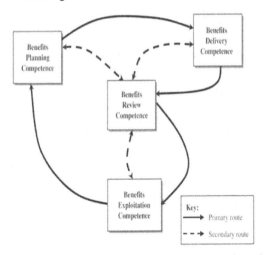

**Figure 3:** Benefits Realization Capability model - Ashurst et al., (2008)

As illustrated in Figure 4, Markus and Tanis (2000) identified four phases in the lifecycle of one of the most complex and potentially the most value-adding IS investment, ERP. The authors define the first phase as the *"chartering phase"*, comprising decisions leading to funding of the ERP project. They define the second phase of their lifecycle as the *"project phase"* comprising system configuration and rollout. The third phase in their lifecycle is called the *"shakedown phase"*, and they define it as the period of time from "going live" until "normal operation" or "routine use" has been achieved. They define the final phase of *"onward and upward phase"* as the on-going maintenance and enhancement of the ERP system and relevant business processes to fit the evolving business needs of the organization.

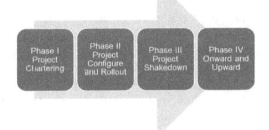

**Figure 4:** Markus and Tanis (2000) IT Value Model

Ward and Daniel (2012) incorporating their earlier research (2006), developed a process-driven model consisting of 5 major iterative steps: 1. Identify and structure the benefits, which results in developing a business case identifying the objectives for the investment and all potential benefits that could be obtained; 2. Plan the benefits realization containing a full benefits plan and a business case for the investment; 3. Execute the benefits plan, which includes the actual conversion and implementation of business process changes and information system implementation; 4. Review and evaluate the results, which takes place after the implementation is completed, as a post implementation review step, to assess performance and adjust accordingly; and 5. Establish the potential for further benefits. Their model is depicted in Figure 5.

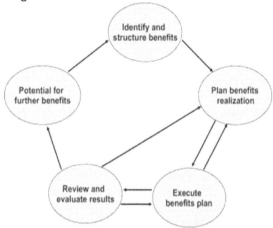

**Figure 5:** The Benefits Management Process Model - Ward and Daniel (2006 2012)

### 2.2.2   Variance theories

Variance theories explain 'why' something happens, and what variables moderate that outcome. A major reason businesses fail to realize business value from their IS investments is their lack of appropriate individual and organizational competencies, and not exploiting certain contextual factors. Mohr (1982) coined the term "variance" to describe the way that researchers view the world when they see it comprised of independent and dependent variables.  In terms of theoretical concepts, the variance approach focuses on properties of entities, often called variables or factors. It is assumed that these properties can have different values even though the property itself has a fixed meaning.  For example, an IT system might have the property "system quality." The meaning of system quality remains fixed over time even though the values for any given system could change over time (e.g., from high to low) and different systems could have different values at any point in time.

In 2000, Marchand *et al.*, surveyed over a thousand senior managers from 169 senior management teams in 98 companies operating in 22 countries and 25 industries to discover how the interaction of people, information and technology affect business performance. The authors proposed their model as a new instrument to measure the effectiveness of organizational information use, comprising the following three elements:

*Information technology practices (ITP)*, which describes the capabilities of a company to effectively manage IT applications and infrastructure to support their business operations, business processes, managerial decision making, and innovation.

*Information management practices (IMP)*, which describes the capabilities of a company to manage information effectively over the lifecycle of information use, this lifecycle includes sensing information, collecting information, organizing information, processing information, and maintaining information.

*Information behaviors and values (IBV)*, which describes the capabilities that promote behaviors and values (information culture) in its people for the effective use of information.

The Marchand *et.al* (2000) model is adjusted in Figure 6 to conceptualize the theoretical constructs of the model. The model is a variance theory linking certain organizational competencies - Hard IT Management (ITP), Hard Information Management (IMP), and Other Soft Behaviors and Values (IVB) - to organizational performance. In order to improve organizational performance (dependent variable), organizations must develop these organizational competencies.

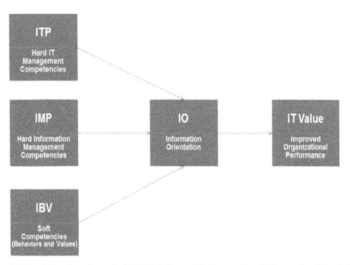

**Figure 6:** The Marchand et al., (2000) Adjusted Information Orientation Model

As Figure 7 illustrates, in the Sambamurthy and Zmud, (1999) model, raw materials (technology, knowledge, data), as well as resource competencies (knowledge of how to apply IT, and knowledge of business activities) enable the creation of intermediate "IT impacts" (new/improved products and services, transformed business processes, enriched organizational intelligence, and dynamic organizational structures. This implies a necessary and sufficient relationship between IT management competencies and "IT impacts": the greater the competencies, the greater the impact. According to the authors, "IT impacts" eventually lead to business value and improved organizational products and services, but the authors do not elaborate on how "IT impacts" create ultimate business value, and what processes or conditions are necessary to create that final outcome. Although the authors mention the need for IT management processes as a condition to create "IT impacts", they do not elaborate on such processes, and therefore, the model appears to be a variance theory of IT management competencies and "IT impacts".

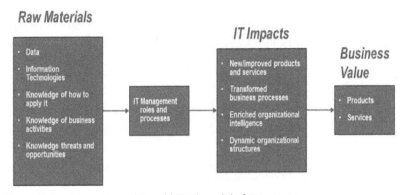

**Figure 7:** Sambamurthy and Zmud (1999) model of IT Impacts

Peppard and Ward (2004) used the Resource-Based-View (RBV) theory of the firm and grounding their research with the prior work done by Peppard *et al.* (2000) developed a model representing the components of what they called "The IT Capability". The model has three levels: the resource level, the organizing level and the enterprise level (see Figure 8). The resource level denotes the resource components that are the key ingredients of the IS competencies. In managing IS, these resources are the skills, knowledge and behavioral attributes of both employees and external providers. The organizing level is concerned with how these resources are mobilized and marshaled via structures, processes and roles to create IS competencies. It is, however, only at the enterprise level the authors contend that the capability actually manifests itself and is ultimately recognized in the performance of the organization.

Compared to the earlier model of IS competencies developed by Peppard *et al.* (2000), this model presents a notable improvement. The "IS capability" in their model is the dependent variable, and all the other factors listed are the independent variables. Organizations mobilize resources and arm these with the proper organizational processes and structures to create an intermediate outcome - IS capability - which in turn may be used by firms to improve their performance.

At first glance, the model appears to be a hybrid model, combining both process and variance orientation. However, a closer look reveals that the process component does not really address how IT value is created, and does not offer a recipe-like sequential process of how value is created.

Although the authors allude to a process construct, they use that more as a factor or variable, and therefore, their model appears to be more of a variance theory, linking various factors, such as individual resource competencies, organizational competencies, and organizational structures as key variables affecting IT value generation (in their case leading to an IT capability).

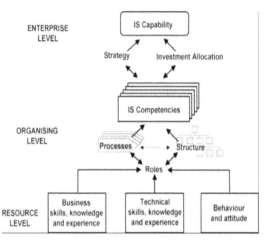

**Figure 8:** A model of the IS capability adapted from Peppard and Ward (2004)

### *2.2.3   Hybrid theories*

In order to provide a more comprehensive explanation of the IT value proposition, in terms of the processes, as well as the factors that enable and maximize business value, a few authors have developed hybrid IT value models (Lucas, 1993; Melville *et al.*, 2004).   Burton-Jones *et al.*, (2011) elaborate the many benefits that hybrid approaches provide to theory-building in IS research, and these include: improving understanding of concepts (whether the state of an entity is affected by events or processes), and improving understanding of relationships (the process by which a relationship among properties occurs).

As Figure 9 illustrates, Lucas (1993) is concerned with how (process) IT increases firm performance.  He proposes two conditions, occurring in sequence, leading to the performance outcome. The first, necessary but not sufficient, condition is that IT be designed in such a way that it fits the firm's task effectively. An effective IT design is not, however, sufficient for organizational performance improvement, because technology cannot improve organizational performance unless the technology is used. Therefore, appropriate use of an effectively designed technology is also a necessary condition for improved organizational performance in Lucas' model. Lucas acknowledges that factors other than appropriate use of an effectively designed technology may influence firm performance (e.g., competitor's reactions).

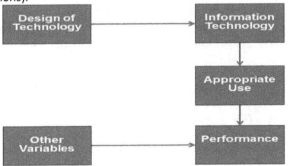

**Figure 9:** IT Value Model – Adapted from Lucas (1993)

In one of the most-cited IT value research papers, Melville *et al.*, (2004) use the RBV of the firm to develop a descriptive model of the IT business value generating process integrating the previous strands of research into a single framework. One of their principal findings is that IT is valuable, but the extent and dimensions are dependent upon internal and external factors, including complementary organizational resources of the firm and its trading partners, as well as the competitive and macro environment. The authors suggest that if the right IT is applied within the right business process, improved processes and organizational performance result, conditional upon appropriate complementary investments in workplace practices and organizational structure and shaped by the competitive environment. The authors'IT Value model comprises three domains. The first of these is the "focal firm", which is the organization acquiring and deploying the IT resource firm. Within the focal firm, IT business value is generated by the deployment of IT and complementary organizational resources such as policies and rules, organizational structure, workplace practices, organizational culture, non-IT physical capital resources, non-IT human capital resources, and what they call organizational capital, e.g., formal reporting structures and informal relationships within and among firms. The authors separate the second domain, "competitive environment" into two components: industry characteristics and trading partners. In industry characteristics, they include competitiveness, regulation, technological change, and other related factors. The authors suggest that when IT spans firm boundaries, the business processes, IT resources, and non-IT resources of trading partners play a role in the IT business value generation of the focal firm. According to the authors, the third domain, "macro environment", denotes country- and meta-country- specific factors, which include government promotion and regulation of technology development and information industries, IT talent, information infrastructure, as well as prevailing information and IT cultures. The model is depicted in Figure 10.

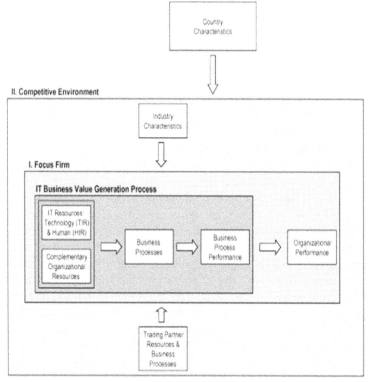

**Figure 10:** IT Business Value Model (Melville et. al 2004)

Schryen (2013) conducted a comprehensive review of the IS Value literature and found that the value creation process remain unclear in terms of how, why and when IS assets and organizational capabilities are transformed into business value. The author indicated that IS business value theory building and testing as one of the key challenges of future research, and argued that the best theories of IS Value are "hybrids", combining the best qualities of "Variance" and "Process" orientation.

## 2.3    Additional factors affecting IT Value Derivation

In the quest to find the "silver bullet" for deriving business value from IT, scholars and researchers have prescribed a number of different cures. Some advocated the use of IT Governance (Marshall et al, 2007; Sambamurthy and Zmud, 1999; Peterson, 2004; Avison et al (2006); Weill and Ross, 2004). Others have suggested the use of formal benefits management processes to manage value throughout the lifecycle of the IT value proposition (Peppard, 2007; Ward and Daniel, 2008).

There is also a large body of research evaluating individual competencies needed by the Corporate IT function and the CIO. Periasamy and Seow (1998) identified five critical success factors for the CIO to deploy IT to deliver optimal value to his organisation promptly and successfully. Lane and Koronios (2007) found that the role of the modern CIO has become increasingly business focused and strategic, and that soft skills dominate the critical competencies. Polansky et al. (2004) presented a 10 Point Leadership Agenda for CIOs, which comprised IT strategy; IT governance; IT organisation and staffing; technology and architecture; technology awareness; corporate governance; business intelligence; business transformation; customer care; and Internet and e-business. CSC (1997) defined six leadership roles for the CIO (e.g. Chief Operating Strategist) and Remenyi *et al.* (2005) used the analogy of the Chameleon to describe the key characteristics of CIOs (e.g. the ability to change). Chun and Mooney (2009) found that much of CIO role has evolved to the executive-level management and is centered on working with other business executives inside and outside of the firm to change the firm's strategy and processes.

A stream of research has looked beyond the individual competencies needed by CIOs and the corporate IT function, and stressed the importance of user-related and other contextual attributes as contributing factors to IS success. Sabherwal et al. (2006) developed and tested a comprehensive theoretical model linking IS success with four user constructs (user experience with IS, user attitude towards IS, user training in IS, and user participation in the development of IS), and two constructs representing the context (top-management support for ISs and facilitating conditions for ISs). Several authors (Armstrong and Sambamurthy, 1999; Feeney and Willcocks 1998; Sharma and Yetton, 2003; Salvage and Dhanda, 2007) emphasized the importance of non-CIO executives taking an active role in the planning of IS. Peppard and Ward (2004) argued that competence is an organizational concept that reflects a bundle of skills and technologies while capabilities are related to the strategic application of competencies in order to achieve business objectives.

Furthermore, a number of researchers have highlighted the impact of human/social factors within business organizations. Nissen (2002) points out that the concept of 'user' may not be a helpful one in the context of an IS value proposition, since it serves to insulate system developers from the needs of real business professionals. Few people, he suggests, would define themselves as users of IT, but as accountants, sales personnel, storemen, etc. Furthermore, they are not simply 'consumers' of information systems, but co-creators. As Ward and Peppard (2002) point out:

*As the benefits management process proceeds, it may cause revision to the specification, and it is assumed that effective change control processes can deal with this. The other related set of activities are organizational changes of many types that have to be made to deliver the benefits. The benefits management process should be the driving mechanism for these change activities. How to bring them about in detail is addressed in the wealth of change management and organizational development literature (2002, p.441).*

While most researchers have concentrated on rational choices involved in IT/IS deployment, this does not always reflect the whole picture. The affective zone can also have an impact on benefit realization, but this factor is often swept up into consideration of 'change management practice'. Argyris (2004) describes how 'defensive routines' can arise in organizational behavior. When faced with the need to address uncomfortable choices or deliver 'bad news', people may wish to avoid awkwardness or confrontation, and thus become quite skilled in what Argyris calls 'skilled incompetence'. In a magazine article, Williams (2007) reported on research commissioned by the IT Governance Institute. 52% of the projects sampled were expected to lead to negative returns, while 31% actually destroyed value for the companies concerned, yet only 3% of projects were abandoned before completion. This suggests that managers were continuing to preside over projects knowing that they would destroy, rather than create business value. Williams reflects that this cannot be accounted for through rational management decision-making, but suggests reluctance by managers to cancel when this might be seen as a sign of weakness and failure.

## 2.4   The country-specific CIO experience

A number of other authors have explored the challenges faced and competencies needed by CIOs within the context of a particular county. For example, to understand the individual competencies required of CIOs in Brazil, Vreuls and Joai (2011) evaluated seven competency models found in literature and used a pure quantitative approach to identify CIO competencies from the perspective of Brazilian CIOs. They concluded that CIOs should possess/develop knowledge of the business; understanding of the organizational context; the ability to influence the organization; technical expertise; external networking; management of the information technology operation and the capacity to innovate using new information technologies. Reviewing 3 large Australian IS projects and their failures, Avison et al (2006) found that managerial IS unconsciousness and failure in IS governance, defined as patterns of authority for key IS activities in firms, including IS infrastructure, IS use and project management can even lead to the bankruptcy of private companies and the waste of millions of dollars of taxpayers' money. The authors also argued that the importance of IS governance is largely ignored in the failure literature (Avison and Wilson, 2002).

Zuo and Maou (2005), carried out the first academic study in China with regard to CIO state and impact. The Chief Executive Officer's (CEO) perspective in that study was that CIOs need to be more business-oriented, requiring soft skills and relationship management skills. Using a different approach, Gottschalk (2000) looked at CIO roles in Norway, which lead to the identification of required competencies. Oracle conducted a study in 2011 and included information from a number of regional CIOs/organizations (e.g. Saudi Arabia, Emirates, Jordan, Dubai, India and other emerging markets). They found that the IT knowledge and competency of non-IT people (general Management and the users) is weak and that CIOs are surrounded by executives who have an inadequate awareness of IT capacity.

# 3. Data collection

The data in this paper has been collected from interviews with the CIOs of the participating organisations. Two interviews with each of the participating CIOs were conducted, followed by an offline collaboration process, using email as the platform to confirm and to prioritize the challenges raised during the interviews. Next, a one day forum was organized allowing the CIOs to meet each other and to collaborate real-time on the key challenges. The forum was also used as an opportunity to plant the seeds for a more permanent platform for CIO collaboration and for future research, which ultimately resulted in the formation of the *"CIO Lebanon Association"* officially approved by the Lebanese Ministry of Interior.

Data from Kompas (2009) was initially used to identify the total population of industries and organizations. Subsequently, a sample was selected to include organizations that represented the four key industries in Lebanon: Banking, Healthcare, Higher Education, and Retail (77% of the sample included such companies). It was also important to choose organizations that had significant experience in IT/IS, and with no prior IS studies to reveal that population, organization size (no. of employees) was used as a substitute to select the participants (35% of large organizations and 8% of medium size organizations in Lebanon were included in the sample), (See Tables 1 & 2):

**Table 1:** Lebanese organizations and sample used

|  | Total for Lebanon | Sample |
|---|---|---|
| No of Organisations > 500 employees | 78 | 26 |
| No of Organisations 250 - 500 employees | 122 | 10 |

**Table 2:** Participating organizations

| Sector | Sample |
|---|---|
| Banking | 11 |
| Healthcare/Hospitals | 6 |
| Higher Education | 6 |
| Airline carrier | 1 |
| Post office | 1 |
| Retail | 5 |
| Telecommunications | 1 |
| Printing | 1 |
| Logistics | 1 |
| Pharmaceuticals | 1 |
| Food & Beverage | 1 |

# 4. Results

A total of 14 key challenges were identified and categorized as either "process-related", i.e. ways and means of deriving value from IT investments, or "variance-related", i.e. factors that affect getting maximum value from IT. Process-oriented challenges included:

## 4.1  Change resistance and the need to manage change

The majority of CIOs indicated that it was very difficult, costly and time consuming to implement business process changes and related behavioral changes in their organizations. This was by far one the most important challenge raised. The CIOs attributed this challenge to a number of factors, including: ownership of IT projects resting upon the IT function; not adopting formal change management processes; lack of IT literacy of users and management; having powerful users with self-serving and hidden agendas; lack of having change champions, and the lack of CIO empowerment.

## 4.2  IT illiteracy of management and users and the need for organizational readiness

While this was generally less of an issue in some sectors (e.g Higher Education), this was a major issue preventing the majority of participating organizations in getting maximum value from IT. The CIOs of organizations that had this issue attributed it to a *"generational gap"* claiming IT illiteracy among their older employees who were still in charge of key management positions. Other CIOs blamed the Higher Education sector in Lebanon for not preparing future managers adequately in the use and exploitation of IT. While most of the participating organizations had developed employee training programs, the training was more oriented to developing general IT literacy competencies, rather than developing IT planning, exploitation, and value extraction competencies.

## 4.3  Inadequate CIO to CxO relations and the need for better relationship management processes

The title of CIO was only given to four of the participants, while others held a number of other titles, including Director of IT, Head of IT, and IT Manager. Three of the CIO positions were in the Banking sector, and one in Higher Education. More than half of the participants reported directly to the top executive. 80% of the CIOs in the Banking sector reported to the Chief Operations Officer (COO), and only one of the CIOs in the Higher Education industry reported directly to the President, the rest reporting to the VP of administration position. In other sectors, it was a mixed bag, with some CIOs having direct access and strong relationships with their CEOs, and others reporting to lower level executives and therefore lesser potential impact on their organizations. Where the relationship was direct, the CIOs enjoyed a strong and productive relationship, resulting in an equal seat at the executive table and a direct involvement and impact to their organization's strategy. Many of the CIOs who did not hold that title, or did not report directly to their CEOs expressed a deep concern and attributed this issue to the lack of appreciation of the strategic value of IT within their organizations.

## 4.4 Lack of formal and comprehensive benefits management processes

None of the participants had implemented a comprehensive benefits management program. While some (25%) had developed formal processes at the early stage of planning IS investments (by using business cases), and others (50%) had formal project management practices during the implementation stage of IS projects, none had any meaningful management practices at the post implementation stage. It also seemed that the majority of companies and their management were not interested or capable of accurately measuring the value of their IS investments. Of those companies that were measuring, the focus was either on project efficiency measures (in-flight, or during IT project implementation metrics) such as: delivery of projects on time, on budget, and according to customer scope and requirements; or the focus was more on IT operational measures (availability, throughput, and response time).

The majority of CIOs were also struggling to convince their users to own or at least co-own the responsibility of deploying information systems and more importantly the responsibility of reaping the benefits from such investments. In addition, the business value of IT was poorly defined and vaguely understood and not common to all stakeholders within the organization. More than 40% of organizations viewed IT as a cost center, rather than as a partner in generating value.

## 4.5 Lack of formal IT governance

While a number of organizations, especially the ones in the Banking sector have instituted structural forms of governance, in the forms of organization-wide IT steering committees to approve and manage enterprise IT projects, IT decision rights were, in the majority of organizations, owned and exercised by the Corporate IT function. Many of the CIOs attributed this to the lack of technology literacy of their Management and users. There was also an emergence of enterprise-wide Project Management Office (PMO) structures in a few organizations, but these were in their very early stages. The PMO function either did not exist (75% of cases), or was just being implemented.

## 4.6 Complex IT applications architectures and the need for IT Architecture Management

The applications architecture (AA) construct is a conceptual model representing departmental and enterprise information systems in support of operational business processes and analytical decision-making. The challenge as described by the CIOs was that their AA was very complex, difficult to support, did not fully support their business strategy, and was not flexible. The most significant issues include:

- Legacy information systems built with antiquated ICT technologies.
- ERP systems that have been heavily customized and no-longer supported by ERP vendors. Almost every CIO indicated at one time or another having difficulty and/or failing to implement enterprise applications. Two of the major retail organizations had customized their ERPs to the point where it was impossible for them to upgrade to a new version of the ERP.
- The majority of CIOs did not have a clear AA roadmap or strategy, and even if such a roadmap existed, it was not a formal planning process linked with their overall business planning process.

## 4.7 IT talent management issues and the need to have better IT Management

This was mentioned as a key issue by more than 70% of the participants, and it was a more acute issue when it came to finding senior level people. A number of the CIOs felt that this was a much bigger issue 5 years ago when talent was being lost to higher-paying markets outside of Lebanon. However, due to the economic problems in the Gulf, and the relative stability in Lebanon, CIOs felt that this issue was more under control.

The list of other "variance-related" challenges included:

## 4.8    Family business ownership

With the exception of organizations that were owned by religious entities (three Hospitals and three Universities), or public organizations (two were involved in this study), or organizations that weren't family owned (two Universities, and two other organizations), all remaining 26 organizations were family-owned, which constituted 72% of the participating organizations.

The predominance of family business ownership is one of the characteristics of the Lebanese economy. In family firms, property and control are so firmly entwined that family members are involved in both strategic and day-to-day decision making, and the firm is shaped by dynastic motive. As evidenced by this research, the family impact extends to large organizations, and many organizations in the thriving banking industry, for example, were closely held by extended families. Five of the family-owned organization felt that family-ownership was a positive situation because it involved leaders who were also owners that cared about the longevity and long-term viability of their firms, as opposed to leaders that were only in these positions to establish short term gains. All remaining family-owned organization CIOs indicated serious disadvantages arising from family ownership, such as unfair and inconsistent human resource policies in the recruitment, selection, and promotion of employees.

## 4.9    Budgetary constraints

This was more of a challenge in the Healthcare sector, as most of the organizations in this sector had cash flow issues due to significant delays in receiving remittances from the Government. The CIOs in the Healthcare sector indicated that the biggest share of their revenues came from government-insured patients (75%), and only 25% of their patients had private insurance. This was also a challenge in smaller organizations.

## 4.10    Political, economic, and social instability

Lebanon has witnessed many devastating wars before and after its independence from France in 1943. The most devastating recent war lasted for over fifteen years beginning in 1975. Another recent war in 2006 resulted in the destruction of the majority of the country's infrastructure. Since 2006, the country continued to experience many additional conflicts inside the country and throughout its surrounding neighbouring countries. Many of the CIOs expressed total frustration and lack of control over these issues and found this to be the most serious challenge they faced.

## 4.11  Telecommunications issues

During the initial interviewing process, this challenge clearly emerged as the top challenge among most CIOs. Issues related to the reliability, availability, and cost of Internet bandwidth was a key concern. This even resulted in three of the organizations having to compromise the architecture of their core ERP system. The affected organizations had several branches in the region, and have deployed an ERP product in a totally de-centralized architecture/approach. Had they had more reliable and affordable Internet access, they would have chosen to deploy these ERPs using a centralized architecture/approach.

## 4.12  Lack of Governmental IT laws

One of the key issues raised by the majority of CIOs is the lack of any governmental ICT legislation regulating and protecting the electronic rights of organizations and consumers.

## 4.13  Local culture issues

This was mentioned by the majority of CIOs as a key and possibly detrimental factor in not only getting business value from IT, but in getting any value from the business. Three of the CIOs that are currently engaged in re-engineering their entire organization spend the majority of their time (one CIO indicated that it is as high as 70% of their time) dealing with and managing cultural transformation. The issue of "entitlement" was dominant in larger organizations, and in organizations that were family-owned.

## 4.14  Immaturity of local suppliers, vendors, and partners

All CIOs indicated their dissatisfaction with local professional services organizations, and expressed a need and commitment to help improve these vendors' service levels. Also of deep concern in the Hospital sector was the lack of ICT competence in doctors, which created a key challenge in rolling out IT applications and services. In the Higher Education sector, there were similar issues with Faculty members who did not want to be involved in the planning, implementation or roll-out of applications, and when it came to using such applications, they abdicated that responsibility to their assistants.

# 5. Conclusions and future steps

The challenges in deriving business value from IT suggest the necessity to develop certain organizational competencies. While these reflect the Lebanese CIO experience, many of these challenges and related competencies have also been found in the extant literature. As Figure 11 illustrates, some of these competencies may be classified as process-oriented (*"how to derive value from IT"*), and others are competencies that require organizations to mind, mitigate, and exploit certain internal and external organizational factors (*"when, how, and under what conditions IT value is derived"*). Process-oriented competencies are critical; however, they are not enough, and should be complemented by variance-oriented competencies. The need for both types of competencies justifies the use of *"Hybrid"* models of IT value. The conceptual model that emerges from this study is preliminary and is grounded in the data gathered from key Lebanese CIOs. Future studies should engage with other CIOs, in and out of Lebanon, and with all the other stakeholders involved in the IT value proposition, be it Management, users, vendors, and other key stakeholders, to refine and adjust the model.

The arrows in Figure 11 refer to the various strands of future research that should be conducted. Arrow 1 suggests identifying the inputs driving the entire value proposition, and investigating the relationships between such inputs and the rest of the model. Arrow 2 calls for investigating three aspects of the process part of the model: identifying the sequence (if any) of activities; identifying additional possible missing activities; and investigating the relationships between these activities. Arrow 3 suggests investigating the relationships between the process and variance components of the model. Arrow 4 calls for investigating the relationships between the various internal factors, and also the need to identify additional such factors that impact the value proposition. Arrow 5 calls for investigating the relationships between the various external factors, and also the need to identify additional such factors that impact the value proposition. Finally Arrow 7 suggests investigating the relationships between the independent variables (process and various components) and the dependent variable, *"IT Value"*. While there is an abundance of literature about the dependent variable itself, additional valuable insights may be gained by continuing the benefits management research agenda developed by Peppard and Ward (2007), and Wards and Daniel (2006, 2012). Finally, future research should also compare and contrast the emerging IT value model with the extant IT value models.

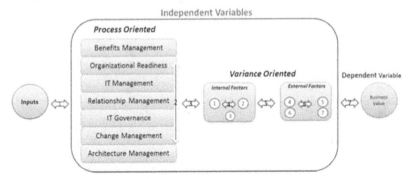

**Figure 11:** A Hybrid IT Value Model

# References

Argyris, C. (2004). 'Reasons and Rationalisations. The Limits to Organizational Knowledge'. Oxford University Press.

Armstrong, C. P. and V. Sambamurthy (1999). 'Information technology assimilation in firms: The influence of senior leadership and IT infrastructures', Information systems research, 10(4), 304-327.

Ashurst, C., Doherty, N. F., and Peppard, J. (2008). 'Improving the impact of IT development projects: the benefits realization capability model', European Journal of Information Systems, 17(4), 352-370.

Avison, D. E., Dwivedi, Y. K., Fitzgerald, G., and Powell, P. (2008). 'The beginnings of a new era: time to reflect on 17 years of the ISJ', Information Systems Journal, 18(1), 5-21.

Burton-Jones, A., McLean, E.R., Monod, E. (2011) 'On approaches to building theories: Process, variance and systems', Working paper, Sauder School of Business, UBC.

Chun, M. and J. Mooney (2009.) 'CIO roles and responsibilities: Twenty-five years of evolution and change', Information and Management, 46(6), 323-334.

CSC (1997). Critical Issues of Information Systems Management - 10th Annual Survey, Computer Sciences Corporation, USA: El Segundo, California.

Cohen, W. M., and Levinthal, D. A. (1990). 'Absorptive capacity: a new perspective on learning and innovation', Administrative Science Quarterly, 38, 128-152.

DeLone, W. H. and. McLean, E. R. (1992). 'Information systems success: The quest for the dependent variable', Information Systems Research, 3(1), 60-95.

Delone, W. H. and McLean, E. R. (2003). 'The DeLone and McLean model of information systems success: A ten-year update', Journal of management information systems, 19(4), 9-30.

Devaraj, S. and Kohli, R. (2003). The IT payoff: measuring the business value of information technology investments, FT Press.

Feeny, D. F. and L. P. Willcocks (1998). 'Core IS capabilities for exploiting information technology', Sloan Management Review, 39(3), 9-21.

Gottschalk, P. (2000). 'Information systems executives: the changing role of new IS/IT leaders', Informing Science, 3(2), 31-40.

Govekar, M. and Adams, P. (2010). 'Hype Cycle for IT operations management 2010', Gartner Research, Stamford. 1-62.

Hitt, L. M. and E. Brynjolfsson (1996). 'Productivity, business profitability, and consumer surplus: three different measures of information technology value', MIS quarterly, 20(2), 121-142

Keen, P. G. (1980). MIS research: reference disciplines and a cumulative tradition: Center for Information Systems Research, Sloan School of Management.

Kohli, R. and Grover, V., (2008). 'Business Value of IT: an essay on expanding research directions to keep up with the times', Journal of the Association of Information Systems, 9(1), 23-39.

Kompass (2009). "Database of Medium-to-Large Organizations in Lebanon". http://lb.kompass.com/

Lane, M. S. and A. Koronios (2007). 'Critical competencies required for the role of the modern CIO', ACIS 2007 Proceedings, 90.

Lucas, H.C. (1993). The business value of IT: An historical perspective and thoughts for future research. In Banker and Kaufman (Eds.), Strategic IT Management. Harrisburg: Idea Group.

Marshall, P., McKay, J., Prananto, A. et al. (2007). 'Business value creation from IT investments: Towards a process theory of IT governance', Australasian Journal of Information Systems, 12(2), 192-206.

Marchand, D.A., Kettinger, W.J., and Rollins J.D. (2000). 'Information Orientation: People, Technology and the Bottom Line', Sloan Management Review. July 15, 2000

Melville, N., Kraemer, K., and Gurbaxani, V. (2004). 'Review: Information technology and organizational performance: An integrative model of IT business value', MIS quarterly, 28(2), 283-322.

Momoh, A., Roy, R. and Shehab, E. (2010). 'Challenges in enterprise resource planning implementation: state-of-the-art', Business Process Management Journal, 16,(4), 537–565.

Nissen, H-E. (2002). 'Challenging Traditions of Inquiry in Software Practice,' in Y. Dittrich, C. Floyd and R. Klischewski (editors), Social Thinking – Software Practice'. Cambridge Mass: MIT Press, 69-90.

Oracle (2011). 'Corporate CIOs in emerging markets an evolving role', Economist Intelligence Unit. The Economist. Accessed 31 May 2015 at http://www.economistinsights.com/

Peppard, J., Ward, J., and Daniel, E. (2007). 'Managing the realization of business benefits from IT investments', MIS Quarterly Executive, 6(1), 1-11.

Peppard, J. (2007). 'The conundrum of IT management', European Journal of Information Systems, 16(4), 336-345.

Peppard, J. and J. Ward (2004). 'Beyond Strategic information systems: towards an IS capability', The Journal of Strategic Information Systems, 13(2), 167-194..

Periasamy, K. P. and A. Seow (1998). 'CIO: Business Executive or Technical Expert', Institute of Systems Science, National University of Singapore, 1998 22.

Peterson, R. (2004). 'Crafting IT Governance', Information Systems Management, 21(4), 7-22.

Polansky, M., T. Inuganti (2004). 'The 21st century CIO', Business Strategy Review, 15, 29-33.

Remenyi, D., Grant, K.A., and Pather, S. (2005). 'The chameleon: a metaphor for the Chief Information Officer', Journal of General Management, 30(1), 1-11.

Sabherwal, R., Jeyaraj, J. and Chowa, C. (2006). Information System Success: Individual and Organizational Determinants, Management Science, 52(12), 1849-1864.

Salvage, I. and Dhanda, I.S. (2007). 'IBM White Paper on IT Service Management', http://whitepapers.theregister.co.uk/search/?q=IBM viewed 11 Nov 2007.

Sambamurthy, V. and Zmud, R.W. (1999). 'Arrangements for IT governance: a theory of multiple contingencies', MIS Quarterly, 23(2), 261-290.

Sharma, R. and P. Yetton (2003). 'The contingent effects of management support and task interdependence on successful information systems implementation', MIS Quarterly, 27(4), 533-556.

Schryen G (2013). 'Revisiting IS business value research: what we already know, what we still need to know, and how we can get there', European Journal of Information Systems, 22(2), 139–169.

Ward, J. and Peppard, J. (2002). Strategic Planning for Information Systems, 3rd edition. Wiley.

Ward, J., Daniel, E., and Peppard, J. (2008). 'Building better business cases for IT investments', MIS Quarterly Executive, 7(1), 1-15.

Vreuls, E. and Joai, L. (2011). 'An Exploratory Model for the Relevant Factors Related to the Professional Performance of the Brazilian CIO', Electronic Journal of Information Systems in Developing Countries, 47(5), 1-20.

Weill, P. and Ross, J.W. (2004). 'IT Governance: How top performing firms govern IT', MIS Quarterly Executive, 3(1), 1-17.

Williams, P. (2007). 'Make sure you get a positive return', Computer Weekly, 13 Nov 2007.

Zuo, M. and J. Y. Mao (2005) 'A Survey of the State and Impact of CIOs in China', proceedings of PACIS 2005, Bangkok, Thailand. Paper 39.

# Digital Archiving, Green IT and the Environment: Deleting Data to Manage Critical Effects of the Data Deluge

Geert-Jan van Bussel[1], Nikki Smit[2] and John van de Pas[3]
[1]Hva Amsterdam University of Applied Sciences, School of Economics and Management, Amsterdam, The Netherlands
[2]BECIS Information Management, Amsterdam, The Netherlands
[3]Saxion University of Applied Sciences, School of Creative Technology, Deventer, The Netherlands

---

**Editorial Commentary**
The phenomenal reach of networks in our modern inter-networked society of the 21st century suggests that we are witness to an exponential growth of data storage across both cloud and localised systems. Moore's law (Moore, 1965) implies a massive increase in requirements for data storage (see e.g. Chip, 2005a). However, given that storage is largely dependent on energy, the inter-networked era is placing an undue premium on the judicious application of limited energy sources. Thus whilst this paper by van Bussel, Smit and van de Pas is not based on a typical IS evaluation problem, it does provide a basis for a new dimension of evaluation. Given that the cost of data storage will decrease as the demand increases, the evaluation of energy costs of IS projects will undoubtedly be necessary. This paper, then, provides a basis on which a new perspective of IS project (ex-ante) should evolve, involving an evaluation of the 'greenness' of the IS infra-structure. The outcomes of such evaluation should assist in ensuring that hardware architecture of IS will draw only minimally on the already con-strained resources of the natural environment.

---

a    Chip, W. 2005.    Kryders Law.    Scientific American, August 1.
[http://www.scientificamerican.com/article/kryders-law/]

---

**Abstract:** The development of the World Wide Web, the emergence of social media and Big Data have led to a rising amount of data. Information and Communication

Technologies (ICTs) affect the environment in various ways. Their energy consumption is growing exponentially, with and without the use of 'green' energy. Increasing environmental awareness has led to discussions on sustainable development. The data deluge makes it not only necessary to pay attention to the hard- and software dimensions of ICTs but also to the 'value' of the data stored. In this paper, we study the possibility to methodically reduce the amount of stored data and records in organizations based on the 'value' of information, using the Green Archiving Model we have developed. Reducing the amount of data and records in organizations helps in allowing organizations to fight the data deluge and to realize the objectives of both Digital Archiving and Green IT. At the same time, methodically deleting data and records should reduce the consumption of electricity for data storage. As a consequence, the organizational cost for electricity use should be reduced. Our research showed that the model can be used to reduce [1] the amount of data (45 percent, using Archival Retention Levels and Retention Schedules) and [2] the electricity consumption for data storage (resulting in a cost reduction of 35 percent). Our research indicates that the Green Archiving Model is a viable model to reduce the amount of stored data and records and to curb electricity use for storage in organizations. This paper is the result of the first stage of a research project that is aimed at developing low power ICTs that will automatically appraise, select, preserve or permanently delete data based on their 'value'. Such an ICT will automatically reduce storage capacity and reduce electricity consumption used for data storage. At the same time, data disposal will reduce overload caused by storing the same data in different formats, it will lower costs and it reduces the potential for liability.

**Keywords:** data deluge, digital archiving, archival retention levels, information value chain, green archiving, green IT

# 1. Setting the stage: Data Deluge, Digital Archiving and Green IT

## 1.1 Data Deluge
The development of the World Wide Web, the emergence of social media and Big Data have led to a rising amount of data (Armitage and Roberts, 2002; Segaran and Hammerbacher, 2009; Manyika, 2011). The seemingly infinite opportunities to process and publish data, global electronic communications, an explosion in devices located at the periphery of the network, including embedded sensors, smartphones, and tablet computers, aerial sensory technologies, software logs, cameras, microphones, radio-frequency identification readers, wireless sensor networks, and a large-scale digitization of cultural heritage such as film, music, art, images, maps, and text, have caused an unprecedented global growth in the amount of

data. This growth has been analysed in several research projects, but the comparison of their results is difficult because of the different definitions and research methods used (Lyman and Varian, 2003; Hilbert and López, 2011; Gantz and Reinsel, 2012). This research agrees on one basic fact: the astonishing growth rate in the amount of data in the world. To summarize the results, it is confirmed [1] that the data storage capacity doubles every 40 months, and [2] that the annual growth rate in the amount of data is almost 40 %, creating a 'data deluge'. This data creates new opportunities for analytics in human genomics, health care, oil and gas, search, surveillance, finance, and many other areas (Golden, 2010), but is also putting great pressure on the infrastructures of information and communication technologies (ICTs) (Van Bussel and Henseler, 2013).

## 1.2   Digital Archiving

The use of collaborative technologies in organizations to streamline business processes also creates huge amounts of data (Jacobs, 2009). These data are used and generated by knowledge workers who engage in peer-to-peer knowledge sharing across organizational boundaries. The storage, dissemination and processing of this data require complex ICT systems. These ICT systems present security and durability challenges that pose a major threat for information quality (Bearman, 2006). Digital data are fragile. They are easily altered without recognition. They require storage media that have relatively short life spans, and access technologies that are changing extremely fast. For some data types, such as multimedia, it is almost impossible to be used outside the proprietary environments in which they were generated (Hodge, 2000). These problematic challenges threaten the trustworthiness of organizational records, that data that are meant to be (and used as) evidence for policies, decisions, products, actions and transactions. Organizations have to respond to increasing societal demands for the trustworthiness of these records, mostly for privacy, accountability and transparency reasons. That is why Digital Archiving (DA) is important for organizations.

DA ensures that the informational and evidential 'value' of records is utilized in business processes to improve performance. It provides an ICT infrastructure to (indefinitely) store (identified and trusted) records and keep them accessible. It ensures that (privacy) laws and regulations are respected and audits periodically the possibility to reliably reconstruct the past. DA manages the four dimensions of information to allow for such a re-

construction. Those four dimensions are [1] quality, [2] context, [3] relevance, and [4] survival. The quality dimension is focused on the quality
requirements of data and records to realize 'immutable mobiles' (Latour,
1990). 'Immutable mobiles' allow for the repeated use of data and records
for consultation and for reconstruction of past happenings. Context provides meaning to the data and records: metadata are captured that give
information about the organizational, technological, and societal environment in which the data and records were generated. Data and records are
only relevant if they fit the organizational objectives of performance and
accountability. The survival dimension concerns the security and durability
challenges, which have to be overcome to realize access, retrieval, and
preservation over time for all 'immutable mobiles' (Van Bussel 2012ab).
DA's purposes are to reduce the costs of transactions, to enlarge the speed
of access to organizational experiences, to help in decision-making, to
share knowledge, and to realize accountability.

The deluge of data is threatening DA's possibilities to realize its purposes
(Van Bussel, 2012ab; Van Bus¬sel and Henseler, 2013).

## 1.3    Green IT

ICT has not always worked to the benefit of environmental sustainability,
although there are many ICTs that have positive environmental effects,
such as GPS systems and online mapping software, which lead to more
efficient travel and, as a result, reduce emissions of carbon dioxide (Tomlinson, 2010). The origins of an environmental approach to ICTs can be
traced back to the beginning of the 1990s, when the reduction of the use
of hazardous materials, the maximization of energy efficiency, and the re-
cyclability or biodegradability of defunct products and factory waste be-
came hot items in computing (Jacob and K.G, 2012; Esfahani et al, 2015ab).

Green IT (Brooks et al, 2012) is defined by Murugesan (2008: 25-26) as 'the
study and practice of designing, manufacturing, using, and disposing of
computers, servers, and associated subsystems - such as monitors, print-
ers, storage devices, and networking and communications systems efficiently and effectively with minimal or no impact on the environment'. ICTs
affect the environment in various ways. Its production requires electricity,
raw materials, chemical materials and large amounts of water, and sup-
plies (often toxic) waste (Robinson, 2009). Computers and peripherals are
changed two or three years after purchase (Murugesan, 2008). In 2006,
global production of E-waste was estimated at 20-50 million tonnes per

year (UNEP, 2006). In rich countries, E-waste represents some 8 percent of municipal waste (Widmer et al, 2005). It is the fastest growing municipal waste stream (EPA, 2011). Most of this E-waste is not recycled, because those items tend to go out with the normal household waste and do not receive special treatment (Ladou and Lovegrove, 2008). Some 80 percent of collected E-waste is exported to poor countries and ends up in landfills and informal dumps (Schmidt, 2006). These dumping sites are poisoned and groundwater is polluted (Murugesan, 2008).

Green IT has been introduced to minimize environmental effects of ICTs, to save costs and for corporate social responsibility (CSR). There are four paths along which the environmental effects of ICTs should be addressed: green use (reducing the energy consumption of ICTs and use them in an environmentally sound manner), green disposal (refurbish and reuse old ICTs and properly recycle unwanted ones), green design (designing energy efficient and environmentally sound ICTs), and green manufacturing (man-ufacturing ICTs with minimal or no impact on the environment) (Murugesan, 2008). Green IT can also develop, according to Donnellan, Sheridan, and Curry (2011), solutions that align IT processes with the prin-ciples of sustainability and stimulate innovative technologies to deliver green benefits across an organization. In that way, end user satisfaction, management restructuring, regulatory compliance, fiscal benefits, and re-turn on investment (ROI) can be addressed. In the opinion of Visalakshi et al. (2013: 64), Green IT may be 'simple, plain, common sense'. The positive effects of Green IT are extensively studied in academic literature (Harmon and Auseklis, 2009; Brooks et al, 2012; Lei and Ngai, 2013; Subburaj et al, 2014; Esfahani et al, 2015ab).

The energy consumption of ICTs (as well as the corresponding energy costs) are growing exponentially as a result of the data deluge. From 2000 to 2005 consumption of electricity in data centers doubled, while electri-city consumption worldwide grew by (only) 16.7 percent per year (Koomey, 2008). From 2005 to 2010, the consumption of electricity in data centres alone jumped with 56 percent (Koomey, 2011; Cook, 2012). This in-crease in electricity consumption results in increased carbon dioxide emis-sions. According to Dubey and Hefley (2011), each PC or laptop in use gen-erates about four tons, each server about eight tons of carbon dioxide eve-ry year, although there are many possibilities to lower those emissions (Boccaletti et al, 2008). The use of 'renewable' energy resources (water, wind, solar, geothermal, tidal, wave, and biofuel resources) could affect these emissions positively (WNA, 2015), but in 2014 the use of renewable energy resources for electricity generation is still quite low. The U.S. Energy Information Administration estimates that in 2012 almost 21 percent of the world electricity generation was from the use of renewable energy resources, with a projection for nearly 25 percent in 2040 (EIA, 2012; EIA, 2014). This means that carbon dioxide emissions will be a problem in the foreseeable future. Curbing back data storage could have very positive effects on energy use. In 2008, storage networks were responsible for 15 percent of total ICT energy costs (HP, 2008). This percentage had, in our estimate, doubled in 2011, given the increasing need for data storage as a result of multiplication of data, social media, and fear of not being compliant (Van Bussel, 2012a). Studies have shown that electricity costs can approach 50 percent of the overall energy costs for an organization (Harmon and Auseklis, 2009). In January 2013, an average in-house server in the USA costs $731,94 in electricity (Hammond, 2013).

Summarizing: ICTs have a large energy footprint. The electricity use for ICTs has shown remarkable growth, which resulted in rising costs for electricity consumption. The data deluge (and the use of more and more ICT resources to manage this deluge) threatens [1] to drown all positive effects of Green IT and [2] to raise energy costs exponentially.

# 2. Research question, objective, and methodology

## 2.1 Research Question
Market research firm IDC estimated in 2007 that the amount of annually generated data exceeded the storage space globally available (Gantz and Reinsel, 2007). The data deluge is threatening to prevent both DA and Green IT to reach their objectives. To keep data and records accessible over time, to allow for Green IT to reach its environmental effects, and to prevent energy costs from rising unnecessarily, it becomes vital to curb data storage.

The bulk of all preserved data and records is stored on hard disks, consuming more electricity than necessary. Although electricity use of servers can be largely reduced by using them efficiently keeping the powered-up servers utilized and keeping as many as possible powered-down, this does not work in archiving and storage infrastructures. Research has shown that search and data mining activities for access will spread fairly evenly across all servers, making it impossible to keep servers powered-down (Adams et al, 2011; Adams et al, 2012). For curbing data storage, it will be necessary to appraise data and records value (over time), to implement data and records value appraising methods and tools, and to completely and permanently delete data and records that have lost their economic, social, cultural, financial, administrative, fiscal and/or legal value (Robyns, 2014; Niu, 2014).

The research question we want to answer in this paper is if it is possible to methodically reduce the amount of stored data and records in organizations based on the value of information, using the Green Archiving Model we have developed. Reducing the amount of data and records in organizations helps in allowing them to fight the data deluge and to realize the objectives of both DA and Green IT. At the same time, methodically deleting data and records should reduce the consumption of electricity for data storage. As a consequence, the organizational cost for electricity use should be reduced.

## 2.2    Research Objective

We have tested the viability of our Green Archiving Model in previous research with two exploratory case studies. In Van Bussel and Smit (2014) we stated that this model could be used to increase awareness in organizations for the environmental aspects of data storage and that the objectives of DA and Green IT could be realized using the model. The objective of this paper is to ascertain that our Green Archiving model can be used to methodically reduce the amount of stored data and records based on their value and that it can be used to reduce the costs for consumption of electricity for data storage.

Green Archiving intends to raise awareness of the environmental effects of ICTs (like increased carbon dioxide emissions) and to the effects of the data deluge on the accessibility of data and records. It tries to define solutions for [1] the rising amount of data and records and [2] the constantly rising costs of electricity. Green Archiving integrates Green IT with two leading theories of DA: the theories concerning the Information Value Chain (IVC) and Archival Retention Levels (ARLs). Both theories can be used to reduce the amount of stored data and records based on assigned information values. Operationalizing Green Archiving, organizations curb power consumption, lower needs for storage capacity by permanently deleting data and records based on their value, and develop 'low power' ICTs (Forrest,

Kaplan and Kind¬ler, 2008). That way, Green Archiving realizes the objectives of Green IT and curbs data storage, allowing DA to realize its objectives of fast accessibility of past experiences, transparent accountability, data and records-driven decision-making, knowledge-sharing, and reducing costs of transactions (Barosso and Hölzle, 2007; Schwarz and Elffers, 2010; Orgerie et al, 2014; Van Bussel and Smit, 2014; Pine and Mazmanian, 2015). Green Archiving is a relatively new subject and is not extensively studied yet within the context of information and archival sciences.

## 2.3    Research Methodology

This paper is based on the research project that was first reported on in Van Bussel and Smit (2014). We are using here the results mentioned in that paper, with additional results from one of the exploratory case studies used. We have added also results from an extensive research in existing case studies on DA, Green IT and data deduplication. Our exploratory research was a combination of desk research, qualitative interviews with information technology and information management experts, a focus group and two exploratory case studies. We researched scientific literature with an ICT, information management and archival science perspective. We collected literature with a key word search in Google Scholar, Microsoft Academic Search and in the Digital Library of the University of Amsterdam (indexes on IT, information science / management, archival science / management). The key words used in this search were: 'Green Computing', 'Green IT', 'IT power use', 'IT power costs', 'information value', 'archival appraisal', 'archival disposal' and 'environmental awareness'. The findings of this desk research were used, discussed and criticized in: [1] individual, semi-structured interviews with ten ICT, information management and archival science experts (three scientists, two consultants, three CTO's, and two storage industry specialists); [2] a focus group, consisted of six (other) experts (two Green Computing consultants, two information managers and two storage managers). We used the information acquired through desk research, interviews and focus group to develop a provisional Green Archiving model. In Van Bussel and Smit (2014), this model was than tested for validity in two small exploratory case studies.

## 3. Exploring the stage: Composing the Green Archiving Model

### 3.1 Green IT Components

Analyzing literature, published case studies, interviews and focus group discussion, we discern six components of Green IT research. The first is product longevity (Visalakshi et al, 2013; Agarwal and Nath, 2011). As Walker (1995: 21) already stated, 'product's longevity is influenced by the durability of its component parts; its capacity to be repaired, maintained and upgraded; and its aesthetic qualities'. Product longevity helps in ensuring an intelligent utilization of resources in manufacturing processes, which account for 70 percent of the natural resources used during a computers lifecycle (Mingay, 2007). The second component of Green IT is software and deployment optimization (Ahamad and Ravikanth, 2012; Badbe, 2014; Choudhary, 2014), that influences the amount of computer resources required for any given computing function. It is a way for saving energy that includes algorithmic efficiency, resource allocation, virtualization, and terminal servers. Virtualization is a very popular method of optimization in archiving and storage environments. With it, many virtual versions of devices or resources (servers, storage devices, networks or operating systems) could be made, using only one actual device or resource, making it much more energy efficient (Ren et al, 2015). The third component is power management (Schlomann et al, 2015; Kashyap et al, 2015; Visalashki et al, 2013). Even with a turned off monitor, a computer will consume as much energy as a powered but idle computer. Almost one-third of the energy consumption of an organization's PC population is wasted as a result of PC's that are unused but still turned on. With power management, it is possible for organizations to annually save up to $60 per computer (Gunaratne et al, 2005). This translates also in a reduction in the pollution emissions from reduced electrical generation. Materials recycling (Shalini and Prasanthi, 2015; Visalashki et al, 2013; Kwon et al, 2006), the fourth component, refers to recycling or reuse of computers or electronic waste, including finding other uses for ICTs, or having them dismantled, allowing for the safe extraction of materials for reuse in other products. Recycling ICTs can keep harmful materials such as lead, mercury, and chromium out of landfills (Murugesan, 2008). Telecommuting, often referred to as teleworking, occurs when paid workers work away from their normal place of work, usually from home. It is not clear if the reduction of a company's energy consumption matches the rise in energy consumption at home in order to work remotely, but reducing the amount of cars moving employees back and forth will produce a carbon dioxide emission reduction (Asgari and Jin, 2015; Srivastava et al, 2015; Thompson, 2009). The last, sixth component, low power IT (or energy-efficient computing) (Hopper and Rice, 2008; Düben et al, 2014; Ahmad and Ranka, 2012; Lee et al, 2013) has been designed to use less electronic power. The increasing electricity costs are forcing hardware developers to rethink their technologies. A variety of approaches have been proposed to trade the accuracy of the hardware fabric in return for savings in resources used such as energy, delay, area and/or yield and, therefore, lead to reduced costs. The components software and deployment optimization, telecommuting, and low power IT are important for reducing power consumption for data storage.

## 3.2    Archival retention levels and information value chain

Information and Archival science are interdisciplinary fields concerned with the analysis, collection, classification, storage, retrieval, dissemination, appraisal, disposal and preservation of data. They use methods and techniques to appraise and select organizational data for long-term (or indefinite) preservation or to permanently delete appraised data (Shepherd and Yeo, 2003; Xie, 2013; Smallwood, 2013). Appraisal is the process of establishing the 'value' of data and records, qualifying that value, and determining its duration. The primary objective of appraisal is to identify the data and records to be continuously preserved for an unlimited period of time (Duranti, 1994). Appraisal establishes the value of organizational data over time, be it economic, social, cultural, financial, administrative, fiscal and/or legal value (Cook, 2013). Many appraisal approaches are based on content evaluation of records (very impractical in an electronic age of information overload), causing a de-contextualization. Shepherd and Yeo (2003: 151) stated that appraisal 'should be based on analysis of organizational purposes and the systems that support them'. The focus of appraisal is moved from the data and records to the organizational contexts that created them. In the appraisal process, 'judgements of value' are made to decide what to keep and what to destroy. Penn (2014) re-interprets appraisal through the philosophical frameworks of axiology and demonstrates that the concept of value has a wider resonance than has been previously considered. Appraisal always results in retention schedules, which assure that all data and records are retained and disposed according to their quantified value: the time (in years) that data and records should be retained, according to considerations of organizational risks and assigned economic, social, cultural, financial, administrative, fiscal and/or legal value. Minimizing risks (especially those of litigation) also means systematic disposal immediately after the expiration of the assigned retention period (Shepherd and Yeo, 2003). Two theories of archival science offer tools for appraising data and records: the theories of Archival Retention Levels (ARLs) (Den Teuling, 2001) and Information Value Chain (IVC) (Van Bussel, 2012ab).

The first theory concerns itself with designating ARLs in organizations to store and retain data that is unique, authentic, relevant and contextual. The ARL theory is part of appraisal methods that consider organizational contexts and purposes more important than the specific content of data and records. ARLs define detailed functional (organizational) responsibilities for the retention, storage and archiving of unique, authentic, relevant, and contextual data and records (Smit, 2012). Data value is appraised according to the organizational level that is responsible for the collection, analysis, processing, and storage of that specific data. This organizational level is the designated ARL. At the ARL the data are retained as long as the retention schedule permits. This schedule makes the economic, social, cultural, financial, administrative, fiscal and/or legal value of the data and records (retained at every ARL) explicit and defines its archival value: a time (in years) after which this information should be irreparably destroyed. Identical data retained at other functional levels within the organization and without a new business objective (duplicates) can be immediately deleted, permanently and irreparably. When using ARL's, it will be necessary (to prepare for litigation procedures) to capture data about the organizational level these duplicates are being kept and the persons who have accessed them (Van Bussel and Henseler, 2013). In digital environments, these duplicates can be stored in different forms and places and in various business processes, not being the designated ARL (Paul and Baron, 2007). The effect of using ARL's on the organizational need for storage capacity will be substantial, as published case studies indicate. In hospitals, for instance, an average organization's duplicate rate in 2009 was typically between 5-10 percent (McClel-lan, 2009). Deduplication lets an organization keep 20 times more data in a given amount of storage (Geer, 2008). The practical experiments of Mandagare et al (2008) show that between different deduplication techniques the space savings amount for almost 30 percent, which was confirmed in Dutch (2008) and Proof point (2013). Using ARL checklists can reduce the amount of data stored up to a minimum of 30 percent, which has direct effects on costs and needed storage capacity. The organizational use of ARLs can be seen as contextual data deduplication.

The IVC theory defines the utilization of the informational and evidential value of data and records in business processes to improve trusted information management and the performance of business processes (Van Bussel 2012ab). The IVC includes all processes of information management and manages data generation, data identification, data capture, data storage, data processing, data distribution, data structuring, data publication, data (re-) use, data appraisal, data selection, data disposal, data retention, data security, data auditing and data preservation. DA uses this chain to reach its purposes: to reduce the costs of transactions, to enlarge the speed of access to organizational experiences, to help in decision-making, to share knowledge, and to realize account-ability. For the purpose of this paper, only the processes of data appraisal, data selection and data disposal are important. In the data appraisal process the short- and long-term (or indefinite) value of data and records is defined in order to retain and preserve them for later (re-)use. As stated above, this data appraisal defines the archival value and results in a retention schedule. In the data selection process, data and records are collected and set aside according to the agreed upon retention schedule. In the data disposal process, the set aside data and records are completely, permanently and irreparably deleted (Shepherd and Yeo, 2003). Organizational retention schedules are used to operate those processes. Almost 75 percent of all data and records in an organization can be permanently deleted over time (Archieflandsverordening, 2007). The value of Big Data, for instance, degrades rapidly over the short term. Retaining that data for a long time, hoping it may become valuable or needed some day, is unnecessarily costly and indefensibly risky (Gascon, 2013). In a retention schedule, such a Big Data data set will be appraised to be destroyed after its last use. Normally that would mean up to one year after the moment that specific Big Data data set was last used.

## 3.3    Green Archiving Model

Combining the components of Green IT with the data reducing components of DA, allowed us to develop a Green Archiving model. As our earlier research showed (Van Bussel and Smit, 2014), that model can be used: [1] to increase awareness in organizations for the environmental effects of the use of ICTs, [2] to reduce the amount of stored data and records, [3] to reduce power consumption for data storage and, ultimately, [4] to reduce greenhouse gas emissions and E-waste in realizing all components of Green IT. This paper concentrates on the aspects [2] and [3] of the model. Aspect [1] was added to the objectives of the Green Archiving Model when conducting interviews with Digital Archiving and Green IT specialists and exploring the research question within a focus group. In their professional experience, the specialists encountered an extremely low organizational awareness of the environmental effects of ICTs and a lack of knowledge about the electricity use needed for storage and the associated organizational costs. Aspect [4] of the model will be part of further research; there are many case studies confirming the fact that Green IT reduces carbon dioxide emissions and E-waste (Murugesan, 2008; Schmidt, 2006). In future case studies we want to research the total effects of the application of the Green Archiving Model. The model of Green Archiving we developed is shown in figure 1.

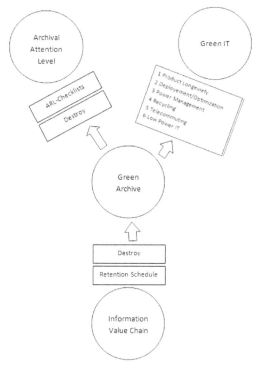

**Figure 1:** Green archiving model: combination of Green IT, ARL and IVC

# 4. Testing the stage: experimenting with the Model

## 4.1 Purpose

The Green Archiving Model has four objectives. In Van Bussel and Smit (2014), we ascertained in a case study in the Dutch Music Institute (Nederlands Muziek Instituut) that the Green Archiving Model was viable and that it could be used in organizations to increase awareness of the environmental effects of ICTs (objective 1). In that paper, we also presented some provisional results in reducing the amount of data (objective 2), and in curbing power use for data storage (objective 3), using a case study in a Dutch international trade organization. We are presenting more definite results of using the Green Archiving Model here, especially concentrating on objectives 2 and 3, following additional research in this trade organization and already published case studies. The fourth objective (reducing carbon dioxide emissions and reducing E-waste) will be addressed in future re-search.

## 4.2 Exploratory research

We organized three different exploratory case studies in a small international trade corporation in Maastricht (The Netherlands), working with subsidiaries in Europe, Asia and South America. These three case studies were: [1] a scan of the ICT infrastructure of the corporation using the model (November-December 2013), [2] a pilot study by the corporation's IT department on the effects of ARL Schedules (March-May 2014), and [3] a pilot study by de corporation's Chief Information Officer on the effects of a Records Schedule on the globally stored data and records (January-March 2015). In [1] the Green Archiving model was enthousiastically received. Green Computing was well known within the IT department, but only the components Software Deployment and Optimization (virtualization of storage servers) and Power Management were implemented. The results of this implementation of these components were comparable to those described by Dubey and Hefley (2011). The IT department admitted that it should be more aware of other Green Computing components. CSR was extremely important for the corporation and implementing other components of Green Computing would be a significant contribution to CSR. The IT department planned to look into the possibilities of Telecommuting and Product Longevity. When we did the exploratory scan, the organization didn't use ARL checklists, but (for this case study) agreed to experiment with them in its corporate headquarters. After a scan of the headquarters' file systems, the IT department estimated that almost 35 % of their IT storage capacity of 18 TB was used for duplicate files. It acknowledged that the use of ARL checklists would have a significant effect on the IT storage capacity. Retention Schedules were used only for the data stored in their document and records management applications, but the IT department acknowledged that both applications were not yet generally in use. Rigorous use of those schedules would certainly have an effect on the IT storage capacity, but the IT department could not quantify those effects yet. In [2] the IT department organized a pilot study on the effects of ARL Schedules in their global information management environment. It analysed all file systems and database management systems, storage area networks ans mail systems in the global operations of the corporation. In this pilot study, the corporation realized the functional responsibilities in the organization structures of their subsidiaries were not clearly defined. It developed a new information management structure based on the IVC theory and integrated it in their business process models. The ARL analysis confronted the IT department with ICTs that were implemented within their subsidiaries without their knowledge. Global data storage capacity was 45 TB (including the headquarters' 18 TB storage capacity). The conclusion of this pilot study was that the use of ARL checklists would diminish global data storage capacity with 30 percent. 37 percent of the company's data storage capacity was used for duplicate files. The IT department calculated that such a reduction of the amount of data would result in less electricity use for data storage and would diminish electricity costs with 25 percent. These results correspond with the results of data deduplication mentioned earlier in this paper. In case study [3} the office of the Chief Information Officer analysed the retention schedules in use in their records and document management applications. They were limited to data and records captured within the document and records management software that was not globally implemented yet. The Chief Information Officer decided to use the European Document Retention Guide 2013 (De Brauw, 2013) as a way to analyse the possibilities of further reducing the data and records stored. The Chief Information Officer concluded that almost 10 percent (3.5 TB) of all data and records stored in February 2015 could be disposed of immediately, because they had no 'value' anymore for the organization as all possible retention periods had passed. Based on the Guide only 5 percent of all data would have to be retained for longer than twenty years. The IT department calculated that using ARLs and Retention Schedules for all data and records in the organization would curb data storage with almost 45 percent and would reduce electricity costs with 35 percent. The conclusion of the Chief

Information officer was that methodical use of the value of information (as expressed within the Retention Schedule used) would improve storage efficiency, reduce the amount of stored data and records, diminish litigation risks, and reduce electricity costs. The Green Archiving model seems to be a viable model for organizational use.

# 5. Conclusions and future work

In this paper, we studied the possibility to methodically reduce the amount of data and records stored in an organization based on their 'value' and using the Green Archiving Model. The case study showed that the model can be used to reduce [1] the amount of data (45 percent, using ARLs and Retention Schedules) and [2] the electricity consumption for data storage (resulting in a (calculated) cost reduction of 35 percent). These case studies indicate that the Green Archiving Model is a viable model to methodically reduce the amount of stored data and records and to curb electricity use for storage in organizations. That way, it facilitates DA and Green IT to reach their objectives. These case studies only provide us with provisional results. They need to be confirmed in further research. We are planning extensive case studies to research the environmental effects of Green Archiving and the scientific viability of our model. The ultimate goal of this research project is the development of a low power ICT that will automatically appraise, select and preserve or permanently delete data and records. Such an ICT will automatically reduce storage capacity and curb electricity consumption used for data storage. At the same time, data disposal will reduce overload caused by storing the same data in different formats, it will lower costs and it reduces the potential for liability.

# References

Adams, I., Miller, E.L., and Rosenthal, D.S. (2011). Using Storage Class Memory for Archives with DAWN, a Durable Array of Wimpy Nodes. Technical Report UCSC-SSRC-11-07, Santa Cruz: University of California.

Adams, I.F., Storer, M.W., and Miller, E.L. (2012). 'Analysis of workload behavior in scientific and historical long-term data repositories', ACM Transactions on Storage (TOS), vol. 8, no. 2, art. 6: 1-27.

Agarwal, S. and Nath, A. (2011) 'Green Computing - a new Horizon of Energy Efficiency and Electronic waste minimization: a Global Perspective', CSNT '11 Proceedings of the 2011 Inter¬national Confe¬rence on Communication Systems and Network Technologies, Washington: IEEE, pp. 688-693.

Ahamad, S.F., and Ravikanth, P.V. (2012) 'Green Computing Future of Liveliness', International Journal of Computational Engineering Research (IJCER), vol. 2, no. 4, pp. 41-45.

Ahmad, I., and Ranka, S. (2012) Handbook of energy-aware and Green Computing, London: Chap¬man & Hall/ CRC,

Archieflandsverordening 2007, MvT, National Archives of the Netherlands Antilles.

Armitage, J. and Roberts, J. (2002) Living with Cyberspace. Technology and society in the 21st century, London, New York: Continuum.

Asgari, H., and Jin, X. (2015) 'Toward Comprehensive Telecommuting Analysis Framework: Setting the Conceptual Outline', Transportation Research Board 94th Annual Meeting, No. 15-0282.

Badbe, V.C. (2014) 'Green Computing Approaches', International Journal of Computer Technology and Applications, vol. 5, no. 6, pp. 3042-3049.

Barroso, L.A. and Hölzle, U. (2007) 'The case for energy-proportional computing', IEEE Compu¬ter, vol. 40, no. 12, pp. 33–37.

Bearman, D. (2006) 'Moments of risk. Identifying threats to electronic records', Archivaria, vol 62, Fall, pp. 15-46.

Boccaletti, G., Löffler, M., and Oppenheim, J. M. (2008) 'How IT can cut carbon emissions', McKinsey Quarterly vol. 37, October, pp. 37-41.

Brooks, S., Wang, X., and Sarker, S. (2012) 'Unpacking Green IS: A Review of the Existing Lite¬rature and Directions for Further Research', Vom Brocke, J., Seidel, S. and Recker, J. (eds.), Green Business Process Management. Towards the Sustainable Enterprise, Heidelberg: Springer, pp. 15-37.

Choudhary, S (2014) 'A survey on green computing techniques', International Journal on Computer Science and Informa¬tion Technology, vol.5, no. 5, pp. 6248-6252.

Cook, G. (2012) How clean is your cloud ? Catalysing an energy revolution, Amster¬dam: Greenpeace International..

Cook, T. (2013) 'Evidence, memory, identity, and community: four shifting archival paradigms', Archi¬val Science, vol. 13, no. 2-3, pp. 95-120.

De Brauw Blackstone Westbroek (2013) European Document Retention Guide 2013, Amsterdam: Iron Mountain..

Den Teuling, A. (2001) 'Selectie in de praktijk', Ketelaar, F.C.J., Den Teuling, A.J.M. and Van Wijn¬gaarden, J. (eds.), Archiefbeheer in de praktijk, Alphen aan den Rijn: Samsom, pp. 4020/1-55.

Donnellan, B., Sheridan, C. and Curry, E. (2011) 'A Capability Maturity Framework for Sustainable Infor¬mation and Commu¬nication Technology', IEEE IT Professional, vol. 13, no. 1, pp. 33–40.

Düben, P.D., Joven, J., Lingamneni, A., McNamara, H., De Micheli, G., Palem, K.V. and Palmer, T.N. (2014) 'On the use of inexact, pruned hardware in atmospheric modelling', Philosophical Transactions of the Royal Society of London A: Mathe¬matical, Physical and Engineering Sciences, vol. 372, pp. 1-16, DOI: 10.1098/rsta.2013.0276.

Dubey, S., and Hefley, W.E. (2011) 'Greening ITIL: Expanding the ITIL lifecycle for Green IT', Pro¬ceedings of Portland International Conference on Management of Engineering and Techno¬logy (PIC¬MET 2011), Washington: IEEE, pp. 1-8.

Duranti, L. (1994) 'The concept of appraisal and archival theory', The American Archivist, vol. 57 (Spring), pp. 328-344.

US Energy Information Administration (EIA) (2012) 'International Energy Statistics'. Online. Available: http://www.eia.gov/cfapps/ipdbproject/IEDIndex3.cfm?tid=6&pid=29&aid=12 (26 May 2015)

US Energy Information Administration (EIA) (2014) 'International Energy Outlook 2013'. Online. Available: http://www.eia.gov/forecasts/archive/ieo13/electricity.cfm (26 May 2016)

US Environmental Protection Agency (EPA) (2009) Electronic Waste Management in the United States through 2009, Washington D.C.: EPA.

Esfahani, M.D., A.A. Rahman and N.H. Zakaria (2015a) 'The Status Quo and the prospect of Green IT and Green IS. A syste¬matic literature review', Journal of Soft Computing and Decision Support Systems, vol. 2, no. 1, pp. 18-34.

Esfahani, M.D., A.A. Rahman and N.H. Zakaria (2015b) 'GreenIT/IS Adoption as Corporate Ecological Responsiveness. An Academic Literature Review', Journal of Soft Computing and Decision Support Systems, vol. 2, no. 1, pp. 35-43.

Forrest, W., Kaplan, J.M. and Kindler, N. (2008) 'Data Centers: How to cut Carbon Emissions and Costs', McKinsey on Business Technology, vol. 8, no. 14, pp. 4-14.

Gantz, J.F. and Reinsel. D. (eds.) (2007) The expanding digital universe. A forecast of world-wide information growth through 2010, Framingham (Ma.): IDC.

Gantz, J. and Reinsel, D. (2012) The Digital Universe in 2020: Big Data, Bigger Digital Shadows, and Biggest Growth in the Far East, Framingham (Ma.): IDC.

Golden, B. (2010) 'Cloud computing: How big is big data? IDC's answer', CIO, May 7.

Geer, D. (2008) 'Reducing the Storage Burden via Data Deduplication', Computer, vol.41, no. 12, pp. 15-17.

Gunaratne, C., Christensen, K. and Norsman, B. (2005) 'Managing energy consumption costs in desktop PCs and LAN switches with proxying, split TCP connections, and scaling of link speed'. International Journal of Network Management, vol. 15, pp. 297-310.

Hammond, T. (2013) 'Toolkit: Calculate datacenter server power usage'. Online. Available: http://www.zdnet.com/toolkit-calculate-data-center-server-power-usage-7000013699/ (26 May 2015)

Harmon, R.R. and Auseklis, N. (2009) 'Sustainable IT Services: Assessing the Impact of Green Com¬puting Practices', Proceedings of Portland International Conference on Manage-ment of Engineering and Technology (PICMET 2009), Washington: IEEE, pp. 1707-1717.

Hilbert, M. and López, P. (2011) 'The world's technological capacity to store, communicate, and com¬pute information', Science, vol. 332, no. 6025, pp. 60-65.

Hodge, G.M. (2000) 'Best practices for Digital Archiving. An Information Life Cycle Approach', D-Lib Magazine, vol. 6, no. 1. Online. Available: http://www.dlib.org/dlib/january00/01hodge.html (26 May 2015).

Hopper, A. and Rice, A. (2008) 'Computing for the future of the planet', Philosophical Transac-tions of the Royal Society A: Mathematical, Physical and Engineering Sciences, vol. 366, pp. 3685-3697, DOI: 10.1098/rsta.2008.0124.

HP (2008) 'Groen computergebruik: energie besparen en helpen de aarde te beschermen'. [Online]. Available: http://m.hp.com/be/nl/hp-news/details.do?id=48932&articletype=news_release (26 May 2015).

Gascon, D. (2013) 'Are you a Data Hoarder? Really, are you?', Compliance, Governance & Oversight Council, CGOc. Online. Available: https://www.cgoc.com/blog/are-you-data-hoarder-really-are-you (25 May 2015).

Jacob, J.S. and P. K.G (2012) 'EDPAC: event-driven power aware pervasive computing for effective power utilization in Green Computing', International Journal of Advanced In-formation Technology, vol. 2, no. 1, pp. 55-64.

Jacobs, A. (2009) 'The pathologies of Big Data', Communications of the ACM, vol 52, no. 8, pp. 36-44.

Ren, J., Li, L., Chen, H., Wang, S., Xu, S., Sun, G., Wang, J. and Liu, S. (2015) 'On the deploy-ment of information-centric net¬work: Programmability and virtualization'. International Conference on Computing, Network¬ing and Communications (ICNC), Proceedings, Gar-den Grove (CA.): IEEE, pp. 690-694.

Kashyap, P., Naik, A., and Patel, P. (2015) 'Green Computing', International Journal of Research, vol. 2, no. 4, pp. 940-944.

Koomey, J.G. (2008) 'Worldwide electricity used in data centers', Environmental Research Let¬ters, vol. 3, no. 034008 (July-September), doi:10.1088/1748-9326/3/3/034008).

Koomey, J.G. (2011) Growth in data center electricity use 2005-2010, Oakland (Ca.): Analytics Press

Kwon, Y.C., Sang, W.L. and Moon, S. (2006) 'Personal computer privacy: Analysis for Korean PC users', Advances in Information and Computer Security, Berlin-Heidelberg: Springer, pp. 76-87.

Ladou, J., and Lovegrove, S. (2008) 'Export of electronics equipment waste', International journal of oc-cupational and environmental health, vol. 14, no. 1, pp. 1-10.

Latour, B. (1990) 'Postmodern? No, simp¬ly amodern! Steps towards an anthro¬polo¬gy of science', Studies In History and Philosophy of Science, vol 21, no. 1, pp. 145-171.

Lei, C.F. and Ngai, E.W.T. (2013) 'Green IT Adoption: An Academic Review of Literature'. PACIS 2013 Proceedings. Paper 95.

Lee, S.M., Park, S-H. and Trimi, S. (2013) 'Greening with IT: practices of leading countries and strate¬gies of followers', Management Decision, vol. 51, no. 3, pp. 629-642.

Lyman, P. and Varian, H.R. (2003) How much information?, , Berkely: School of Information Management and Systems, University of California.

Mandagere, N., Zhou, P., Smith, M.A. and Uttamchandani, S. (2008) 'Demystifying data dedu-plication', Proceedings of the ACM/IFIP/USENIX Middleware'08 Conference Companion, Leuven (Belgium), pp. 12-17.

Manyika, J. (ed.) (2011) Big Data. The next frontier for innovation, competition and productiv-ity, Mc¬Kinsey Global Institute.

McClellan, M.A. (2009) 'Duplicate Medical Records: A Survey of Twin Cities Healthcare Or¬gan¬iza¬tions', AMIA Annual Symposium Proceedings, Bethesda (Mi.): AMIA, pp. 421-425.

Mingay, S. (2007) Green IT: The New Industry Shock Wave, Gartner.

Murugesan, S. (2008) 'Harnessing Green IT: Principles and Practices', IEEE IT Professional, vol. 10, no. 1, pp. 24-33.

Niu, J. (2014). 'Appraisal and Selection for Digital Curation', International Journal of Digital Curation, vol. 9, no. 2, pp. 65-82.

Orgerie, A.C., De Assuncao, M.D. and Lefevre, L. (2014) 'A Survey on Techniques for Improving the Energy Efficiency of Large Scale Distributed Systems', ACM Computing Surveys, vol. 46, no. 4, pp. 1-35.

Paul, G. and Baron, J. (2007) 'Information Inflation. Can the legal system adapt?', Richmond Jour¬nal of Law & Technology, vol 13, no. 3, pp. 1-41.

Penn, ESM (2014) Exploring archival value: an axiological approach. Doctoral thesis, UCL (University College London). Online. Available: http://discovery.ucl.ac.uk/1455310/ (26 May 2015)

Pine, K. and Mazmanian, M. (2015) 'Emerging Insights on Building Infrastructure for Data-Driven Transparency and Accountability of Organizations', iConference 2015 Proceedings, Newport Beach (Ca.), pp. 1-13

Proofpoint (2013) 'Archive and Governance ROI Tool'. Online. Available: http://www.proofpoint.com/pro-ducts/archive-governance/roi-tool/index.php (26 May 2015).

Robinson, B.H. (2009) 'E-waste: an assessment of global production and environmental im-pacts', Science of the total environment, vol. 408, no. 2, pp. 183-191.

Robyns, M. C. (2014). Using Functional Analysis in Archival Appraisal: A Practical and Effective Alternative to Traditional Appraisal Methodologies. Plymouth: Rowman & Littlefield.

Schmidt, C. W. (2006) 'Unfair trade e-waste in Africa', Environmental Health Perspectives, vol. 114. no. 4, A232.

Shalini, K., and Prasanthi, K.N. (2013) 'Green Computing', Journal of Telematics and Informatics, vol. , no. 1, pp. 1-13.

Schwarz, M., and Elffers, J. (2010) Sustainism is the new modernism. A cultural manifesto for the sus¬tainism era, New York: Distributed Art Publishers.

Segaran, T. and Hammerbacher, J. (2009) Beautiful Data: The Stories Behind Elegant Data Solutions, Sebastopol (Ca.): O'Reilly Media.

Shepherd, E. and Yeo, G. (2003) Managing records. A handbook of principles and practice, London: Facet Pub-lish¬ing.

Schlomann, B., Eichhammer, W., and Stobbe, L. (2015) 'Energy saving potential of information and communication tech¬nology', International Journal of Decision Support Systems, vol. 1, no. 2, pp. 152-163.

Smallwood, R.F. (2013) Managing electronic records: Methods, best practices, and technologies, Hoboken (NJ): John Wiley & Sons, Hoboken (NJ), chapter 7.

Smit, N. (2012) Green Archiving. Digitale archivering en het milieu, Amsterdam: Reinwardt Academy (BCM Thesis).

Dutch, M. (2008) Understanding data deduplication ratios, SNIA Data Management Forum.

Srivastava, K., Sethumadhavan, A., Raghupathy, H., Agarwal, S., and Rawat, S. R. (2015) 'To Study the Indian Perspective on the Concept of Work from Home', Indian Journal of Science and Technology, vol. 8, no. S4, pp. 212-220.

Subburaj, S., Kulkarni, S. and Jia, L. (2014) 'Green IT: sustainability by aligning business requirements with IT resource utilisation', International Journal of Communication Networks and Distributed Sys¬tems, vol. 12, no. 1, pp. 30-46.

Thompson, J.T. (2009) 'Three approaches to green computing on campus', EDUCAUSE Quarterly Magazine, vol. 32, no. 3. [Online]. Available: http://www.educause.edu/ero/article/three-approaches-green-computing-campus (26 May 2015).

Tomlinson, B. (2010) Greening through IT. Information Technology for environmental sustainability, Cambridge (Ma.): MIT University Press.

UNEP (2006) Call for Global Action on E-waste. United Nations Environment Programme, s.l.

Van Bussel, G.J. (2012a) Archiving should be just like an AppleTM en acht andere, nuttige (?) stellin¬gen, Amsterdam: Amsterdam University Press.

Van Bussel, G.J. (2012b) 'Reconstructing the Past for Organizational Accountability', The Electronic Journal of Information Systems Evaluation, vol. 15, no. 1, pp. 127-137.

Van Bussel, G.J. and Henseler, H. (2013) 'Digital Archiving and e-Discovery: Delivering evidence in an age of overload', John, B., Nkhoma, M. and Leung, N. (eds.), Proceedings of the 4th inter¬national confe¬rence on Information Systems Management and Evaluation (Ho Chi Minh City, May 2013), Reading (GB): ACPI, pp. 281-288.

Van Bussel, G.J. and Smit, N. (2014) 'Building a Green Archiving Model: Archival Retention Levels, Information Value Chain and Green Computing', Devos, J. and De Haes, S. (eds.), Proceedings of the 8th European Conference on IS Manage¬ment and Evaluation. ECIME 2014. University of Ghent, 11-12 september 2014, Reading (GB): ACPI, pp. 271-277.

Visalakshi, P., Paul, S. and Mandal, M. (2013) 'Green Computing', International Journal of Modern En¬gineering Research (IJMER). Proceedings of the National Conference on Architecture, Software sys¬tems and Green computing (NCASG), Paiyanoor (India), May 3, 2013, pp. 63-69.

Walker, S. (1995) 'The environment, product aesthetics and surface', Design Issues, vol.11, no. 3, pp. 15-27.

Widmer, R., Oswald-Krapf, H., Sinha-Khetriwal, D., Schnellmann, M. and Boni, H. (2005) 'Global per¬spectives on e-waste', Environmental Impact Assessment Review, vol. 25, no. 5, pp. 436-458.

World Neclear Association (WNA) (2015) 'Renewable energy and electricity'. Online. Available: http://www.world-nuclear.org/info/Energy-and-Environment/Renewable-Energy-and-Electricity/ (26 May 2015).

Xie, S.L. (2013) 'Preserving Digital Records: InterPARES findings and developments', Lemieux, V. (ed.), Financial Analysis and Risk Management. Data Governance, Analytics and Life Cycle Manage¬ment, Berlin-Heidelberg: Springer, pp. 187-206.